The Pandora
PROBLEM

Facing Narcissism in Leaders & Ourselves

E. JAMES WILDER

Published by Deeper Walk International.

First Printing November, 2018 / Printed in the United States of America

ISBN: 978-1-7327510-1-9

Deeper Walk International
13295 Illinois St. #223
Carmel, IN 46032

www.DeeperWalkInternational.org

Endorsements

"Transformation is never as clear as when a predator becomes a protector or an enemy becomes a friend." Dr. Wilder's insights into personality disorders challenges past theories claiming that change is not possible. Deep character transformation can occur in a group environment that can share each other's pain thus generating spontaneous love for one's enemy. This book is a must read for mental health professionals, Church leaders, and all who desire to instill hope with the suffering.

Dr. Christina Lynch
Director of Psychological Services
St. John Vianney Theological Seminary, Denver, CO

Dr. Wilder and I have been friends and colleagues for many years. He has an amazing and unique brain, and he comes up with amazing and unique insights. His teaching regarding maturity and maturity skills has changed my life. Anything Jim comes up with is worth paying attention to.

Dr. Karl Lehman
Board Certified Psychiatrist
Author of *Outsmarting Yourself* and *The Immanuel Approach*

This book challenged me at so many levels I lost track of them all. Jim doesn't just challenge narcissists to change. He challenges all of us to a deeper understanding and practice of what it means to love our enemies.

Dr. Marcus Warner
President
Deeper Walk International

In *The Pandora Problem* Dr. Wilder brilliantly, poignantly, and practically responds to the mystifying question posed by his friend and Rwandan priest, "How could anyone be a Christian and not be deeply transformed?" If that question eats away at your soul, whether for yourself or your church, this book is for you.

Howard Baker,
Denver Seminary

The Pandora Problem, though one might not at first realize, is a follow up to the revolutionary Rare Leadership book written by Dr. E. James Wilder and Dr. Marcus Warner. In Rare Leadership, these gentle soul doctors challenged our traditional Western mindset about how human beings learn best, authentically mature and have our identities more deeply transformed into the image of Jesus Christ. They taught us how to access and build up the infrastructure that God has embedded in the right hemisphere of our brains that is fundamental to getting our whole brains to work in harmony, to renew our minds in Christ and to create joy cultures through our ways of leading others. It felt like they were training us to high jump 7 feet. In this volume, Dr. Wilder now comes along and challenges us to learn to pole vault 17 feet! At least he hands us a pole - the hesed community of Christ, which can take us all higher into God's kingdom than we have imagined. He might have called this book Rare Love, for the grace of God will not have had its full work realized in our lives and faith communities until we spontaneously love our enemies and learn to restore people given over to narcissism. This is a human condition that our culture, but not Christ, teaches us to give up on. However, to do this, we must first courageously face any hidden narcissism still at work in us. Lord, have mercy!

Pastor Michael Sullivant
CEO
Life Model Works

Table of Contents

Introduction

In this groundbreaking book, *The Pandora Problem*, my good friend Jim Wilder has given us a much needed gift. Perhaps no problem has elicited more universal cries of hopelessness than the Pandora problem of narcissism.

Just as the young woman of Greek mythology panicked at what she let out of the infamous box, slamming the lid shut on hope, so most of us are afraid of lifting the lid on the problem of narcissism, and we too have left hope locked away.

Jim Wilder has not simply given us hope in this book, he has pointed the way to solving the problem of narcissism. Historically, we have tried to solve this dreaded issue through one-on-one therapy with people who don't think they have a problem. It hasn't worked, and most therapists won't even see narcissists anymore.

With his usual insight and precision, Jim has placed his finger on the core issue of what makes narcissism appear so hopeless. It is the fear of those surrounding the narcissist to speak up and engage. This fear is caused by having no tools – no game plan – no understanding of how to interact as a group with the narcissist in the middle.

Jim has not only unpacked the problem of narcissism with fresh biblical and clinical perspectives, he has identified the solution and provided both exercises and guidance on the path to recovery. In the process, he has taken us beyond the mere issue of narcissism (as if that were not large enough), and pointed us toward a solution to what is broken in the way the the church makes disciples.

More than any book I have ever read, *The Pandora Problem* strips away the veneer and helps us see what the calling to love our enemies is all about.

I hope you will read this book from cover to cover several times. I hope you will gather a group together to go through the exercises and discussions. This is a book worth pondering and it presents a process worth pursuing. Don't cheat yourself or those around you by skimming through these pages. This book may just change your life.

Marcus Warner
President
Deeper Walk International

I dedicate this book to

Me

or you

if you insist

CHAPTER ONE

"Better Not Say Anything"

**Nothing will hurt or destroy in all my holy mountain,
for as the waters fill the sea, so the earth will be filled
with people who know the LORD.**
Isaiah 11:9 (NLT)

The ancient Greeks told a myth about Pandora's Box, a container in which human illnesses, death, and many terrible things were sealed. In the original story, this container was a jar that was kept in a cave and carefully guarded by a family. However, one brother stole fire from the gods for people to use. As a punishment, the god Zeus then sent the insatiably curious Pandora to them, knowing she would open the jar. When Pandora lifted the cover, evils began flying out, so she slammed it shut leaving Hope trapped inside. She never opened the jar again.

Just as Pandora's experience made her fear ever again opening the dreaded box, we fear troubles will begin to fly if we open certain topics. Yet, like Pandora, if we keep the cover on these same topics, we leave hope trapped in the silence.

What Pandora let out of the box had consequences for everyone. Likewise, when we speak about opening Pandora's Box what follows brings consequences on far more people than the speaker. A whole group can know what was left unsaid but stay silent. Some must bite their lips to stay quiet while feeling amazing amounts of pressure. We know that saying anything only makes it worse!

We all know of Pandora problems that just get worse if we talk about them. We say there is an "elephant in the room" or we are "opening a can of worms." Everyone sees the problem, but great dread comes upon all who consider mentioning it. We have learned from experience that these topics are explosive and best left untouched.

Pandora problems

At the center of every "Pandora problem" is a person or a tight cluster of people. Surrounding a Pandora problem there is always a group – and not just any group. We almost always find a rather caring group around a Pandora problem, yet this group feels hopeless. They know nothing can save them from the consequences if any one of them opens Pandora's Box.

But we're not really talking about boxes are we? We are speaking of people who will suddenly feel more like enemies than friends when we mention a problem to them. We know of no way to deal with the person in the middle of the Pandora problem that will bring us all joy. Instead, something about the person in the center creates dread. We do not expect that what we say will make things better. Nothing the group knows how to do will help. Speaking just makes it worse.

What kind of problem could produce such dread in a group? We show no hesitation when addressing issues we can handle. A group with solutions would actively discuss and address their problems. Yet, as we will see, dread of addressing problems shows up in all kinds of places. Pandora problems flourish in businesses, schools, national governments and all kinds of rich, educated, artistic and enlightened groups. It is amazing how many people experience Pandora problems and stay silent.

Pandora problems are also found in most churches, Christian families, institutions, and schools. We might expect Christians to live in truth and freedom but instead we find more Pandora problems in churches than in the average population. The transforming power of God seems missing.

Christian silence attests to issues we do not believe our Christian faith can handle or solve. If we knew and trusted Christian solutions we would joyfully speak up saying, "This is just the sort of thing that gets changed and healed in our church." We would be loaded with stories of Pandora problems that were transformed.

Most Christians I meet do not believe Christianity can save their marriages, keep singles from sex before marriage, remove tempers, correct their internet usage, or alter their food cravings. When Christianity does not profoundly change bad character everyone from our children to our neighbors wonders, "Why bother being Christian?" The group around each Pandora problem stays silent thinking the same thing.

This book is written to people who think Christianity should be more transformative than it generally is. We will think together about things that Western culture generally does not understand or value. We will need to change church culture as well. We, who are dissatisfied with the degree of our transformation, must become the change agents.

Pandora problems happen in a group.

To understand the dynamics of a Pandora problem we need to understand the kind of issues a group fears will only become worse. The group must have confidence that there really is a way to make changes or a Pandora problem will result. Groups do not fear issues they can change for the better.

Let us compare and contrast two Christian leaders and how they dealt with their Pandora problems. In each case the Christians needed to help a man love his enemy – the person who had killed the man's mother.

As I watched Father Ubald hugging the man who murdered Ubald's mother, I studied their faces. Both men were smiling and calm. Some deep transformation had happened in their character to transform enemies into friends. I glanced beside me where Fr. Ubald sat as we watched the Rwandan genocide documentary[1] together. His face was peaceful. How had this African priest guided his congregation of predatory killers and traumatized victims into loving relationships? In particular, what changed the predators?

---

1   "Forgiveness: The Secret of Peace" - an award-winning documentary. www.secretofpeace.com

My mind went back to Dr. R, another great Rwandan leader I know. Like Fr. Ubald, Dr. R taught and practiced forgiveness after the genocide. But in the Christian community where Dr. R served, the genocide became a Pandora problem. No one would speak of their part in the killing. Participation in genocide was known by all and spoken by none. Even here I cannot mention my friend's name because it will only make things worse.

Dr. R told me how once, as he stood speaking, the very man he had watched kill his mother sat in the front row. The man in the front row was just another Christian pretending he knew nothing. Dr. R went on speaking as if he knew nothing. While Dr. R silently forgave the man, there was no change of character for the killer, no smiles of reconciliation in the church, and no joy in the community. Saying anything would just make matters worse.

Both Dr. R and Fr. Ubald are amazing leaders who bravely address the issues of genocide. Both leaders are very experienced in teaching and practicing forgiveness. Both men faced a personal encounter with the one who had killed their mothers. Both sons had the Christian character to forgive enemies. The difference in these two encounters was in the group that gathered around them.

Causes at the center of Pandora problems

We all know we can address issues some places and in other contexts the same topic creates a huge problem. Why can the same people examine and correct problems in one place when in another it becomes a Pandora problem and they all stay silent? Sometimes it only takes one person walking into the room and the conversation stops. To understand the explosive or corrosive nature of Pandora problems we need to examine the person (or cluster of people) in the center.

There is no silence about what lies at the center of Pandora problems. Thousands of books, psychological studies, and almost endless material on the internet help us see causes, identify conditions, and isolate the character flaws or disorders at the center of every Pandora matrix.

These problems are classed as personality disorders. Personality disorders such as narcissism, psychopathy, and sociopathy are common. Severe forms are found in pedophiles, abusers, molesters, rapists, and serial killers. Many personality disorders are considered untreatable. We generally isolate ourselves from severe cases we identify.

Moderate forms of personality disorders are quite common. One smiling case I will call Joe came to my office in a nice suit. "Look," he said to me. "I'll pay your full rate a month ahead of time. You can do what you want with the hour. Just tell my wife I am coming for counseling." Joe was an obvious narcissist, and I could do nothing to help him. God knows what he told his wife.

Joe wanted his wife's loyalty without offering loyalty in return. He wanted to look like a friend but operate like an enemy. How often do we wonder if the people who want our loyalty are really looking out for us? Have we been hurt or exploited by someone we thought would protect us?

Have we ever threatened someone to get our way or feel more secure? "Well, it wasn't a threat really," we tell ourselves. "It was more of a warning and justified under these conditions." What else could we do? We needed action!

Character defects emerge under pressure for most of us. Marriage conflicts, custody battles, church leadership, business demands, and government power reveal milder character flaws and create problems that might only get worse if we say anything. We are about as unsuccessful changing these milder forms of personality disorders as we are with severe ones.

In this book, we will examine Bible accounts and current Christian experience in various parts of the world and find what is needed for a Pandora problem to yield real character change instead of silence. Studying how severe character issues have been corrected can help us find solutions to the smaller ones that keep us quiet.

Something lacking

The easily identified person in the center of a Pandora problem distracts us from a corresponding deficit in the surrounding group.

Pandora problems exist because the group around the person with a personality disorder lacks a working solution. Correcting personality disorders requires solutions that take the surrounding group into account. The group must move from silent dread to active engagement. This poorly understood solution for the group will be the topic for our book.

People in the center of Pandora problems seem to lack something needed to be fully human. Scripture says that what is missing is "hesed/agape" (חֶסֶד/ἀγάπη). *Hesed* is attachment love.

What are the signs of hesed attachment? We can test hesed levels three ways. First, where there is hesed there is joy and lots of it. Second, as hesed rises so does one's spontaneous love for one's enemies. Third, low hesed results in low compassion. Compassion is how we translate "splagchnon" (σπλάγχνον) from the Greek. Hesed people splagchnon, that is, they share the pain of others, including any pain they might have caused themselves.

Godly character is built on hesed attachment love. Therefore, character transformation requires us to grow the hesed we lack. People do not begin their Christian life with love for enemies. God does not choose followers based on who loves enemies. Christian discipleship should therefore focus on growing hesed. Disciples should show very large increases in hesed.

"Love your enemies," Jesus said.[2] The prophet Isaiah announced, "The lion will eat straw like the ox,[3]" and "They shall not hurt nor destroy in all My holy mountain.[4]" Jesus and Isaiah expect God's Kingdom will profoundly change people's character for the better. Can that really happen?

As Fr. Ubald and I fixed breakfast together it became clear he was mystified by something. How could anyone be a Christian and not be deeply transformed? He had experienced untransformed congregants, seminarians, and church leaders. 45,000 of his parishioners were murdered in the genocide. Many of the killers were also his parishioners and claimed to be Christians.

As Fr. Ubald wondered aloud how some Christians avoided transformation, I realized that most Christians I knew wondered if anyone could be transformed! Watching Fr. Ubald, I knew that teaching enemies to love each other could be done. After the genocide, Fr. Ubald and his parish saw to it that killers, who thought they were Christians, were transformed.

---

2   Luke 6:27ff
3   Isaiah 65:25a
4   Isaiah 11:9a and 65:25b

The main effect of Christian life is (or should be) growing love in people who are less loving, less joyful, and less protective than people should be. Without transforming power, the Christian life is a miserable way to live and offers little to the world. Without character transformation, we are running out the clock until we die because the Kingdom of God seems ineffective here and now.

NARCISSISM IN CHURCHES

The first Pandora problem we must examine is narcissism in the church. A 2015 study estimated that somewhere between 96,300 and 112,350 churches in the USA currently have a narcissistic pastor.[5] Virtually all Christians will experience a narcissistic pastor during their lifetime. These extraordinarily high levels can only be explained if churches actively seek, support, sustain, promote, and propagate narcissistic leaders.

The most common reaction to *Rare Leadership*, the book about mature leadership and building a loyal and responsive group identity that I wrote with Dr. Marcus Warner, has been, "What do I do if there is a narcissistic predator in the leadership group at church?"

To a very significant extent, Christian churches are unable to recognize personality disorders and may even find these disorders desirable in leaders. If, as one study suggests, 30% to 90% of churches in the West are run by narcissists[6] we should not be surprised that these churches cannot correct the problem.

Consider the study by Zondag[7] that 90% of Dutch pastors were high scorers in narcissism. Not only do churches make good places for narcissistic predators to prosper, but churches often actively seek predators for leaders by favoring narcissists in the selection process.

Doctors Ball and Puls[8] found that both men and women pastors in Canada were 500% to 3,000% more likely to be narcissists than the general population. They state that, "While the statistical likelihood of a pastor regaining mental health after suffering NPD

5   "Frequency of Narcissistic Personality Disorder in Pastors: a Preliminary Study," R. Glenn Ball, D.Min, Darrell Puls. DRS., A Paper Presented to the American Association of Christian Counselors, Nashville, TN, September 26, 2015.
6   Ball and Puls.
7   Zondag, H. 2004. Just like other people: Narcissism among pastors. *Pastoral Psychology, 52,* 423–437.
8   Ball and Puls.

[narcissistic personality disorder] is small, it must be remembered that all things are possible with God."

Instead of suggesting character change through either therapy or Christian practices, Ball and Puls recommend that narcissism be treated like cancer and aggressively screened out of church ministry. Most churches do the same with pedophiles.

Do we expect narcissistic leaders will cure themselves or teach us to notice their problems? The Christianity churches practice seems more likely to feed victims to the predators than to change predators into protectors. Could it be there are flaws in the way we practice Christianity or does it simply not work for severe problems?

CHARACTER CHANGE IS A GROUP PROCESS.

Years of involvement in the places where character change happens (or doesn't) have led me to the solutions we will explore in this book. Solutions to Pandora problems come from changes in the group standing around the elephant-sized character problem and thinking, "It will only get worse if I say anything."

Sure enough, it will get worse if only one person speaks while the others wait in silent dread. A group-wide identity change is needed. The first essential character change is correcting group identity. Transformation of character requires a group who knows how to transform character.

Notice we are now talking about how to change the group before looking for ways to change the person in the middle. The Pandora problem exists and persists because the surrounding group has no answers. We will explore ways to enrich the group's options and strengthen the group's identity.

I have spent the last forty years trying to understand how people transform and sustain transformation. My search has led me to examine cults, abuse, mind control, terrorism, and government torture. I have studied crime scene investigation, serial killer profiling, and the children who kill. I have learned to help war veterans, trauma survivors, refugees, survivors of Jewish, Armenian and Tutsi genocides, political or religious mass killings in southern Sudan, Uganda, Nigeria, Colombia, Sri Lanka, and Southeast Asia. Exploring this suffering has revealed how people change for the better and worse in the presence of their enemies.

Transformation is never as clear as when a predator becomes a protector or an enemy becomes a friend. Many saints began life as narcissistic sociopaths. These individuals were deadly or pleasure-seeking, self-justified, and hardened. St. Paul, St. Francis, St. Augustine, and St. Ignacious of Loyola were all harmful individuals before they were transformed.

The popular song "Amazing Grace" was written by a sociopathic slave trader. John Newton was responsible for the torment, devastation and deaths of many slaves and families. Of course, on the surface John Newton was a sea captain and clergyman. In time he came to see a "wretch" inside. More than thirty years after leaving the slave trade he denounced it and slowly began to emerge as a protector. Charles Colson's transformation is still in the memory of older Americans. Beginning as a hard man, he emerged as an advocate for people in prison.

What are the factors I observed in these transformations? In every case, I see an interactive encounter with God. There are meaningful relationships with God's people who are willing to love their enemies. The person with character weakness begins to share the pain of others then shows a great increase in hesed. The very weaknesses that once were exploited become the places for attachments to grow. Instead of justifying themselves, people who transform accept shame for their previous way of life and become members of a new people and way of life.

Sustaining character change is more than simple transformation. Once again I learn from people who live with weakness and love their enemies. Understanding how people sustain character in terrible situations illuminates sustainable character with common problems we all have. The families of martyrs who love their enemies can teach us to love irritating people in church. We all have a tendency to start treating others like "enemies" when we are hurt. We tend to stop sharing their pain and withdraw. Examining Christians who came to love the predators that tracked and tried to kill them sheds light for me on how transformation is sustained.

By learning how transformations occur we discover why our current methods are not working well.

I entered the counseling profession at the time that culture was becoming aware of clergy molesting their constituents. The initial response from the churches was to ask clergy to repent, send them to counseling, and move them to a new community. The results were "repeat offending" in most cases – certainly all the cases I witnessed.

Western solutions have not done well treating sexual predators, pedophiles, narcissists, and sociopaths. Churches routinely run background checks to screen out perpetrators among volunteers, but where are churches offering transformation to the perpetrators they have caught? Yet, the history of the Christian church is built around stories of transformed lives. We will see that the solutions to narcissism and personality disorders use mechanisms in the brain that are ignored and even demonized by Western culture and American values.

Understanding hesed

One of the best researched topics across cultures and species is the powerful force of attachments. In biblical language, it is "hesed" in Hebrew or "agape" in Greek. Hesed can best be called "secure attachment" or "enduring love."

Attachment love is the kind of force that can form and transform character. Attachment love is the sort of love that bonds us for life to our parents, children, brothers, sisters, partners, and pets whether these prove to be worthy or wretched. It is the nature of attachment love to spring from much deeper in the brain than those elements that control our will. Therefore, we cannot simply will ourselves to love or, in the case of an abusive partner, to stop attachment by making a better choice.

Hesed is loyal, but hesed loyalty is built by joy. In Pandora problems loyalty brings very little joy. Pandora problems require loyalty around keeping quiet, not triggering trouble, and keeping the person in the center less dangerous.

Governments run by tyrants require great celebrations where participants who fail to smile enthusiastically disappear – never to be seen again. When loyalty is built through fear, strengths are good and weakness is bad.

Raising hesed levels changes the character of all human and spiritual interactions much like raising the level of water in a reservoir raises all the boats. While hesed is difficult to perceive directly, it is reflected in the degree of relational joy that is present.

Hesed is loyalty built around weakness. Discovery of a weakness in a hesed group brings help. Weakness creates places to help each other grow. Sharing weaknesses builds joyful, sheltering bonds. Loyalty grows out of joy to be together.

Winners and losers

Attachment love endures, so hesed is often translated "enduring love." Yet, for attachment to be good love it must not simply endure but also be deeply kind. Thus, hesed is also translated as "loving kindness."

Martha Stout from the Harvard Medical School and author of The Sociopath Next Door says, "If you take loving kindness out of the human brain, there's not much left except the desire to win."[9]

Without the power to produce loving kindness (hesed attachment) in people who are not hesed, Christianity can only hope to produce winners. However, this is a VERY peculiar kind of winner. Without hesed, winning amounts to making sure others lose. Narcissism and sociopathy are closely related this way. Each of these character disorders is driven to see others lose as its way to win.

Many people have attended church for years and never seriously considered loving their enemies.

This impulse to make others lose is suppressed when people have a strong group identity and normal social fears. Individuals who genetically are less fearful, along with those who actively produce fear to gain power, readily track and exploit weaknesses in others in order to win. Have you met them or seen them in the news?

The most notorious outlaw in the wild lumberjack days of the North Woods was John Sornberger aka Jack McWilliams. Jack was wanted by the law on 42 different criminal counts. Jack had the reputation as the most feared and hated predator in the state of

9   Stout, Martha. *The Sociopath Next Door: The Ruthless Versus the Rest of Us*. New York: Broadway Books, 2005.

Minnesota. His reputation as a fighter began at age twelve and he progressed to prizefighter, thief, thug, and pimp. McWilliams took great narcissistic pleasure in tormenting the cowardly sheriff of Bemidji. Stories about Jack lived on in Northwood's lore.

Years later, I attended school in Bemidji and came to know Jack's story through a book by Dr. Harry Rimmer.[10] Dr. Rimmer was a teacher and pastor both known and admired by my parents. Harry, himself a former prizefighter who grew up in lumber camps, recounts how the people of Minnesota watched Jack's character be profoundly changed after becoming a Christian. Jack, now John once again, received a pardon from Governor Johnson and went on to become as well known for his evangelism as he had been for his criminal ways. John no longer did whatever it took to win.

The vision given through Isaiah that, "They will not hurt or destroy in all My holy mountain,[11]" requires a religion capable of creating hesed (loving kindness) in predators. Nonetheless, many people have attended church for years and never seriously considered loving their enemies. Most predators are not changed by going to church. Instead, predators prosper in many churches where they find better hunting. Predators think good hunting is winning. In God's way of life, wolves who lie down with lambs win. Winners do not destroy.

To maintain its claim of being the fulfillment for Isaiah's prophesy, the church must produce changed predators (pedophiles, rapists, killers, narcissists, and psychopaths) whose new capacity to hesed/agape has changed their lives and destiny. Very few churches, pastors, or congregants express confidence that the Christianity they know and practice will transform narcissistic sociopaths, killers, abusers, or even an ordinary bad temper. Yet these very problems characterize people with low levels of hesed/agape love.

Why we fail to see transformation

This book proposes some reasons why the church in the West has failed to grow hesed/agape in predators and has become a religion for nice people. Churches rarely see character transformations if they . . .

---

10   *The Last of the Giants*, Harry Rimmer LL.D., copyright Research Science Bureau, Inc. 1948 and reprinted 2001 by Northern Canada Mission Distributors, Prince Albert, SK Canada.
11   Isaiah 11:9a NASB

1) Lose a group identity.

2) Focus on beliefs (will) over relationships (hesed).

3) Misuse the power of shame and emotions.

4) Accept self-justifications.

5) Hide weakness.

6) Do not love their enemies.

Expectation of transformation has been fading in America. The Greatest Generation did fairly well at managing their issues until they got really old. The wealthier Boomers found fewer things they needed to manage and more ways to express themselves. The Boomer's children saw Christianity as nice ideals that no one could actually follow in real life. By the end of the last millennium most elements of Christian character became unreachable ideals. Why even have impossible ideals?

It is way beyond the realm of this book to explore the factors from philosophy, technology, industrialization, migration, legal systems, economics, and many other sources that shaped the Western mind. We have come to rely on being civilized, affluent, educated, and legal rather than transformed. We resort to education, jobs, insight, correctional facilities, medication, and better choices to manage problems but rarely transform our inner selves.

This "Christian sin management" has neither convinced our children or our neighbors that Christians have answers. Christian self-management has not removed lust, anger, pornography, food cravings, debt, conflict, or anxiety. The result is a solid veneer we call our "image" that we must maintain together. Few even think to ask how we are doing at loving our enemies.

Most literature reviews declare that curing narcissism is hopeless.

Professional counselors achieve limited to no success treating narcissists. Counseling schools often tell students not to accept narcissists as clients. If we apply the reasons for counselor failures with narcissism to why churches rarely see transformation we discover some overlap.

1) Counseling is almost exclusively done in the absence of a community. Confidential sessions do not

effectively utilize or restore group identities or help the group around a Pandora problem.

2) Talk is cheap and claiming beliefs does not require any hesed attachment. Narcissists can affirm whatever makes them look good. With their brains in a non-relational mode, narcissists do not share the pain others feel and so have no guilt and will justify whatever it takes to make others lose. Cognitive interventions and talk therapy are particularly ineffective with personality disorders.

3) Few people, counselors, or communities are skilled at recovering from shame. Counselors are largely unable to stop narcissists from using emotions coercively outside the office.

4) Self-justification is the narcissist's specialty. Most counselors support and accept self-justifications that fit community values rather than recognizing self-justification as the worst of evils. Instead of accepting other people's explanations, narcissists feel attacked and must then defeat the enemy. Others will be condemned so that the narcissist is justified.

5) When they have problems in relationships, most people express how they were hurt. Expressing pain does not work with a predator who does not plan to share pain and will exploit weakness.

6) "Feeling therapy" makes predators more predatory and more effective. Expressing pain attracts an attack from narcissists who must be sure others lose. Narcissists punish rather than love those who do not treat the narcissist "right." If counselors identify the narcissism they will usually advise terminating relationship rather than loving an enemy.

Finding solutions that transform

If raising hesed levels builds disciples of Jesus, do we know how? We are admonished by churches to love but how much time have we spent in church practicing? Few discipleship programs focus on raising hesed levels. If spontaneous love for our enemies is the measure of success, do we check our results?

Since low hesed characterizes character disorders, it leaves in its wake narcissism, psychopathology, domination, predatory behavior, and greed. These character flaws will be passed from generation to generation of Christians rather than be corrected.

Change agents wonder why they are not more deeply changed by Christian practices. They know something more should be possible, but they don't know what it looks like. When change agents look at themselves, think about Jesus, wonder where life is going, or take time to pray, they become dissatisfied with who they are and what churches produce. Although they have grown and healed, they know they have not transformed enough. They need a hesed that transforms character.

Hesed is not choice.

The commonly preached idea that agape (hesed love) is a choice will not work in a living human brain. A Western Christian will focus on making better choices, building stronger beliefs, Bible studies and Christian practices such as prayer, attendance to church and small groups. Without trying to make an encyclopedia of these activities, we need to notice that they depend almost entirely upon improving beliefs and choices.

If the human brain was a tree, beliefs and choices would be the leaves on the top branches. Hesed would be the tree roots. Leaves are the last thing to grow on a tree and the first to fall off. Leaves feed the tree but support almost nothing. Without leaves a tree will eventually die and hesed love also dies without good choices. Yet, we are anchored by our love.

A will that is not nourished by love is a weak will. Attachment love is at the base of the brain while the will is in the top neurons. Hesed is not under the will's control. Even in the moment-to-moment operation of the brain, all the hesed motivation and character elements load in first, long before we reach the top branches of the brain where our beliefs and choices hold on like birds on a windy day.

Tenacity can be achieved through choice (by some people some of the time) but attachment love works differently. The brain centers that produce attachment love are way below the cortex and out of willful control.[12]

---

12   See *The Solution of Choice* by Warner and Wilder.

We intuitively know that attachment is not a choice when we observe lovers, enemies, blended families, and parents with babies. We know that attachment cannot be ended by choice as we watch deaths of loved ones, divorces, abusive relationships, and church splits. What we all understand (but struggle to explain) is that our brain does not ask our permission to love, to attach, or to stop loving.

Hesed is not built alone.

Attachment love for others cannot develop individually. How do we attach when there is no one there? Growing the healthy hesed of a group identity requires a group that practices with us. Likewise, we do not learn hesed for our enemies without group practice. The group around a Pandora problem is in the right place to practice loving enemies.

The extent to which the Western mind becomes individualistic is hard to exaggerate. The bigger the problem the more we deal with it one-on-one. Saying something makes a problem worse when we expect solutions to be private. Places where Christianity changes people's character are less focused on individualistic solutions and more focused on becoming a people who love their enemies.

Fr. Ubald taught his parishioners to believe in love for ten years only to see his parish members kill each other. After the genocide he changed his approach. The parish community prepared both the survivors and perpetrators to love each other. Together they became a people who confessed, loved, and forgave. We will need to learn a great deal about hesed groups before we can duplicate his results. Most churches teach people what to believe but allow them to stay hidden enemies.

Hesed is necessary but not enough.

No transformation into the character of Christ will happen without raising hesed. Hesed is missing in people with personality disorders. Yet, raising hesed by itself is not enough to create good character. Raising hesed is like watering the ground – something will grow but we might get big weeds and still have nothing to eat unless our farming includes more than watering. Character transformation requires healthy shame messages, rejecting self-justification, and other elements we will consider in later chapters.

Transformation cannot be done alone.

If you are still reading this book you are almost certainly a change agent. You are dissatisfied with the amount of transformation you have achieved. If you could change on your own you would have done it by now, but there are things we cannot do alone. To change our character so we love our enemies requires help from our identity group. An identity group is made up of those who are our kind of people. For Christians, our identity group is intended to be the church. Our Christian identity group needs some changes.

We will need to make some deep changes in our Western Christian ways if we are to be a group that can change character. To face the narcissistic Christian in us we need to rethink things we thought we understood. The group study guide companion to in this book was written and tested by Barbara Moon to help create that change.

Books that make us think are not easy to read. This book requires us to see something in the ancient spiritual life that we do not see well as a culture. You may wonder at first how some chapters contribute to our progress because the conclusions come together in later chapters. We will work our way through one topic at a time. Some ideas we must take apart while other ideas we must put together.

Understanding character change

Our Western solutions to building Christian character do not fit the way that the brain runs or how the brain makes changes. Western theology is built around medieval models of the human mind that were modified to be more individualistic by the Enlightenment. Christians in other cultures read the same Scriptures we do and see different solutions. Our individualistic culture makes Christianity more of a *faith* we believe than an *attachment group* we love. We fail to see ourselves as a people, a tribe, or a new family. When we read that we are a family we smile and say "that is true," but our bond seems more like a metaphor than a glue.

What makes Christianity stand out from other religions is how we are to love our enemies.

Understanding how hesed group identity will transform character for the better is going to be a stretch for most of us. The process isn't perfect. Group identities have issues. Villages form character with defects. Strong group identities are needed to change character, but every identity group has defects.

Consider how many times your family has migrated over the last few centuries. At one time in the past, your family lived in a village that knew all four of your ancestor's grandparents. It was impossible to imagine life that was not connected to everyone we knew – they were our people. We are that number of generations away from intuitively understanding how a group identity works.

Church groups become an expression of culture.

Churches are a lot like car dealerships – they keep the customers coming back and offering attractive choices but they do little to design and build a different kind of transportation. Dealerships do not produce better power plants – engines are all designed somewhere else.

In the same way, churches use existing fears and desires people developed outside the church as the motivational power plants. Hesed character requires quite different motivation than what we bring to church from our outside life. Character and motivation are not created by what we hear, believe, or choose. Transformation requires a new kind of identity group that's not what culture gave us. Loving enemies requires churches to become more like designers than sales people.

The small groups in Western churches are better suited for building narcissism than for loving enemies. If we attempt to transform character using the average Christian church group, that group would disintegrate. As our culture values comfort, groups will stay comfortable and resist transformation. Groups will amplify pooled dysfunctions, resentments, and even hatred. Groups will generate affairs, take sides listening to self-justifications, spread shared biases, and dislike weakness. Groups will fall apart when real issues requiring transformation arise. Mostly, groups will conclude they have a Pandora problem, and things will only get worse if something is said.

RAISING HESED IN A GROUP IDENTITY CHANGES CHARACTER.

We have already seen the first principle in character change is a transforming group identity. People around a Pandora problem must see an opportunity for something new to emerge.

The second transformational principle is that identity groups must raise hesed. What makes Christianity stand out from other religions is how we are to love our enemies. The most effective way to raise hesed is learning to love our enemies.

Jesus instructs us that "you (plural) love your (plural) enemies. "The plural "you" in Matt 5:44, Luke 6:27, and Luke 6:35 suggests that hesed be done as a group. While the plural could simply come from addressing a group of individuals, brain function suggests a reason the passage might intentionally be plural. For the human brain, the path to loving our enemies depends upon our group identity. We learn to love enemies because that is what "our people" do.

Character is transformed while raising hesed levels in our identity group. How we hesed others becomes a practical topic in communities that produce transformation. Our character is open for discussion, our weaknesses are expected, and we learn to love at those moments when people we normally love feel like enemies.

In the next chapter we will expose the way narcissism becomes camouflaged in church culture. At the center of each Pandora problem is someone who claims to be our friend but can act more like an enemy.

If You Are Ready

Group Exercises

Knowing information and applying concepts are different realities. *If You Are Ready* guides groups through a laboratory experience designed to equip the group around a Pandora problem. *If You Are Ready* exercises follow a clear progression but do not match the topics in the chapters directly. Instead, the *If You Are Ready* exercises have six goals:

1) Experience finding a group identity.

2) Experience strengthening a Christian group identity.

3) Experience building hesed.

4) Experience correcting of self-justification.

5) Experience being helped to love an "enemy."

6) Building loyalty around weakness.

This is not an introductory book or a manual on how to form and run groups. These exercises will be helpful if you are ready, but let me suggest other helpful resources. Running this group exercise will be easier if you have experience with:

- **Building relational skills** – *Transforming Fellowship* by Chris Coursey, *Relational Skills in the Bible* by Coursey & Brown, or THRIVE Today Training

- **Building joy** – *Joy Starts Here* by Wilder, Khouri, Coursey, & Sutton

- **Building awareness of God** – *Joyful Journey* by Wilder, Kang, Loppnow & Loppnow

- **Building Christian community** – *Living From the Heart Jesus Gave You* by Friesen, Wilder, Bierling, Koepcke, & Poole

- **Building belonging** – *Connexus*

- **Leadership** – *Rare Leadership* by Warner & Wilder

If You Are Ready is designed as a ninety minute experience in group identity with a group size of about fifteen to thirty. For the most creativity, do exercises in multiple small groups and then compare the results as a whole group.

If You Are Ready

Group Exercise for Chapter One

1. As a group create a list of as many characteristics of a Christ-like group identity as you can in fifteen minutes. The list should complete the phrase, "We are people who . . . "

2. Take the assessment on the next page titled "My Group Identity Awareness Level." Keep in mind that some of these topics have not been covered in the first chapter so you will answer from what you understand today.

3. Gather in groups of about five people. Keep in mind that some of these topics have not been covered in the first chapter so you will work from what you understand today to discuss the answers to your questions.

4. After you discuss your answers to the assessment consider where this group is starting on the following issues:

    a.   Do we need to notice who we are more carefully? If so, what steps will we take in this group?

    b.   Do we need to be more active in sharing each other's pain? What help will I want from this group?

    c.   How well do we currently practice healthy shame messages?

    d.   How well do we currently notice self-justification?

    e.   How well do we notice when our mind is reacting to others as though they were against us?

    f.   How do we expect our group will respond to weakness and, in particular, character weakness?

5. As a whole group decide if we are ready to try this group experience together.

My Group Identity Awareness Level

1. Group identity

How many times in the last week have I felt I belonged with a group? _____

How many factors can I name right now that make the group where I belong unique? _____

How many times in the last week have I thought of ways to strengthen my group? _____

2. Shared pain

How often in the last week have I felt the pain of someone who is important to me? _____

What three things most make me uncomfortable and want to withdraw from others?

    1.

    2.

    3.

What one thing most makes me think "They had that coming (deserved it)"?

3. Exchange of healthy shame messages

How many healthy shame messages have I received this last week? _____

How many healthy shame messages have I delivered this last week? _____

How many times have I expressed appreciation for a healthy shame message this last week? _____

4. Combating self-justification

> How many self-justifications have I noticed myself make this last week? _____

> What seems to be my main area of self-justification this week? _____

> How many self-justifications have I noticed others give this week? _____

5. Loving enemies spontaneously

> How many times this week did I notice my mind switching into a less than loving state? _____

> What most made me feel that someone was against me this week? _____

> How long does it take me to become consciously aware that I (or someone else) have switched into a mental "enemy mode"? _____

> What relational weakness causes the most "shutdowns" with people I usually like? _____

6. Building loyalty around weakness

> How many times this week have I noticed someone had a weakness and I stepped in to help him or her? _____

> This week did I do more to hide my weaknesses or to let others see my limitations? _____

> How many times this week did I have helpful conversations about weakness? _____

CHAPTER TWO

The Narcissism Trap

"Will you really annul My judgment? Will you condemn Me that you may be justified?"
Job 40:8 (NASB)

The current popular trend in writing dictates that every chapter should start with a catchy story illustrating the author's point. The story that needs to open this chapter is your experience with a Pandora problem. Stop and think of a situation that really bothers you but would get worse if you said anything.

Take a moment to remember your Pandora problem because we will spend this chapter analyzing it together. We begin with these questions:

- Would you be reluctant to talk openly about your story?

- Will someone else get hurt if you talk?

- Are people afraid of repercussions if someone speaks?

- Would a group know who you were talking about if you didn't mention names?

- Do you feel like you are dealing with an enemy at times?

- Is someone very good at justifying her or his position?

- Will someone in the group always lose?

- Does it feel like there is meanness involved somehow?

- Is there no hope for a solution?

- Do you know of other Pandora problems?

When your life has been touched by narcissism you feel like the mouse between the cat's paws. Sometimes you may feel you are watching a cat play with your heart, your church board, a department in your company, a neighborhood school or your grandchildren's lives. You know that your life (and perhaps the lives of those you love) has become someone's game. This chapter will help us understand your story.

What is narcissism?

The word "narcissism" came from the Greek fable told by Ovid about Narcissus who fell in love with his own reflection in the pond. Real life narcissists do not like looking at themselves at all – they like looking good to others.

In modern culture, narcissism is a term for being self-centered and self-absorbed. Yet narcissism is more than being centered on "me." It is a dynamic game that works according to predictable rules. As long as the narcissist sets the rules of the game, the narcissist is unbeatable. The options are . . .

- Play a narcissist's game by narcissist rules. The narcissist wins.

- Play like a narcissist. When narcissists play against each other the best predator generally wins.

- Don't play.

- Change rules.

Why doesn't everyone simply quit the narcissist's game? There are consequences. When a family member (or something we deeply value) is hostage to a narcissistic game, the losses from walking away can be huge. It is hard for any individual to leave the game if the whole community or family system is still playing.

"The only winning move is not to play." This is the conclusion reached by the computer in the movie *WarGames*[1] when it computes the total mutual destruction its game of global thermonuclear war produces. Most of what we are likely to read about narcissism will conclude that if we don't play we must simply have nothing to do with the narcissist. Instead of abandoning difficult people in order to make our lives easier, let's consider changing the group around a Pandora problem.

---

1   WarGames, a 1983 motion picture nominated for three Academy Awards written by Lawrence Lasker and Walter F. Parkes. UAA Films.

Group rules

Perhaps nothing makes the topic of narcissism more difficult to understand than the extent to which narcissism mimics human nature, social values, and group rules. We will look at three narcissistic game rules that hide easily in our values: 1) the best justification wins, 2) I should not have to suffer, and 3) weakness is bad. We will examine the first rule in this chapter and the other two rules in Chapter Three.

Let's start with the central rule that keeps narcissists in charge, makes most marital and family counseling with narcissists futile, and dominates in most group conflicts.

RULE ONE: THE BEST JUSTIFICATION WINS.

Self-justification refers to any tactic we use to keep from admitting wrong or taking blame. A narcissist is always self-justified. We believe justifying our actions is a good thing. We will see how self-justification creates a trap that almost 100% of people believe cannot catch them. Everyone who believes they cannot be caught will still be trapped at the end of this book and trying to figure out the right thing to do to escape.

We expect people to justify themselves if they can. From childhood we appeal to "fair" and "not fair." In playgrounds or the principal's office, the best justification usually wins. When a better justification (in our view) does not win, we think it should have won. Consequently, whoever justifies himself/herself best gains greater power. Courts and public opinion are heavily swayed by whomever justifies their case the best. We hold presidential debates and, while we are sure all of them are lying to us, we vote for the ones who justify themselves the best in our eyes. Self-justification is just so common, comes so easily, and so fits our expectation that we wonder, "What else could you say?"

Humans spend a great deal of time, money, and energy on their "image management" as Dr. Dallas Willard called it.[2] A major part of image management is justifying one's actions. Justifying oneself in a way that looks good greatly improves the chances of getting one's own way. Even people who claim their position is justified by truth, fairness, and honesty frequently use these values to make themselves look better.

---

2   Dallas Willard, "Spirituality Made Hard," The Door, May/June 1993. p.129.

Church fights, like marital conflicts and divorces, are dominated by the people who make themselves look best. Often the winner speaks in very spiritual terms and cites all the values people hold dear. Yet, what justifies a thing for one person often does not work for another. To a millennial, "That makes me uncomfortable," may be enough justification to oppose the government while an appeal to authority may justify supporting tyrants to another person. Either way, we are listening to people justify themselves.

Self-justification is at the center of the narcissist's game. Narcissists are skilled at it. Let's break down how self-justification creates a Pandora problem and a group trap.

SELF JUSTIFICATION TRAPS THE GROUP.

The trap that holds a group around a narcissist has three elements: 1) self-justification, 2) trusting our own judgment (sense of good or evil), and 3) the avoidance of shame. Together, these elements create the perfect trap. Examining this trap will help us understand the ancient wisdom and reveal a way of escape.

Narcissism TRAP element one – Self-justification

The first element in the trap that ensures "it will make things worse if I say anything" is a group that accepts self-justification. Allowing self-justification empowers the narcissist's game rule that "the best justification wins." Before we go further, what are the justifications you remember hearing in your Pandora example for this chapter? Did the group take time to listen to justifications or take them seriously? Did those justifications stop the group in its tracks? The answer is almost always "yes."

Narcissists justify themselves very well, but narcissists are not the only ones to justify themselves. Talk radio reveals how people listen to self-justification as though it contains value. Notice that "what I am doing is right" is the heart of self-justification. Nothing provides better self-justification than having God, psychology, expert opinion, authority, reason, and all other good things back "me."

"Doing what was right in their own eyes" is the worst thing God can say about people. The very thing that God considers the worst element of society – doing what you think is right based on your justifications – is highly valued by people.

If we accept self-justification we are stuck. The moment we counter the narcissist by justifying ourselves (either proving we are good or avoiding shame) we are playing into the narcissist game. If we reply to self-justification with our own self-justification we are trapped. The narcissist wins.

The ancient figure of Job is considered to be a model for human life by Muslims, Jews, and Christians. In Job's dialogue with God, God tells Job that self-justification is annulling God's judgment.[3] When we justify ourselves, we condemn someone else. Human judgment about who is good justifies me at the expense of condemning you and God. This is a deadly trap.

Understanding the consequences of self-justification will take most of this book. We will consider common experiences, statistical proofs, and biblical evidence that people cannot calculate the right thing to do and therefore can never really justify themselves. Yet, humans continue thinking, "There must be a right way to justify myself." Every side in a war, every partner in a domestic fight, and every party to a lawsuit argues that they are right. Parents and rebellious children justify what they do and say. Parents justify killing a fetus. The medical establishment justifies killing a patient with cancer by lethal injection and not killing a serial killer using the same injection because it might cause pain.

> **If we reply to self-justification with our own self-justification we are trapped.**

The winners in self-justification fights will usually be the ones who offer the "least painful path" as their justification. Look a little deeper and we see that self-justification promotes whatever I find least painful. Therefore, the process of self-justification pits what is painful to me against what is painful to you.

While they love the game, experienced narcissists will make sure they have hostages who will get hurt if their self-justification fails. Narcissists want to be sure others lose. It is not enough simply to prove they are right. Because people are easily persuaded that the least painful way is "right," narcissists want victims who will be hurt if the narcissist does not win.

The narcissist will make sure to argue that if someone (whoever the group values) is hurt, it is the group's fault. Had the group

---

3   Job 40:8

listened, the pain would all have been prevented. How good of them to warn us! Narcissists portray themselves as friends while acting like enemies, exploiting weaknesses, and refusing to share any pain they create. In Chapter Three, we will see how dangerous it can be to block shared pain.

Narcissism TRAP element two – My own judgment

The best justification wins means the self-justified narcissist must always be good. One narcissist will be a good liberal while another is a good conservative, one will be a good atheist and another a good shaman, one a good gambler and another a good Bible believer, but each narcissist will want to be good and determine group standards.

Self-proclaimed goodness sets up an almost irresistible invitation to an argument. Whoever is being hurt by the self-justification, dropping in the public's opinion, or looking like the bad one will want to prove the opposite is true. Now we are in a trap and locked into the narcissist's game.

Narcissists will insist that problems be decided on the basis of who deserves condemnation and will come armed with proof it is not them. Any audience foolish enough to trust its own judgment will become the power-base for the narcissist's win. An audience is all that the narcissist needs to dish out the judgment and condemnation. The group around a Pandora problem always hosts and empowers the game – be it a community, a counselor, a church, friends, or foes. Church groups will hear justifications that sound spiritual, but a narcissist will readily switch justifications in another group with different values.

The camouflage around the trap

Most Christians, (along with most people) think we can judge what is right by adding what our religion or culture believes is good into our own judgment system. Most people believe so strongly they can tell good from evil that it is hard to believe I am questioning the obvious. They can figure out what is right using the Bible and experience! Therefore, most Christians will not believe what I am going to say next.[4] ***Every time we use our own judgment to decide good and evil, we get it wrong.*** Every time!

---

4   For a more complete discussion of knowing good and evil see the discussion on true and false knowing in chapter five of *Living from the Heart Jesus Gave You*, Friesen et al 1999.

Adam and Eve's desire to decide for themselves what was good and evil is what theologians call "original sin." We want to believe that the original sin can be sanctified and justified if we soak it in prayer, Scripture, theology, meditation, logic, or some form of spiritual practice. Perhaps by properly soaking our thoughts in truth we will know the right thing to do?

Let us examine the size of the task involved with knowing good and evil in real life situations. While this mathematical discussion may seem long and detailed, we need to reach total certainty that self-justifications are always wrong and a worthless waste of time.

The first element in knowing the right thing to do is to determine "how many things govern what is right that are true at the same time." We will start with the Jewish answer that there are 613 laws in the Old Testament that are true at the same time.[5]

These 613 laws create 2^{613} possible combinations of sacred laws that must be considered for every situation. That number is approximately 33,992,831,540,273,094,316,133,645,219,358,000,000,0 00,000,000,000,000,000,000,000,000,000,000,000,000,000,000,0 00,000,000,000,000,000,000,000,000,000,000,000,000,000,000,0 00,000,000,000,000,000,000,000,000,000,000,000,000,000,000,000 with the last 153 places rounded off to zero. We have a minimum of this many options to consider for every "right thing to do" decision.

The mind has trouble with numbers that large so let's simplify this number to the scientific notation of 3.4 times 10^{184}. Next, let's ignore the 3.4 times and only consider the multiplier. To put 10^{184} in perspective, let's compare this multiplier to things we know. We have 10^{13} brain cells. There are fewer than 10^{24} known stars. There are 10^{80} atoms in the observable universe. Thus if every atom in the universe was one nerve cell in our brain we would not have enough brain cells to have one for each option we must consider to calculate the right thing to do. Calculating the right thing to do requires a brain larger than the whole universe and larger by a lot!

Let us suppose that every single atom in the known universe became another universe the same size as our universe. All those universes together would have 10^{160} atoms – still quite a bit short of the 10^{184} options we are considering. If we repeat the process of

---

5   There are a few more laws in the New Testament but we will leave them aside for this discussion. To keep numbers simple (and smaller) we will not consider the possibility that some of God's laws have more than two possible responses. When laws create multiple possibilities then the number of alternatives is much, much greater. But let's stay simple.

creating a universe of universes as many times as there are stars in the universe we now have enough atoms to multiply by 3.4 and have one atom for each possible answer. A universe of universes multiplied as many times as there are stars multiplied again by 3.4 would produce enough atoms for each atom to represent one choice your brain must consider to calculate the right thing to do.

If you still think that you or the narcissist of choice is capable of making this calculation correctly and justifying him or herself, let me propose another thought.

Suppose what is right and wrong is actually cosmic? That is, good is about how everything in the universe should work together over time. If so, we actually need to consider the right answer for everyone and not just for me. Whatever makes all things work together for good is what is right. The right thing to do must work for the good of all the people who love God across all history and not simply comply with 613 true principles at any given moment.

Is there a biblical reason to believe that good is cosmic? St. John heard in a vision that only one Being in the universe was able to understand and bring all history into harmony.[6] This is the Bible's standard for what is good. Humility is in order when dealing with more people than we can know, in a universe much bigger than we can grasp over a history much longer than we can track. We can never justify ourselves intelligently.

If God provides an active presence that engages our thoughts and guides us to truth, then there is an alternative way to know what is right. If God is inert, and religion is a set of true beliefs and practices, then we are left with no higher appeal than our own judgment. Without God's active intelligence in our lives, religion becomes people quoting God to justify themselves. The narcissist wins.

The simple math reveals that viable, human self-justification is impossible. We are therefore extremely unwise to accept self-justification from anyone. We should not listen to the narcissist's judgments and justifications or be guided by our own. We should not play by self-justification rules. Before we believe anyone's justification let's be sure to check if his or her head is bigger than the universe.

---

6   Revelation 5

Narcissism TRAP element three – Avoiding shame

The best justification wins is built around justifications that avoid pain. Shame is painful and a natural response to a loss of joy. Shame is a pain narcissists will not accept. When someone is not glad to be with us we hang our heads and our smiles run away.

Healthy shame is a very helpful corrective state if we use it to create better relationships. Shame is a major force in socialization and character formation. Hesed communities use healthy shame for growth.

Shame is not helpful if we lack a clear way to return to joy. While healthy shame is needed for self-improvement, it quickly becomes toxic in the absence of compassion. Narcissists cannot tell the difference between a healthy invitation to change character and toxic shame. Narcissists treat all shame as though it was toxic. Narcissists have not learned a relational recovery mechanism, so they stay in shame and the shame turns toxic. Avoiding shame is the driving power behind narcissism.

Recovering from shame is a learned response. We must learn how to recover joyful relationships after a "joy killer" breakdown. Recovering from shame becomes a relational "reset." If we had screens on our foreheads they would read, "Your relationship link needs to restart." Correcting ourselves and restarting joyful engagement in 90 seconds or less is optimal.

Narcissists treat all shame as though it was toxic.

When families, groups, and cultures do not use shame relationally, bad things happen. Toxic shame does not raise hesed in relationships. Instead of self-improvement, toxic shame condemns us. Judgment that decrees who is "bad" is condemnation and always produces toxic shame. Our sense of identity becomes "I am bad." Alternately, we condemn whoever is causing us "shame pain," and they become our "bad enemy." Toxic shame becomes a weapon against the "enemies" who cause the narcissist shame. Toxic shame is easily created where people accept self-justification and condemnation.

Without healthy shame there is no transformation. A healthy shame message reminds us that we are not acting like our best selves and calls us back to our identity group. Without an identity group around us to teach us to love our enemies, we make enemies suffer and lose using toxic shame.

Without healthy shame there is no transformation. Take a moment to review your Pandora story for this chapter. Was there a sick and sinking feeling when the person in the center heard something that should trigger healthy shame? Did the person in the center learn from the shame and become a better person? Did the person in the center create toxic shame in return?

Learning from healthy shame requires a hesed community.

The relational pain when our identity group is not glad to be with us helps us change. Relational shame does not break hesed love. We are not isolated even when we feel healthy shame. Hesed people will see our shame and teach us to be our best self. We can learn to recover from shame.

Building loyalty (hesed) means helping each other to grow a new and stronger self in the places we are weak. Where we are weak we frequently don't express Christ-like character. Even loyal people are not very glad to be with us when we have forgotten to embody Jesus. Instead of joy, our identity group will give us a healthy shame message saying, "It is not like us to act that way."

A community that does not use healthy shame to build more authentically joyful relationships is the seedbed for future narcissism. Without practice using shame to build character in a hesed identity group the next generation does not learn how to return to joyful relationships when corrected. The results are that all shame messages will feel toxic rather than being a way to discover our Christ-like selves.

It is time to ask how well we receive a healthy shame message.

- Do others have their stomachs tighten at the thought of correcting me?
- Do I resent when people say I have character weaknesses?
- Does my mind fill with why others are wrong when they complain about me?
- Do I think others should have known better or gotten out of my way when they say I hurt them?

46

We may have found our inner narcissist – and we all have one. Will our group listen to our justifications or teach us how to hesed our enemies? Can I tell you why I am not glad to be with you right now? Can you tell me? Does our group need some practice with healthy shame? Most of us could use improvement.

TWO VARIETIES OF NARCISSISM

As we explore narcissism we should know that narcissism manifests in two forms. Both forms of narcissism can be noticed when narcissists discover someone is not happy with them. In the more familiar form, a narcissist will turn the problem back on others saying, "No, you are the problem! I am justified being unhappy with you right now!" We call this form that attacks others *peacock narcissism*.

In the second form, a narcissist reacts to shame by exaggerating how bad we think the narcissist is. We will call the response *skunk narcissism*. The skunk will keep beating him or herself until we "take back" what we said. We must convince the skunk narcissist that he or she is quite wonderful before the self-beating stops. This second form of narcissism sometimes passes for humility. Peacock and skunk patterns often alternate generations in families. As you reflect on your Pandora story which patterns do you see?

Our people do not accept justifications – we love our enemies.

We have looked at the number one rule of narcissism: the best justification wins. We examined evidence that self-justification is nonsense and harmful. Self-justification blocks us from using shame for self-improvement. Self-justification produces severe character weakness. Self-justification results in condemnation of others that makes others feel like enemies.

Building better character requires healthy shame messages from a hesed identity group. We are loyal people who are learning to hesed our enemies instead of rejecting their weaknesses. When we hear self-justification we see weakness. We help others accept healthy shame.

Self-justification by itself does not create a Pandora problem. What makes something a Pandora problem is how it just gets worse when we say something. In the next chapter we discover why.

If You Are Ready
Group Exercise for Chapter Two

Today's group identity affirmation

Repeat together, "We are a people who see what God is building in others."

In groups of about five people tell each other why this characteristic matters to you. (5 minutes)

Today's healthy shame message practice

In groups of about five people create a healthy shame message for me when I exaggerate my achievements slightly. (5 minutes)

Note: A healthy shame message states "we do not" and then states who we are with a Christ-like character response.
"We do not _____, we _____."

Tell each small group's statement to the whole group. (5 minutes)

Today's withstanding self-justification practice

Self-justification: I don't need to pray about it. I know what God is going to say.

In groups of about five people make a list of the weaknesses that lie behind this self-justification. What would a hesed community do to be sure these weaknesses do not prevail? (10 minutes)

Report each small group's conclusions to the whole group. (5 minutes)

Today's loving my enemy practice

This exercise is like texting with God. Write the impression that comes to your mind. Start with something that makes you grateful then your impression of God's response. Next read the question and write your impression of God's response that gives you peace. (5 minutes)

1. Dear God, I am thankful:
2. My dear child:
3. God, when has someone felt like an enemy to me this week?
4. What do You want me to know about loving them?

Read what you have written in groups of about five people. Do not explain what you wrote. Check for a sense of peace after you read. (5 minutes)

Group identity: Exercise 1

1. Discuss the following three problems as a group. (15 minutes total for the 3)

   a. What events or topics make us shudder to say we are Christians?

   b. What are the characteristics others will attribute to us if we say we are Christian?

   c. What impact have the conflicts between Christians produced during your lifetime?

2. Discuss the following three possibilities as a group. (15 minutes total for the 3)

   a. When have I been proud to be a Christian?

   b. What Christian characteristics do I long to see in a group where I belong?

   c. What is the closest I have come to belonging to a Christian group I admire?

3. What characteristic do I most have to offer to a Christian group identity? Write one word or phrase naming the Christian characteristic you embody on a card or name tag. For the remainder of the exercise time (about 15 minutes) stand and go around the group asking others about their main Christian characteristic and explaining your main characteristic to them.

Repeating today's group identity affirmation

Repeat together, "We are a people who see what God is building in others."

CHAPTER THREE

When Narcissism Becomes a Choice

The merciful (hesed) man does himself good,
But the cruel man does himself harm.
Proverbs 11:17 (NASB)

Families or communities that justify themselves will also avoid shame, giving narcissism every possible chance to develop. Does this make narcissism the fate of a poor victim? Self-justified families rarely use shame to build joyful identities. Is narcissism Mother's fault because she would not give us a healthy shame message?

Blake and Jake are twins. From birth, Jake screamed when he didn't get his way. When Blake could crawl he did anything to keep Jake happy. Blake gave Jake his own food, toys, clothes, or whatever Jake wanted. When they were adults, Blake would buy shoes and food for homeless people while Jake would buy houses for himself. When deciding who will suffer, some people choose "you" and some choose "me." In a much-related way, some will fight their own narcissism while others enhance theirs. No external cause explains the difference. How much I will suffer for the sake of others governs the development of narcissism as a lifestyle.

RULE TWO: I SHOULD NOT HAVE TO SUFFER.

I should not have to suffer. Is this truth self-evident? If so, every person, system, or belief that makes me suffer is bad. Whatever I do to stop my suffering is at least partially justified. What could be more obvious?

Avoiding suffering provides a central cultural value whether we are discussing starving children or death row. Medicine and therapy reduce suffering. I should be able to buy marijuana, receive heroin, be euthanized, get a divorce, not have to listen to people who disagree with me, and have this tooth pulled to reduce my suffering. Almost every divisive issue in culture can be justified by reducing suffering for some group.

At least two things are missing from the statement, "I should not have to suffer." The first is a sense that I am larger than a single individual, and the second is the sense that some suffering carries value. A better statement would be, "We should not have to suffer needlessly."

When who I am (thus who I protect from suffering) only includes me as an individual then social pain no longer produces better relationships. I become unbothered by the pain experienced by anyone who is not serving my interests. In fact, their pain helps me win. A narcissist or someone with sociopathic tendencies saying, "I should not have to suffer" means "Don't get in my way." When narcissists add "needlessly" it means, "If you don't want to suffer then let me win." People who let others suffer justify their narcissism.

What turns narcissism into a noxious force is choosing "Better you be hurt than me." Preferring that others do the hurting also results in a rejection of shared pain. Without shared pain the brain operates in a predator configuration taking advantage of the pain others feel. Self-justification without sharing pain quickly becomes predatory. For predators, life is "I win and you lose."

We call people who are unperturbed by others' suffering *sociopathic* if those who are undisturbed by others' suffering are anxious and *psychopathic* if they are fearlessly cold. Either way, without sharing the pain others feel, our minds place them in a "not my people" category used for prey, enemies, and threats. In general, we share the pain of our people but use our enemy's pain and weaknesses against them.

RULE THREE: WEAKNESS IS BAD.

Almost every human culture agrees that it is dangerous and therefore bad to be weak. Do we want a weak pastor or weak parent? Do we want to be a weak employee or work for a weak firm? Weaknesses frequently draw shame messages which create additional risks for narcissists.

Weakness is quickly noticed. If we think we might be attacked or exploited, we want to hide our weakness. Predators look for weakness they can use to their advantage. Protectors also look for weaknesses. Protectors see weaknesses as something to defend, heal, and nurture in order to create growth.[1] Predators build loyalty around strengths, and protectors build loyalty (hesed) around weakness.

Predator survival favors the top predator. Success requires learned predator skills. Predator skills generally involve becoming stronger, noticing weaknesses in one's prey, and learning to exploit those weaknesses. What causes pain to the prey helps the predator win.

Consider the predatory habits of a fellow mammal – the orca – sometimes called a killer whale. The lead predator in the pod is usually a grandmother orca who is leading a group of her daughters. Grandmother searches for a mother gray whale with a baby. The grandmother orca uses her understanding of mother-baby relationships and the need for the baby whale to breathe to find a way to drown the baby gray.

PREDATORS
build loyalty around
strengths.

PROTECTORS
build loyalty around
weakness.

The orcas have found several weaknesses to exploit. Together the orcas separate the mother and baby gray and then use their bodies to keep the small baby gray from surfacing as the orcas know they all need to breathe. The orcas feast on the baby's tongue (a sort of delicacy) and often leave the rest of the baby whale uneaten. The mother gray's loss is not shared pain for the predator orca mothers and grandmothers.

Our brains are born already wired to see the world through predator eyes. "Babies are not predators!" we might say. But to the baby, the world is there to eat. All the baby's brain needs to figure out is how to get it into the mouth. Eating everything within reach is what babies need to do, but we must outgrow this response as our power and control increases.

Learning self-control is mostly about learning to protect others. We learn to wait instead of immediately eating everything. We

---

1   For more see *Joy Starts Here*, Wilder, Khouri, Coursey and Sutton, Shepherd's House, 2012 – chapters 3 and 4.

are learning to become protectors. After years of training, our protector responses can become stronger than the prewired predator responses. This growth is not automatic and is greatly shaped by the group where a child develops. Groups with a protector group identity provide the best training.[2]

Learning deception

Predators generally pick the weakest prey and are more successful when undetected. Prey will attempt to escape once they spot a predator. Narcissists are predators toward their own group so narcissists need to deceive others. To hide weakness, avoid shame, and cover their predatory ways, narcissists must lie.

An excellent way for a human predator to hide is to announce and even believe, "I am benevolent." This self-justification sounds even better if wrapped in spiritual, psychological, educational, financial, and social values.

Narcissists eventually believe many of their own lies! Deceiving oneself is not difficult. Once I believe my own justifications I can sincerely convince others of my benevolence. Narcissists rewrite history, spin stories, redefine words, and color actions to justify themselves. But can a person really con themselves? Can someone not care or share the pain he or she produces? Can a person bond with other people and then use that relationship to take advantage of them? The answer is yes. About 15% of the population does exactly that.[3] We are now talking about psychopathic traits.

A leading expert on psychopaths, Professor Robert Hare, PhD., says that psychopaths follow a three step predatory process in which they use attachment to bring their victim within range without guilt about who gets hurt. Psychopaths:

1) Find the weaknesses in people they think are useful.

2) Manipulate others to bond with them so they get what they want.

3) Abandon the victim and move on or (in organizations) move up.[4]

---

2   For more see *Joy Starts Here*.

3   http://www.bakadesuyo.com/2016/10/how-to-deal-with-psychopaths/ This Is How To Deal With Psychopaths And Toxic People: 5 Proven Secrets, Eric Barker, Barking Up The Wrong Tree, ©2016.

4   Robert Hare PhD. *Without Conscience* Guilford Press, New York, 1993 as quoted by Professor Erik Barker. Ibid.

Narcissist + psychopath (no shared pain) = self-justified predator

Let us take a moment to piece together what we have seen. Narcissists don't use healthy shame to build better identities, so they avoid the pain shame creates. To manage life and keep others from giving them shame messages, narcissists must 1) justify themselves thus becoming controlling, combative/angry, or oppositional or 2) learn to not care using the "no shared pain" option for life – and sometimes they do both.

Adding a psychopathic tendency is a real temptation for a narcissist because it gives the narcissist a "free pass" for all shame messages. Now the narcissist can lead a "no worries" life with Teflon coating. Choosing to avoid pain creates the predator/psychopath version of narcissism.

Parents who do not teach their children to handle healthy shame relationally are setting up a nest for predatory narcissists in their home. Pastors who do not teach their flock to handle healthy shame relationally are preparing for the highest yield of religiously predatory narcissists emerging from their church programs.

Understanding narcissists who have a psychopathic tendency

Adding a subclinical (mild) psychopathic response to narcissism creates a perfect but deadly blend of harmful factors. This blend is extremely common and a major reason why many people despair about helping narcissists. Further, this combination does not operate the way people imagine.

It is commonly believed that predators (like psychopaths) do not have empathy. This is very misleading. Psychopaths use their empathy to improve their predatory success. Predators are very tuned into what causes pain to others and what their prey feels. Psychopaths use their ability to read and understand feelings to control their victims. While their empathic accuracy is not impaired, psychopaths simply do not share the pain they track or create in others. In one study, the rate of re-offending by violent psychopaths increased by twenty percent (20%) after receiving therapy. Therapy improved their empathy and honed their predatory skills.[5]

Empathic sensitivity without shared pain is useful for a wide range of activities from torture to advertising. About fifteen percent

5   *The Psychopath Test*, Jon Ronson, Riverhead Books NY 2011, as quoted by Baker. Ibid.

(15%) of the general population (and a higher percentage of leaders) avoid shared pain on their predatory (psychopathic) road to success. Most readers will feel their stomachs tighten because they have met more than one of these self-justified people.

Making the predatory choice

It takes a conscious choice to reject shared suffering and develop a predator lifestyle. While this choice can be as subtle as an inner vow, "I am not going to let them hurt me again," it can also be quite calculated.

The ability to block shared pain falls across a wide range.

Some Narcissistic Patterns

Restricted Pain Sharing

1. Controlling
2. Combative/Angry
3. Oppositional

No Pain Sharing

4. Disengaged
5. Predatory
6. Psychopathic

1) All these patterns are predatory to some extent, but predatory behavior is more pronounced as you read down.

2) All six patterns occur in both peacock and skunk versions.

For some people (clinical psychopaths) it is ridiculously easy. For others it is nearly impossible. Those who chose the narcissistic path work to become better at blocking shared pain. Many kinds of training (including medical and military) and violent media or games can greatly improve people's ability to block shared pain. Drugs, nicotine, pleasure, thrill seeking, distractions, multiple sexual partners, over-focus, and drivenness also help block others' pain.

Whether being a psychopath comes easily or not, narcissists will improve their deception skills.[6] For some it is super easy and others have to work much harder to believe their own lies. Narcissists do develop one brain habit that makes self-deception much easier.

The secret to excellent self-deception is to keep the "group identity" region in the right prefrontal cortex from sending information to the left-brain system that explains our reality.

---

6 Genetic tendencies, practice, intelligence, wealth, resources, role models, and age create a wide spectrum of blends of narcissism with psychopathology. Scott Peck discusses this spectrum in *People of the Lie*. At the most extreme end are those who lie, hurt, and even kill simply because they like it – even when they gain no advantage by their actions. M. Scott Peck, M.D., *People of the Lie*, Touchstone, NY 1983.

This "explainer" system has been dubbed the Verbal Logical Explainer (VLE)[7] by Karl Lehman, MD. Once the VLE is cut off from relational input it can (and always will) rapidly justify any self-serving explanations. What is more, we will always believe the VLE explanations ourselves. The VLE may not persuade others, but we will buy our own lies.

Teaching the brain to avoid shared pain

To keep relational input away from the VLE requires disruption of our group identity center functions. Without group identity activity in the brain, no message will reach the VLE. The VLE starts freewheeling and making up self-serving justifications.

The stories (lies) told by the freewheeling VLE easily change in an instant. This allows the mind to rewrite history as needed to justify whatever self-interest is in motion – and it is fast! Explanations and justifications can be created or changed in just under a second without the speaker noticing inconsistencies.

Readers familiar with the Life Model[8] will recognize terms like the VLE and the right prefrontal identity center but perhaps not in the context of narcissism. Readers who are having their first look at brain development from a spiritual point of view will begin to see how the brain learns the skills that create character.

One simplified way to think about the brain is to think of the right side of the brain as more dedicated to relationships and the left side as more dedicated to explanations. I have discussed this division in my book with Dr. Marcus Warner called *RARE Leadership*.[9] We detail the "fast track" identity process in the right brain as compared with the "slow track" explanations in the left.

Dr. Lehman points out that some of these right brain processes form relational circuits (RCs). These RCs do many things including creating group identity and sharing pain with others. The RCs are a large portion of the fast track in the brain.

The group identity system in the brain determines when we will willfully share pain. ***We share pain when it is like our people to share pain***. We especially share pain with members of our identity group. We must determine if this is "our pain" or just "your pain."

---

7   Karl Lehman, M.D., *Outsmarting Yourself*, 2011.
8   The Life Model is a comprehensive picture of human maturity with Christ-like character from birth to death. See lifemodelworks.org for more.
9   Warner and Wilder, *Rare Leadership*, Moody Publications, 2016.

Once the brain decides this is "your pain" and not "our pain" the predatory system easily converts "your pain" into "my advantage." When our group identity system determines this is "our pain" we move to protection. Sharing pain stops predatory responses by rendering them painful and abhorrent.

Deciding "this is not my people" is not the only way to block shared pain. A second method people learn is to make their whole relational circuits shut down. Jamming the RCs blocks shared pain. Once a narcissist learns how to shut down his or her group identity center the awareness of shared pain is gone.

There are side effects to this method. With our group identity blocked our moral restraint disappears as does our self-awareness. Self-awareness alerts us to our part in a situation. Without "my part" the situation becomes "your problem" and not something I share or want to share. "My part in this situation" is conspicuously absent for self-justified narcissists.

How does someone jam the brain's relational circuits? Loading in unresolved, bitter, hateful, hurtful, and hostile memories, condemnations, and judgments about others disrupts the relational circuits. We enter a non-relational mental mode reserved for dealing with enemies. In essence, interrupting the relational circuits blocks the group identity input from reaching our conscious thoughts. When the RC system shuts down, self-justification (and believing all one's own lies) takes over the brain *without any self-awareness*. We have a narcissistic predator (psychopath) brain on the loose.

PLAYING THE NARCISSIST'S GAME IS NOT THE SOLUTION.

As we understand the narcissistic game it becomes clearer why the average family member, therapist, pastor, or counselor plays into the narcissist/psychopath's game. Most interventions are little more than "Stop it! You are hurting people." "Stop it!" may delay a predator but it will not change one. "You are hurting people," makes a narcissist's attacks more likely. Counseling generally makes things worse and opens Pandora's Box.

What does the Bible tell us?

In the ancient literature the prophet Isaiah speaks of God's land as a place where no one will "hurt or destroy."[10] This means an

---

10   Isaiah 11:9

end to predatory behavior of any kind as, *"The wolf and the lamb will graze together, and the lion will eat straw like the ox; and dust will be the serpent's food. They will do no evil or harm in all My holy mountain,' says the LORD."*[11]

A spiritual life that does not change predators into protectors is not an effective spiritual life. At best, the Christianity we practice motivates people to control their predatory urges creating the characteristic pattern of intermittent failures and periodic relapses. We need better solutions than self-control and current therapies to change narcissists – particularly those with a psychopathic flair.

The kind of character we now call narcissistic is evident in Bible stories, and biblical writers had terms for it. Understanding of the terms used two to three thousand years ago will help us with the Bible text. Biblical writers knew nothing of modern psychology and did not use the words *narcissist*, *psychopath*, or *sociopath*, but they did describe people.

The ancient wisdom literature said low hesed people[12] were not loyal, could not be trusted, treated others unkindly, lied, and were unmerciful and cruel. Let us consider a few texts.

> *Many a man proclaims his own loyalty* (hesed),
> *But who can find a trustworthy man?*
> Proverbs 20:6 (NASB)

> *What is desirable in a man is his kindness* (hesed),
> *And it is better to be a poor (needy) man than a liar.*
> Proverbs 19:22 (NASB)

> *The merciful* (hesed) *man does himself good,*
> *But the cruel man does himself harm.*
> Proverbs 11:17 (NASB)

Low hesed[13] patterns can be found in Christians. St. Paul warns the Corinthians that they might think themselves spiritual but if their hesed (agape) is low, their spirituality is worthless. He reminds them that hesed is patient, kind, not jealous, arrogant, self-serving, indecent, easily provoked, or vengeful. Hesed shares

---

11   Isaiah 65:25 NASB
12   See how hesed transforms character through meaningful fellowship in Chris Coursey's book *Transforming Fellowship*, 2016. See also chapter 7 of *Rare Leadership* by Warner and Wilder for hesed group identity.
13   *hesed* can be translated as *agape* in Greek

the pain of others and bears all things preferring to suffer than to make the other person suffer.[14]

Hesed is also central to the group identity of the church. Jesus tells the church at Ephesus (through St. John) that their doctrines are right but they are low on hesed (agape). If this low hesed continues, Jesus says He will take His Spirit from that church.[15]

When hesed is high people respond to shared pain at a "gut" level. St. John indicates that blocking one's gut reaction (he uses the Greek word splagchnon – meaning intestines[16]) to shared pain is proof that we have no hesed. *"But whoever has the world's goods, and sees his brother in need and closes* (κλείω kleiō) *his heart* (σπλάγχνον splagchnon) *against him, how does the love* (agape) *of God abide in him?"[17]*

What is clear from this text is that deliberately closing off our intestinal reaction to the pain and needs of others means we have no hesed (agape). We are talking about the willful decision to shut down and block shared pain.

St. Paul tells us that hesed creates mercy. *"But God, being rich in mercy, because of His great love…"[18]* cites God's hesed as the reason for mercy. Jesus teaches that mercy blocks self-justification as we will see in Chapter Eight when we look at the story of the Good Samaritan. For now, we will note that Scripture gives higher hesed and shared pain as part of the solution for personality disorders.

Understanding of how narcissism operates in the human brain and how narcissism operates in culture lets us see how ancient cultures escaped from Pandora problems. We discover that our escape is about an identity group that will not play narcissistic games.

---

14   1 Corinthians 13
15   Revelation 2:1-7
16   The word *splagchnon* is often translated "heart" making it hard for the English reader to understand the "gut reaction" that is indicated in the original.
17   1 John 3:17 NASB
18   Ephesians 2:4 NASB

Why this book will take an extensive look at biblical stories

This book may contain more Bible stories than you are expecting. The ancient texts include extensive discussions and solutions to personality disorders. By looking at stories that are two or three thousand years old we gain perspective.

Little has changed on the problem side and yet much has changed on the solution side. The old stories offer an alternative we struggle to understand. For example we tend to think of individuals with a "problem" rather than groups without a "solution."

We will need to bridge languages, cultures, and time to discover and implement those solutions. In the next chapter we will learn the message a transformative identity group must send to every narcissist.

If You Are Ready
Group Exercise for Chapter Three

Today's group identity affirmation

Repeat together, "We are a people who spontaneously love our enemies and return blessings for cursings."

In groups of about five people tell each other why this characteristic matters to you. (5 minutes)

Today's healthy shame message practice

In groups of about five people create a healthy shame message for me when I point out my unique and special qualities that place me above others. (5 minutes)

Note: A healthy shame message states "we do not" and then states who we are with a Christ-like character response.
"We do not _____, we _____."

Tell each small group's statement to the whole group.
(5 minutes)

Today's withstanding self-justification practice

Self-justification: We should just forgive and overlook these little things and not bring problems up to shame others.

In groups of about five people make a list of the weaknesses that lie behind this self-justification. What would a hesed community do to be sure these weaknesses do not prevail? (10 minutes)

Report each small group's conclusions to the whole group.
(5 minutes)

Today's loving my enemy practice

This exercise is like texting with God. Write the impression that comes to your mind. Start with something that makes you grateful then your impression of God's response. Next read the question and write your impression of God's response that gives you peace. (5 minutes)

1. Dear God, I am thankful:
2. My dear child:
3. God, when has someone felt like an enemy to me this week?
4. What do You want me to know about loving them?

Read what you have written in groups of about five people. Do not explain what you wrote. Check for a sense of peace after you read. (5 minutes)

Sharing other's pain: Exercise 1

The following exercises can be done in either the full group or smaller groups. (45 minutes)

1. Describe what Bible story makes you feel most "splagchnon" (gut reaction) and give a non-verbal expression of your reaction.

2. If you have seen a group of Christians *"weep with those who weep"* (Romans 12:15) tell what you saw and the effects.

3. When did I think, "I wish it could have been me instead" about something painful?

4. When did I think "They deserved it"? How did that influence my motivation to share their pain?

5. Who in my life has been a great listener?

6. Take a minute together for each person to individually and silently thank God for and pray a blessing on their good listener.

Repeating today's group identity affirmation

Repeat together, "We are a people who spontaneously love our enemies and return blessings for cursings."

CHAPTER FOUR

"We Are Not Pleased With You"

Turning Glory into Shame

How long, O you sons of men, will you turn my glory to shame? How long will you love worthlessness...?
Psalm 4:2

"We are not pleased with you" is a phrase that should swing freely like an oiled gate. We should be at ease receiving or giving this message as an invitation to better relationships. Any freezing at the thought of hearing or saying these words is a sign that something is wrong. A Pandora problem may lurk behind that gate. Like Pandora herself, we fear more problems will escape and start flying around.

"We are not pleased with you" is the beginning of a healthy shame message intended to activate the brain's group identity center. Healthy shame messages are an invitation to more joyful relationships for those with relational skill. Shame messages are an axe to produce misery for the unskilled.

A healthy shame message starts with "you are not acting like your people" but ends with an accurate vision of how your people act. Toxic shame messages can be worded many ways but summarized as "you are bad." A healthy shame message helps us notice our defective response and encourages us to learn how our identity group does it. A healthy shame message can be summarized as a realistic "you can do better than that."

"We are not pleased with you" will produce three results when spoken to a narcissist: 1) self-justification, 2) a denial of the narcissist's part of the problem, and 3) something painful (present or future) for the speaker. As we might expect, opening a Pandora problem has made things worse. So far nothing has changed.

The same old game has started. The narcissist now views us as enemies. We must show that we hesed our enemies before the narcissist's character weakness can be transformed.

Those who will not receive a shame message

Throughout the Bible we read how God has faced people who would not receive a shame message. God faced people who 1) justified themselves, 2) would not see their part in the problem, and 3) struck back blaming God for the pain. Scripture stories reveal both how God understands and resolves this issue.

The Old Testament uses a visual symbol to distinguish responses to a shame message from God. Those who receive correction will bow. Those who do not receive a shame message keep their heads up and their necks stiff. People who will not bow justify themselves.

GLORY AND SHAME

Much of our destiny hinges on how we respond to shame messages. Biblical characters that embody narcissism do not receive a shame message in ways that lead to joyful relationships. Instead, stiff-necked people give glory to themselves and turn shame on others. God says they turn glory into shame.

Most things in the Kingdom of God work quite opposite of how we think it ought to work. We naturally like glory and avoid shame. It seems logical that if we avoid shame we will have glory. How we achieve glory or shame with God does not work that way. By accepting shame when we fail to bring joy to God we are returned to being glorious, joyful people.

Psalm 4:2 gives a clear shame message. God is not pleased: *"How long, O you sons of men, will you turn my glory to shame? How long will you love worthlessness and seek falsehood? Selah."* Turning God's glory into shame is not something most of us intend to do. This song indicates the paths to glory and shame have become reversed in our thinking.

Glory and shame before the Garden

Wanting God's glory is how the conflict between good and evil began. In Isaiah 14:12-14 we learn that Satan wanted to take God's glory. Satan also wanted the glory that belonged to humans. In the Garden he incited humans to take forbidden glory (both fruit and knowledge). Adam and Eve took the path they thought led to glory.

Having glory is not bad – God designed us to have glory. The problem arises when we try to steal God's glory. Adam and Eve had malfunctioned in a big way. At the first televised debate from Eden, God said to them, "What happened here?" Adam and Eve went directly to determining who should receive shame and blame. Their response to God was the same three points we see with narcissists: 1) self-justification, 2) failure to see their part, and 3) a hint that God should feel badly about what God had done creating such a woman and a serpent.

Very few people are able to admit they did something shameful and are part of the problem. Even worse, our reactions to shame often contribute to the mess. God does not play this game, but God does help restore glory. Accepting shame with bowed heads brings God's grace that restores glory. The other option is to get our glory back ourselves by some anti-grace method.

Most of us here on Earth think the way to restore our glory is to "look good." We work for glory and approval. Political debates are good examples. Each politician wants to be a champion in the eyes of the nation. Each claims the glory for economic growth while making sure that the other side gets all the shame. The last thing leaders want to admit is that their spending contributes to debt. Very few admit they or their party contributed to bad decisions.

God designed us to have glory. The problem arises when we try to steal God's glory.

The truth is that most of our "fig leaf" solutions are not glorious. Grabbing glory is shameful. Hiding and blaming are always temptations. Even a fender-bender brings out self-justifications. Church boards, businesses, and families spend extensive resources shifting blame, shame, and glory. This narcissistic response does not restore relationships or glory.

This human inclination to take the glory and shift the blame is behind the Lord, saying, *"How long are you sons of men going to turn my glory into shame?"* By seizing glory for ourselves, we are a huge embarrassment to God. Thus the Psalmist asks, *"How long will you love worthlessness?"*

What is worthlessness?

Worthless is what God calls things that *we* think will give us glory by making us look good. Even our piety can fall into worthlessness.

I grew up just as the old translation of the Bible was being replaced by a new one. A change in the wording of 1 Peter 3:3 led to huge and acrimonious debate in churches. The old version said "curly hair" while the new version said "braided hair" made women evil. You see, all the pious women (pastor's wives particularly) had worn their hair in braids for years to avoid having curly hair. Now, this new Bible version said that braiding hair is what evil women did!

May I say that the hair debate was worthless? As intense as the whole debate became, it missed the point. The topic in Scripture is glory not hair. Scripture says that a woman's hair is her glory.[1] But are hair styles the way to get glory? Making the way our hair looks the path to glory is the wrong road to glory. Finding glory through hair is what the traditional pastors were doing by insisting their wives have braided hair.

Hair is not the ultimate glorious thing about a woman; her highest glory is the grace she received. The way Jesus sees her as really special is the most glorious thing in her life. She might think, "Yes my hair is as nice as it can be BUT did you notice who I am with?" She will be like a woman with a new engagement ring. She always manages to show she is chosen. Grace means, "You are special!"

Once her perspective is right, a woman will glory in the wonderful company she keeps. "Me! I am princess daughter of the Most High King of the Universe!" After that, who could care much about hair, clothes, or jewelry? When we get glory backwards, we do not accept our shame but try for the praise of people instead. We also make spiritual sounding rules about appearance. Worthlessness!

So God asks us, *"How long will you love worthlessness?* If you really want the things that make you glorious, the most glorious thing you could have is that you are a reflection of Me. When you are a good reflection of Me, then whatever else you want to put on is pretty inconsequential. Admit it! The things you do to get glory

---

1   1 Corinthians 11:15

are shameful. How long will you love the worthless things?" God's grace makes us glorious.

Do we bow?

Men love positions of power, good names and titles, being the ones in front, the ones everyone bows to, the ones who others think are great. That is loving worthlessness. Showing the world how God transforms us from predators to protectors is glorious. We are becoming hesed! People's praise

In God's Kingdom, accepting shame with bowed heads restores our glory.

is inconsequential by comparison. So why are we fighting for a parking spot or to be top of the list for front-row seating?

Do we want glory instead of worthlessness? God says, "If you will admit your faults and malfunctions, I am faithful and just to forgive them. I will cleanse you of shameful things."[2] God cannot give us the glory and honor when we refuse shame and do not confess our wrongs. Narcissism is a worthless way to restore glory.

God gives glory.

God did mean for us to have glory; both the Old Testament and the New Testament speak to that. Psalm 8:5 says, *"For you have made him a little lower than* elohiym,[3] *and You have crowned him with glory and honor."* We see this repeated in Hebrews 2:7, *"You have made him a little lower than the angels; You have crowned him with glory and honor, and set him over the works of Your hands."*

God's original plan was to crown us with glory and honor. He made us want glory and honor so we would appreciate glory and honor. God does not want us to be grabbing glory when it is not ours – although He allows that option. He does not want us to steal our neighbor's glory and honor and certainly does not want us to take His. Pretending we have glory and honor will fool us and others at times but makes us an embarrassment to God.

Avoiding shame

Families hate it when a family member will not admit they are part of the problem. When the brain's self-awareness is off and

---

2   1 John 1:9 paraphrased
3   The Hebrew transliteration of what is translated "angels" in the NKJV

does not share pain, we feel like we are dealing with an enemy in the family. It is easier to deal with brain damage or schizophrenia than a self-justified person. Joy and glory stay out of that home no matter how hard people try to look good.

The principle reason why we do not want to admit we are part of the problem is because we do not want to feel shame. Shame is the feeling we have when we realize someone is not glad to be with us. We want to bring joy to others, so shame hurts.

In communities that know how to build hesed, shame means our behavior, attitude, or character is not godly and needs to be improved. Shame stops as we return to our glory-filled identities and others can be glad to be with us again.

We avoid shame when we do not understand that shame is the path that brings joy and restores glory. By avoiding shame we bypass correction and become narcissistic. This is worthless.

GOD'S GAME AND HESED RULES

Narcissists give God the same response they give to everyone. Their self-awareness is so low and their self-deception so high that they think God will play their game by their rules. Narcissists cannot understand a God who will bring them shame and then share it with them. They calculate the reason God would cause them shame is to take their glory not to restore it.

Thinking that God follows rules is completely wrong. God has no rules. God acts according to who God is. We tend to think of God having rules so our Verbal Logical Explainer (VLE) can explain God's ways, but this explanation is no closer to reality than a charcoal caricature on paper is to a person's face.

God is hesed. It does us little good to follow hesed "rules" without being hesed inside. God is totally hesed. We can learn to become hesed instead of being self-justified predators. Our character is transformed as God's family gives us healthy shame messages while we learn to hesed those who feel like enemies.

Hesed versus narcissist paths to glory

The hesed path to glory: Restore group identity so we belong to a peaceful, protective, joyful people. We live honorably. We use shame to build a better identity and stronger relationships.

Finding glory God's hesed way is an effect of becoming God's people. We are God's people by God's grace. We readily admit when we have not acted like God's children. We share the pain of others to help us become better protectors. Our solutions are relational and honest. We see things as God does.

The narcissist's path to glory: Make problems go away. Hold on to glory by deception and force. If required, defend honor to the death – preferably yours. Reject all shame. Here are examples:

- I am not responsible for bad things.

- It's your fault. You should fix it. (problem-focused solutions)

- The problem does not exist. (Teflon coating of lies)

    o That is not a problem. That is a feature!

    o That is good not bad.

    o You are crazy – nothing went wrong.

    o You have me confused with someone else.

    o This problem is insignificant and our engineers will have it fixed tomorrow.

Seeking glory in narcissistic ways means earning approval from others, avoiding problems, transferring failures to someone else, and "spinning" the best justifications. A narcissist has already decided that if anyone is going to look bad it will be someone else. We all know people who take credit for other people's work and find somebody to blame when things go wrong. Results and achievements replace hesed. The more our families, organizations, businesses, schools, churches, and institutions focus on results the easier it is to be conquered by narcissists and become their breeding ground.

God lets His people lose their glory.

God speaks over and over to His people about their tendency to claim glory and refuse shame. Hosea 4:7 says, *"The more they increased, the more they sinned against Me; I will change their glory to shame."* The people had become wealthy. King Solomon had made silver as common as stones in the street. People thought this wealth came from their accomplishments. Does this feel familiar? Certainly better cars, better cell phones, and better looks will bring us the glory we deserve!

God exposes fake glory.

In Habakkuk 2:16, we read, *"You are filled with shame instead of glory. . . . Utter shame will be upon your glory."* When we fill our lives with shameful things but call them glorious, God gives a healthy shame message. Because He is hesed, God will let us lose our false glory in order to find real glory – even when it makes God look bad for a time.

Society builds glory out of things that are shameful. We can see this in Philippians 3:19, *"whose end is destruction, whose god is their belly, and whose glory is their shame – who set their mind on earthly things."*

God's character shows us that He only gives good gifts. But when we try to get glory separately from Him, we end up glorying in our body, our money, and even how much we can get away with without getting caught like lesser people would be.

God takes on "spin doctors."

In Jeremiah we see that people who want glory for themselves refuse to feel shame. This time the spiritual leaders are making people happy and trying to help their flock avoid pain and shame. Jeremiah 6:14 tells us, *"They have also healed the hurt of My people slightly, saying, 'Peace, peace!' When there is no peace."*

God says His people can blush.

> *"Were they ashamed when they had committed abomination? No! They were not at all ashamed; nor did they know how to blush. Therefore they shall fall among those who fall; at the time I punish them, they shall be cast down," says the LORD.* Jeremiah 6:15

These shameless religious leaders are setting the identity for God's people. The leaders also embodied two other common narcissistic patterns in that they were also oppositional and defiant.

> *Thus says the LORD: "Stand in the ways and see, and ask for the old paths, where the good way is, and walk in it; then you will find rest for your souls. But they said, 'We will not walk in it.' Also, I set watchmen over you, saying, 'Listen to the sound of the trumpet!' But they said, 'We will not listen.'"*
> Jeremiah 6:16-17

People who want glory for themselves refuse to listen. They will ignore warnings, reject corrections, and deny they are part of the problem. Christian leaders may say their cover-up is helping God, saying, "We don't want to bring disgrace on the church or organization, so we will keep this hidden. We must look good because we serve God. Donors will not support God's work if they hear about this."

Taking what God says is shameful and using it to make God look good is not going to end well.

> For they have healed the hurt of the daughter of My people slightly, saying, 'Peace, peace!' When there is no peace. Were they ashamed when they had committed abomination? No! They were not at all ashamed. Nor did they know how to blush. Therefore they shall fall among those who fall; in the time of their punishment they shall be cast down," says the LORD. Jeramiah 8:11-12

God repeats the healthy shame message based on group identity.

We can see God repeating the same thing over and over again talking to narcissists. God will keep giving narcissists shame messages even when the narcissists do not get the point. If we try to look good and do not feel shame, we are not acting like God's people. God's people feel healthy shame."[4]

Every healthy shame message contains the information of how "our people" act, otherwise the result is toxic shame. God is working on the group identity region of our minds to help narcissists remember they are to be God's people. God clearly says how God's people do and do not act. *"Even the stork in the heavens knows her appointed times; and the turtledove, the swift, and the swallow observe the time of their coming. But My people do not know the judgment of the LORD."* Jeramiah 8:7

Our people listen to correction.

To avoid the loss of our glory, we must humbly listen to correction. In the history of Christian organizations, the ones that turned out

---

4   1 John 1:8 says, *"If we say that we have no sin, we deceive ourselves, and the truth is not in us."* We may confess our sins in one area and be totally blind to them in another. St. John is giving a strong admonition to look at whether or not our life is Kingdom life. Bowing and blushing with shame for our sins brings changes and healing in order to walk with God as He commands.

the worst had leaders who would not take correction. Someone said, "I think you have a problem here. We think your judgment is off. You need to rethink what you are doing. Look at how you are affecting your students, employees, or family. You have a problem with your anger, your spending, or how you try to control people. Joy is low." Or perhaps, no one said anything because it would only make things worse!

God loves those who blush at the realization they do not bring God any joy. When God's people persist in creating their own glory, God is serious about the consequences. In Hosea 4:6-7 we read,

> My people are destroyed for lack of knowledge. Because you have rejected knowledge, I also will reject you from being priest for Me. Because you have forgotten the law of your God, I also will forget your children. "The more they increased, the more they sinned against Me; I will change their glory into shame."

When leaders teach glory through worthless things, God appeals to the group identity of His people lest they raise children who are not His people. The people of other gods give themselves glory. People of the Lord of Glory let His glory shine through their character. Both systems promise glory, one way seeks glory by performance and the other finds glory through belonging. One is living by the flesh (σάρξ sarx), the other is living by the Spirit. These two paths are in complete conflict.

Hosea points out predatory patterns in verse eight: *"They eat up the sin of my people. They set their hearts on their iniquity."* Building our own glory means feeding on the sins of others. When we support narcissism we feed on sin. To follow a "glorious" leader and be among the great ones, the followers must eat the leader's sin. Leaders must eat the sin of followers in order to have their admiration. How is that for glorious?

QASHEH: THE HEBREW WORD הֹשׂק

God has a word for taking glory and avoiding shame. The word is qasheh (kaw-sheh'). It is translated: *stiff-necked, hard, cruel, severe, obstinate, difficult, fierce, intense, vehement, stubborn,* and *rigorous of battle.* Qasheh is used across the Old Testament for anyone who will not feel shame, blush, bow down, and say, "That is my fault, my problem." The qasheh kind of person says, "I am proud! I will look good!"

Older versions of Scripture translated qasheh as "stiff-necked," and in fact, *stiff-necked* is a physical picture of narcissistic body language. A person who is feeling shame hangs his or her head in shame, and the person who will not feel shame is stiff-necked.

The Bible stories that use the word *qasheh* give us a sense of a predatory and sociopathic character who will not share others' pain. We read of those who do not feel shame and become hard, cruel, strong, obstinate, difficult, and impossible to correct. People who are qasheh are intense, fierce, and vehement. They do not sit back mildly when there is a problem but stubbornly demand that others back down.

A picture of the stiff-necked

We can get a vivid picture of qasheh from Isaiah 48:4. *"Because I knew that you were obstinate (*qasheh*), and your neck was an iron sinew, and your brow bronze."* In Isaiah's day the people had left the Stone Age, just passed through the Bronze Age, and were now in the Iron Age. Everyone knew an iron sword could break a bronze sword. Isaiah is describing their necks to be as hard as iron, the hardest thing discovered up to that time. God is using an analogy from the latest weaponry. Their necks were a high-tech version of hard! Their necks were like titanium steel or some space-age metal. Nothing yet known was harder than their necks. Their brows were the next thing to it! The picture is built of the two hardest substances of the time. God is saying they are as stiff and hard as anything they know.

Qasheh and Egypt

God says many places that His people are hard and have stiff necks. *"And the LORD said to Moses, 'I have seen this people, and indeed it is a stiff-necked (*qasheh*) people!'"*[5] Moses tells the people, *"Therefore understand that the LORD your God is not giving you this good land to possess because of your righteousness, for you are a stiff-necked (*qasheh*) people."*[6]

But Moses is not the first we hear of stiff-necked people. When Joseph was sold into slavery in Egypt by his brothers, years passed

---

5   Exodus 32:9
6   Deuteronomy 9:6

and Joseph became a ruler. His brothers came seeking food and, although Joseph recognized them, he treated them like strangers, speaking to them roughly (qasheh). When they returned to Canaan, they told their father, *"The man who is lord of the land spoke roughly* (qasheh) *to us, and took us for spies of the country."*[7] Joseph was acting as though his brothers were not his identity group.

Egypt becomes a biblical icon for qasheh. Egypt gave the Israelites all the bad and kept all the good. Every kind of meanness known to mankind can be summarized as, "If anything bad is going to happen, it is going to happen to you and not to me." The Egyptians' treatment of Israelite slaves was qasheh. *"And they* (Egyptians) *made their* (Hebrew) *lives bitter with hard* (qasheh) *bondage – in mortar, in brick, and in all manner of service in the field."*[8] Qasheh shows up again in Deuteronomy 26:6, *"But the Egyptians mistreated us, afflicted us, and laid hard* (qasheh) *bondage on us."*

Shame is toxic when it aims to control rather than restore honor.

The problem with qasheh is that it is contagious. *"So Moses spoke thus to the children of Israel; but they did not heed Moses, because of anguish of spirit and cruel* (qasheh) *bondage."*[9] It is very hard to receive qasheh without wanting to return qasheh. The children of Israel (a name meaning *victorious with God*) were raised with qasheh, became qasheh, and then took qasheh character with them when they left Egypt. *"And the LORD said to Moses, 'I have seen this people, and indeed it is a stiff-necked* (qasheh) *people!'"*[10]

We can see from these examples that what happens in our "Egypt" affects us so that we act hard, cruel, obstinate, difficult, stubborn, stiff-necked, and severe. Throughout the Old Testament, if people become like Egypt they have abandoned God.

How do we counter this decline: people treat us qasheh, we become qasheh, treat others in qasheh ways, and find ways to justify ourselves for being qasheh. That is how narcissism spreads. The answer comes from being a people who hesed our enemies. This is going to be an epic battle!

---

7   Genesis 42:30
8   Exodus 1:14a
9   Exodus 6:9
10 Exodus 32:9

THE PATH TO GLORY INCLUDES ENDURING TOXIC SHAME.

To be a people who lower qasheh means growing a group identity that can endure some toxic shame. In Mark 8:38, Jesus said,

> *"For whoever is ashamed of Me and My words in this adulterous and sinful generation, of him the Son of Man also will be ashamed when He comes in the glory of His Father with the holy angels."*

As we look at all these verses concerning shame and glory, it brings us face to face with toxic shame. Shame is toxic when it aims to control rather than restore honor. Toxic shame is what narcissists pour on those who do not play their game.

The path to glory in our present lives brings shame here on Earth from people who think poorly of us because we love God's ways. On earth we might avoid toxic shame if we had better cars, more money, more hair or curves.

Those who are not ashamed of Jesus now will not make Him blush when He comes back. If we avoid shame from God's enemies, He will say, "You all have gone around pretending that you are one of Mine. It's just an embarrassment for Me to have you call yourselves My people. You are stiff-necked, have to be right and to make yourselves look good." Then we will be ashamed.

Instead of avoiding shame, we identify with our people who endure shame, listen to correction, and even look like fools so that we will share in the glory of God the Father and of the angels when He returns. That is our strange path to glory.

A QUICK REVIEW

So far in this book we have seen that character change requires us to switch from an individual approach to a group identity focus. Instead of focusing on the person in the middle of a Pandora problem, we address the group that lacks a solution. The group around a Pandora problem must be transformational.

Secondly, we found that the group around a Pandora problem must raise hesed if there is to be a change in the group identity. The group must become people who raise hesed until we even love our enemies.

Thirdly, the group identity around a Pandora problem must lower qasheh. Narcissistic people who do not use healthy shame to build a better identity do not please God. God's identity group is willing to blush and bow rather than become qasheh.

We become a people by raising hesed and lowering qasheh until we spontaneously love our enemies.

We ask, God, that Your glory would shine upon us. Give us the courage to not be ashamed of You even when we have lots of reasons to be ashamed of ourselves. May we let You transform those things we normally hide. Help us be open to Your work and Your touch, so that You are glorified in our lives. Take our qasheh and make us hesed, we pray.

If You Are Ready

Group Exercise for Chapter Four

Today's group identity affirmation

> Repeat together, "We are a people who easily forget what God sees. This weakness makes others look like enemies until we are no longer blind."

> In groups of about five people tell each other why this characteristic matters to you. (5 minutes)

Today's healthy shame message practice

> In groups of about five people create a healthy shame message for me when <u>I keep looking for admiration and affirmation.</u> (5 minutes)

> *Note: A healthy shame message states "we do not" and then states who we are with a Christ-like character response.*
> *"We do not _____, we _____."*

> Tell each small group's statement to the whole group. (5 minutes)

Today's withstanding self-justification practice

> Self-justification: I am not justifying myself! You are!

> In groups of about five people make a list of the weaknesses that lie behind this self-justification. What would a hesed community do to be sure these weaknesses do not prevail? (10 minutes)

> Report each small group's conclusions to the whole group. (5 minutes)

Today's loving my enemy practice

This exercise is like texting with God. Write the impression that comes to your mind. Start with something that makes you grateful then your impression of God's response. Next read the question and write your impression of God's response that gives you peace. (5 minutes)

1. Dear God, I am thankful:
2. My dear child:
3. God, when has someone felt like an enemy to me this week?
4. What do You want me to know about loving them?

Read what you have written in groups of about five people. Do not explain what you wrote. Check for a sense of peace after you read. (5 minutes)

Healthy shame messages: Exercise 1

Note: A healthy shame message states, a) "we do not" and then states who we are, b) "we (fill in the blank with a Christ-like character response)." We do not return curses for curses, we bless.

1. In small groups of about five, create healthy shame messages for the following: (35 minutes)

    a. Have someone write down the healthy shame messages for:

        i. Children laughing at a person who stutters

        ii. Someone refusing to make room for others to pass

        iii. Two ladies expressing contempt for your pastor

        iv. Someone who keeps talking loudly during church

        v. Men making off-color jokes at the church's BBQ

    b. Each small group reads their healthy shame messages to the whole group.

    c. Let each group member take a healthy shame statement and practice saying to the group with a warm tone and smile.

    d. The group thanks the speaker for the shame message.

2. Asking for a healthy shame message in groups of about five. (10 minutes)

   a. We should not simply wait for someone to help us improve our character. An active stance starts with asking people to give us healthy shame messages in the areas where we are learning God's perspective. Many Christians have trouble listening well while others have trouble speaking up.

   b. Consider which side fits you more often – needing to listen better or needing to speak up.

   c. Each member should practice asking the group for help with either listening or speaking. Example: "Could we work together to remind me when I need to (listen better/ speak up)? I would appreciate that."

   d. Where can this request be made in our existing identity groups?

Repeating today's group identity affirmation

Repeat together, "We are a people who easily forget what God sees. This weakness makes others look like enemies until we are no longer blind."

CHAPTER FIVE

Loving Worthlessness

How long, O you sons of men, will you turn my glory into shame? How long will you love worthlessness...?
Psalm 4:2

Character change is a group process and not an individual achievement. We can now consider why we need to focus our efforts on the group around a Pandora problem rather than focusing on the individual in the middle.

The group identity system in the brain provides a mental model for our responses to life. Our mental role-models shape our character. Those who raise us have the first input into our identity, but, starting at puberty, we select our own identity group. Who we select as identity group members shapes our adult identity and character.

A narcissist will want to be the most glorious person in his or her identity group. This would ensure that comparisons will bring glory to the narcissist and avoid shame. In contrast, people who use shame for self-improvement will fill their identity group with people they admire – the best of hesed and humble folk.

Shame finds a proper use every time our identity group (people we know love us) alerts us we are not acting like "us." A healthy shame message also includes a reminder of how "we" would respond.

We already know people who do not use shame for self-improvement will justify themselves. But how does self-justification impact the choice of a group identity for a stiff-necked (qasheh) person? The best option is to avoid a group identity that has people in it! Strange as a group identity without people may sound, it is not hard to achieve if we substitute a vision, goal, or ideal for people. World evangelism, healing, animal rights, Bible study, sports, classic cars, causes, activities, and possessions can become our identity reference.

Notice how easily leaders can become absorbed in causes at the expense of those around them. By becoming people of vision or accomplishments one identifies with objectives rather than God and people. In the place of "our people" we now have our goals, our mission, and our performance graphs. We need not associate with lesser beings or compare unfavorably with better ones. But what of our character? *Things* and *goals* do not grow hesed or decrease our qasheh. Causes and visions are worthless substitutes for a group identity made of people.

To see how an identity filled up with things becomes worthless we turn to one of the best-known examples from the Bible – a young ruler who had done everything right. He came to Jesus with the objective of eternal life. We read, "*Jesus, looking at him, loved* (agape/hesed) *him*" and told the young man to sell all his objects. The young man went away sad because he had great possessions.[1] Jesus loved him. The young ruler loved things. Good things were his identity reference rather than a hesed people. His identity was tied to "rich" and "ruler" rather than to Jesus and God's family. He loved worthlessness.

HESED AND QASHEH GROUP IDENTITIES

Moses has a conversation with God about group identity in Exodus 34:6-9 that provides a comparison between hesed and qasheh identities. A hesed God receives a qasheh people.

> And the LORD passed before him and proclaimed, "The LORD, the LORD God, merciful and gracious, longsuffering, and abounding in goodness [hesed] and truth, keeping mercy for thousands, forgiving iniquity and transgression and sin, by no means clearing the guilty, visiting the iniquity of the fathers upon the children and the children's children to the third and fourth generation." So Moses made haste and bowed his head toward the earth, and worshiped. Then he said, "If now I have found grace in Your sight, O Lord, let my Lord, I pray, go among us, even though we are a stiff-necked [qasheh] people; and pardon our iniquity and our sin, and take us as Your inheritance."

---

1   Mark 10:17-24

God's character is intended as the model for the character of God's people. Instead we read the three main effects of a qasheh group identity that continue spreading for generations. These three characteristics of a qasheh group are 1) iniquity, 2) sin, and 3) transgressions. A hesed God forgives iniquity, transgression, and sin – but how are these three effects different?

Iniquity is the word for deformity. We have been shaped into twisted identities and bodies. The ways that qasheh in our family have shaped us are not exactly God's identity for us. God watches over deformities that are passed from generation to generation.

Sin is the falling short of a standard God has for our group identity. Loving our enemies is something we frequently don't achieve even when we try. Failing to hesed our enemies is sin. God forgives this sin so we will learn to love our enemies.

Transgression is breaking a commandment. We either do what we were not to do or fail to do what we should do. God forgives transgression and returns us to our eternal identities.

Although Moses was the spiritual leader, he makes haste to bow. He humbly intercedes for the people, recognizing that they do not have the character their God demonstrates. When we will bow, God restores our identity including the ways we have been warped, do not measure up, and disobey intentionally. The qasheh show contempt for deformities, condemn others who break their rules, and punish anyone who does not measure up but allow their favored ones to get by with whatever they want. God does not overlook anything.

Hesed	Qasheh
Merciful	Merciless, harsh, judgmental
Gracious	Unkind
Longsuffering	Impatient
Abounding in goodness	Wicked
Abounding in truth	Liar
Keeping mercy for thousands	Vengeful
Forgiving	Holding a grudge

FULL COLOR QASHEH IN THE BIBLE

We can expand our understanding of the group identities who avoid shame and produce qasheh by looking at passages where qasheh is used. Because English translations often use many different words while translating one concept from Hebrew or Greek it is difficult to recognize when the Bible is repeating a word. Here are Scripture references that use qasheh and how they are translated:

- Rebellious – Deuteronomy 31:27
- Corrupted – Judges 2:19
- Doing things their own way – Judges 2:19
- Rough/rude – 1 Samuel 20:10
- Fierce – 2 Samuel 2:17
- Heavy/grievous/severe/burdensome – 1 Kings 12:13ff
- Not listening – 1 Kings 12:15
- Disrupting – Psalm 60:3
- Jealous – Song of Solomon 8:6
- Cruel – Isaiah 19:4
- Treacherous – Isaiah 21:2
- Punishing and pursuing – Isaiah 27:1
- Harsh – Isaiah 27:8
- Obstinate – Isaiah 48:4
- Impudent – Ezekiel 2:4
- Hardhearted – Ezekiel 3:7

When we know that the same word is being translated it helps us understand how large the meaning of qasheh really is. The Bible stories around the word help us understand the lifestyle and characteristic effects of qasheh groups.

Let us examine the stories of narcissistic leaders and people who rejected healthy shame.

Some of the most blazing examples of high levels of qasheh emerge when Israel asks for a king. Human rule over the short-lived United Kingdom of the twelve tribes of Israel started and ended with narcissist kings with predatory, sociopathic traits.

The first and last kings are clearly labeled as qasheh – character disordered.

We will start with King Saul who won the people's choice award fulfilling their dream to be like every other nation.

King Saul

Saul was the first king of Israel. Saul was stiff-necked, ruled his own way, hunted David like a predator would, took religion in his own hands, and he justified it all. As Saul hunted David, a conversation occurred between David and Jonathan that uses our word qasheh,[2] *"Then David said to Jonathan, 'Who will tell me, or what if your father answers you roughly (qasheh)?'"*

Saul's qasheh answer matches the three rules of the narcissist game: 1) self-justification, 2) let someone else suffer, and 3) weakness is bad. Notice how often shame is used or mentioned in the passage:[3]

> *Then Saul's anger was aroused against Jonathan, and he said to him, "You son of a perverse, rebellious woman! Do I not know that you have chosen the son of Jesse to your own shame and to the shame of your mother's nakedness? For as long as the son of Jesse lives on the earth, you shall not be established, nor your kingdom. Now therefore, send and bring him to me, for he shall surely die." And Jonathan answered Saul his father, and said to him, "Why should he be killed? What has he done?" Then Saul cast a spear at him to kill him, by which Jonathan knew that it was determined by his father to kill David. So Jonathan arose from the table in fierce anger, and ate no food the second day of the month, for he was grieved for David, because his father had treated him shamefully.*

Saul's anger is aroused at Jonathan. He gets angry, blames Jonathan, turns shame back on his son, uses swear words and nasty phrases meaning Jonathan is the son of a whore and having sex with his mother. These well-known nasty phrases are intentionally obscured by the translation. People do not like to see those words in the Bible, but God does not make narcissism sound or look better than it is.

---

2   1 Samuel 20:10
3   1 Samuel 20:30-34

To make things worse, although Saul is the one showing the bad character, he accuses Jonathan, Jonathan's mother, and David of bad character. This gives us a glimpse into Saul's group identity – his family is not a part of it. Saul attacks them all and refuses to share their pain.

Saul makes his wife, son, and son-in-law into his enemies. Now Saul's predator thinking declares that David should surely die. When Jonathan dares to answer back and question Saul, Saul throws a spear at him trying to kill his own son. Because the brain will always see the survival of the identity group as more important than one's own life, we can be sure that Saul's son and son-in-law David are not "Saul's people" in his mind – either that or Saul's relational circuits are totally off.

Family violence and name calling is justified by narcissists as "taking care of the family." Saul says, "*For as long as the son of Jesse lives on the earth, you shall not be established, nor your kingdom.*" Saul tries to make himself look good by implying that he is helping Jonathan when the opposite is true. Saul's sense of group identity has removed family and substituted power. Saul's mind has changed family into enemies, and he does not love his enemies.

Does Saul's nasty talk – trying to kill his son and son-in-law – restore Saul's glory and honor? No, Saul loves worthlessness. He does not bow his forehead to the ground. He loses his kingdom to someone hesed who accepts shame.

Rehoboam

The last king of the United Kingdom was Rehoboam. The people came to Rehoboam asking him to lighten their load, lower taxes, and stop treating them like slaves. Rehoboam consulted with the elders who said to lighten up and listen to the people.

The king went to the younger advisors who said to lay it on harder. Show them you are the boss. Don't show weakness.

> Then the king answered the people roughly (qasheh), and rejected the advice which the elders had given him; and he spoke to them according to the advice of the young men, saying, "My father made your yoke heavy, but I will add to your yoke; my father chastised you with whips, but I will chastise you with scourges!" So the king did not listen to the people. 1 Kings 12:13-15a

Rehoboam did not bow so he lost ten of the twelve tribes for his hard-headed ways. The people of the land were not "his people" whose pain he would share. He loved his worthless power and position.

Some qasheh is harder than others.

It has probably crossed your mind that some people are more qasheh than others. As group identities become increasingly tied to objects and objectives, people's qasheh becomes harder. God describes hardened qasheh as *bronze foreheads*[4] or, *"You have had a whore's forehead; you refuse to be ashamed."*[5] Prostitutes were no one's people and had to ignore shame in order to work. God compares His people to whores with foreheads that will not bow down. But foreheads, including the bronze and whore foreheads, were not the extreme high end of qasheh. The winners were weaned on worthlessness.

SONS OF WORTHLESSNESS (BELIAL)

An identity that is totally worthless has no place for God or people. "Son of belial" means the "son of worthlessness," and Scripture tells the stories of many.

As we have seen, the only part of the brain that can overcome narcissism is the group identity region. Four stories about sons of worthlessness will reveal the condition of these group identities. We begin with Nabal.[6] We could have called Pandora problems Nabal problems instead. He is the poster child for narcissism.

Nabal

As David fled from King Saul, the narcissistic predator, he encountered a qasheh son of belial. David's men helped Nabal's shepherds guard sheep in the wilderness. David's men asked to be included in a feast Nabal planned for his workers.

> Then Nabal answered David's servants, and said, "Who is David, and who is the son of Jesse? There are many servants nowadays who break away each one from his master. Shall I then take my bread and my water and my meat that I have killed for my shearers, and give it to men when I do not know where they are from?" 1 Samuel 25:10-11

4   Isaiah 48:4
5   Jeremiah 3:3
6   1 Samuel 25

Clearly David and his men were not Nabal's people. A servant hears all of this and goes to Nabal's wife, Abigail.

> Now one of the young men told Abigail, Nabal's wife, saying, "Look, David sent messengers from the wilderness to greet our master; and he reviled [went off on] them. But the men were very good to us, and we were not hurt, nor did we miss anything as long as we accompanied them, when we were in the fields. They were a wall to us both by night and day, all the time we were with them keeping the sheep."
> 1 Samuel 25:14-16

The servant further reported that David did not put them to shame but offered them respect and protection. No desert bandit did that. Their master had treated David like a bandit, returning evil for good. The servant warned Abigail:

> Now therefore, know and consider what you will do, for harm is determined against our master and against his entire household. For he is such a scoundrel [literally son of belial] that one cannot speak to him. 1 Samuel 25:17

Nabal created a Pandora problem! Saying anything would only make things worse. Nabal didn't allow people in his group identity. No one was hesed enough to tell Nabal when he was wrong. He and his family were about to be wiped out for Nabal's self-justified and worthless answer, yet no one could speak to him.

We have all met people we just cannot correct. Stiff-necked people put their family at risk by aggravating, provoking, yelling at, disagreeing, and attacking others. Nabal would say (as Saul did), "I am defending the family honor and protecting my things (objects and objectives that have taken over his group identity) by not feeding David's worthless people."

Would the identity group around Nabal deal with the Pandora problem? This servant and Abigail provide our first clear example of dealing with a narcissist. The servant quickly and clearly spoke to Abigail who received the shame message about her husband. Abigail quickly spoke with David:

> On me, my lord, on me let this iniquity be! And please let your maidservant speak in your ears, and hear the words of your maidservant. Please, let not my lord regard this scoundrel Nabal. For as his name is, so is he: Nabal is his name, and folly is with him! 1 Samuel 25:24b-25b

Abigail first called her husband's folly what it was without justifying anything. She went to David, expressed her shame relationally, and then reminded David of his group identity and saved them all.

Predatory men in Judges

In Judges we find more sons of belial. We read of a man and his concubine who are traveling through Judea where they stop for the night.

> *While they were celebrating, behold, the men of the city, certain worthless fellows [sons of Belial], surrounded the house, pounding on the door; and they spoke to the owner of the house, the old man, saying, "Bring out the man who came into your house that we may have relations with him."*
> Judges 19:22-25 (NASB)

The master of the house sent out his own daughter instead, along with the guest's concubine, and the sons of belial raped them, killing the concubine. It is clear these predators did not see the women or the traveler as part of their group identity. None of the men in this story are hesed.

Sons of Eli

The sons of Eli the chief priest were priests at Shiloh and part of the family that reared Samuel the prophet. *"Now the sons of Eli were worthless men [sons of Belial]; they knew not the Lord."*[7] They were the leaders known for their greed.

After sacrificing at Shiloh, the meat was given to the worshipers who cooked it and sat with their families to eat. The sons of Eli would go trolling to get the meat out of the worshipers' pots. As part of the priesthood, they had eating rights from each sacrifice. Whatever meat came out on their hook was theirs. Until this time, priests had a single hook, but these sons of belial made triple hooks so they could get the choice meat in everyone's pot. Because of their triple-hooks they were very overfed. On top of that, these priests lay with the women who came to worship.

God rebuked Eli for saying nothing about their narcissism. *"Why do you kick at [bring shame] My sacrifice and My offering which I have commanded in My dwelling place, and honor your sons more*

---

7   1 Samuel 2:12 (NASB)

than Me, to make yourselves fat with the best of all the offerings of Israel My people?" 1 Samuel 2:29

Eli did nothing to correct worthlessness – a very common pattern in churches. Eli's identity with his natural family was stronger than his identity in God's family.

Two false witnesses

King Ahab wanted property that belonged to Naboth. When Naboth refused to sell, King Ahab and Queen Jezebel showed their sociopathic, predatory narcissism. Jezebel hired two sons of belial as false witnesses against Naboth.

> *And two men, scoundrels* [sons of belial], *came in and sat before him: and the scoundrels* [sons of belial] *witnessed against him, against Naboth, in the presence of the people, saying, "Naboth did blaspheme God and the king." Then they took him outside of the city, and stoned him with stones, so that he died.* 1 Kings 21:13

The king and queen here are low hesed, attached to things, and dangerous. Who wants to stand up to narcissistic leaders? When the identity group does not act, however, then narcissistic predators will kill.

More on false witnesses

Remembering others' faults, shortcomings, and defects of character is a favorite tactic of stiff-necked narcissists. Qasheh people create their own history and impose this false witness on others. By changing history and re-coloring the details, narcissists create their own reality. We could call this lying and hypocrisy.

Eventually, creating one's own reality leads to believing one's own lies. The next step is to come down hard on others who do not agree. Changing reality is particularly useful for narcissists after they have hurt others. Instead of sharing pain with those they have hurt, narcissists change the story and then blame their victims.

From the self-justified leaders in Jesus' day to people at the top of churches, businesses, education, and politics today we spot stiff necks that do not bow. In every case we find low-hesed group identities full of objects and objectives that God sees as worthless.

Nowhere in Scripture does a cause become more important than hesed. Yet, in the Western church we follow visionaries, causes, and missions. We unite behind goals and justify our campaigns as the right thing to do. Huge crowds surround some preachers who put their "spin" on events, who use people while promoting their highly attractive causes. These groups and movements produce little transformation. Do not mistake a cause for hesed or let a vision blind you to narcissism.

Keeping our necks flexible

The Bible reveals a God who frequently addresses stiff-necked narcissistic actions done in His name. Making ourselves look good while dragging triple-hooks through other people's sacrifices will invite a strong shame message from God.

Worse yet, we think God will cover up bad behavior for us. Is God a narcissist who needs us to look good so He will look good? No, God lifts up the humble.

In Psalm 3:3, the Lord is called *"the lifter of my head,"* which means, "If I will hang my head, He will lift my head." If we do not bow our heads, we have chosen the path of worthlessness. Worthlessness happens a lot.

To build the character of Christ we must . . .

    1) Admit faults and hang our heads.

    2) Focus on group identity rather than individual choice.

    3) Build hesed in our group identity.

    4) Reduce qasheh in our group identity.

Lord, we ask You to be the one who lifts our head. Teach us to be the people who bow our heads easily; people who worship You because we really appreciate the joy that comes from being with You. Make Your people our people.

If You Are Ready
Group Exercise for Chapter Five

Today's group identity affirmation

Repeat together, "We are a people who are readily ashamed when we fail to be our true selves. We rapidly return to our joyful sense of holding God's hand."

In groups of about five people tell each other why this characteristic matters to you. (5 minutes)

Today's healthy shame message practice

In groups of about five people create a healthy shame message for me when I feel entitled to special treatment and priority. (5 minutes)

Note: A healthy shame message states "we do not" and then states who we are with a Christ-like character response. "We do not _____, we _____."

Tell each small group's statement to the whole group. (5 minutes)

Today's withstanding self-justification practice

Self-justification: You are out of line, rebelling against God's authority, and should not speak about me that way.

In groups of about five people make a list of the weaknesses that lie behind this self-justification. What would a hesed community do to be sure these weaknesses do not prevail? (10 minutes)

Report each small group's conclusions to the whole group. (5 minutes)

Today's loving my enemy practice

This exercise is like texting with God. Write the impression that comes to your mind. Start with something that makes you grateful then your impression of God's response. Next read the question and write your impression of God's response that gives you peace. (5 minutes)

1. Dear God, I am thankful:
2. My dear child:
3. God, when has someone felt like an enemy to me this week?
4. What do You want me to know about loving them?

Read what you have written in groups of about five people. Do not explain what you wrote. Check for a sense of peace after you read. (5 minutes)

Resisting self-justification: Exercise 1

Luke 16:14-15 (NASB) Now the Pharisees, who were lovers of money, were listening to all these things and were scoffing at Him. And He said to them, *"You are those who **justify yourselves** in the sight of men, but God knows your hearts; for that which is highly esteemed among men is detestable in the sight of God."*

Luke 18:9-14 (NASB) And He also told this parable to some people who **trusted in themselves that they were righteous**, and viewed others with contempt: *"Two men went up into the temple to pray, one a Pharisee and the other a tax collector. The Pharisee stood and was praying this to himself: 'God, I thank You that I am not like other people: swindlers, unjust, adulterers, or even like this tax collector. I fast twice a week; I pay tithes of all that I get.' But the tax collector, standing some distance away, was even unwilling to lift up his eyes to heaven, but was beating his breast, saying, 'God, be merciful to me, the sinner!' I tell you, this man went to his house justified rather than the other; for everyone who exalts himself will be humbled, but he who humbles himself will be exalted."*

Luke 20:19-26 (NASB) The scribes and the chief priests tried to lay hands on Him that very hour, and they feared the people; for they understood that He spoke this parable against them. So they watched Him, and sent spies who **pretended to be righteous**, in order that they might catch Him in some statement, so that they could deliver Him to the rule and the authority of the governor.

They questioned Him, saying, "Teacher, we know that You speak and teach correctly, and You are not partial to any, but teach the way of God in truth. Is it lawful for us to pay taxes to Caesar, or not?" But He detected their trickery and said to them, *"Show Me a denarius. Whose likeness and inscription does it have?"* They said, "Caesar's." And He said to them, *"Then render to Caesar the things that are Caesar's, and to God the things that are God's."* And they were unable to catch Him in a saying in the presence of the people; and being amazed at His answer, they became silent.

Galatians 5:4 (NASB) You have been severed from Christ, **you who are seeking to be justified** by law; you have fallen from grace.

1. Read Luke 16:14-15 aloud.

    a. How many ways does this passage connect to what you have been reading in this book?

    b. What things are "highly esteemed by men" that are used to justify oneself and to scoff?

2. Read Luke 18:9-14 aloud. How many ways does Jesus deal with self-justification in this story?

3. Read Luke 20:19-26 aloud. How do we fool ourselves pretending to be righteous?

4. Read Galatians 5:4 aloud. This passage addresses Christians who try to justify themselves using Scripture and their own actions.

    a. What forms does self-justification using Scripture take in our experience?

    b. What can we learn from how Paul addresses self-justification in the church?

Repeating today's group identity affirmation

Repeat together, "We are a people who are readily ashamed when we fail to be our true selves. We rapidly return to our joyful sense of holding God's hand."

CHAPTER SIX

"This Is Too Hard for Me!"

The Sons of Zeruiah

"...The sons of Zeruiah are too harsh (qasheh) for me ..."
2 Samuel 3:39

King David was a warrior who, even as a lad, was not afraid to take on Goliath. David overcame the narcissists Saul and Nabal but backed down in the face of the narcissism of his nephews. Four of his nephews held important military positions for David who, like many rulers, brought relatives into government hoping that strong family loyalty (hesed) would protect his power.

When family hesed is corrupted by qasheh (as it is for narcissists), family bonds create a special kind of hell. We will see how this corrupted hesed produced David's dying wish, "Don't let my nephew live."

King David was a hesed man. Much of what we know about hesed comes from the worship songs he wrote. David's leadership in worship is still felt after 3,000 years. Yet, neither David's hesed nor his worship was able to correct the qasheh in the family that worshiped with him.

David had a group identity flaw mentioned repeatedly in Scripture. David's group identity was a "man of war." In war, David was hesed and very attached to other warriors, but it was an unpurified hesed. In the company of warriors David wanted to be a winner.

If we think back to Chapter One we will remember that when we remove loving kindness (hesed) from the brain we are only left with the desire to win. Low hesed characterizes a sociopathic personality. When individuals with low hesed and high qasheh dominate a group identity there will be trouble. We should consider carefully that if hesed becomes less important than winning, loyalty (hesed) will be used to eliminate enemies by qasheh people like narcissists, sociopaths, and psychopaths. This is a very dangerous inversion.

Leaders who place family members in power are prone to see God as another government supporter. We already saw how Eli the priest was confronted by God for honoring his sons more than God. In David's warrior band, loyalty (hesed) was based on valor and family ties rather than love of God. Nowhere is this more evident than with the three sons of David's sister.

Due to David's "man of war" identity, he placed victory above a pure heart with his nephews. The combination of family ties (unpurified hesed) and "man of war" identity kept his nephews in power. David's worship did not correct this predatory pattern and his group identity as *Winning Warriors Who Worship* continued in deadly ways. After all, they had enemies!

STIFF-NECKED NARICISSISTS IN POWER

In this chapter we will look at some classic examples of stiff-necked (qasheh) people seeking glory for themselves. Stories about these characters take up many more pages in Scripture than the story of the Fall or Creation. One reason for such an enormous amount of Scripture devoted to the topic is what happens when people share rule with God.

As we look at 1 Samuel, we see King Saul described as stiff-necked. No one could tell Saul he had a problem because he would stick a spear in them. Talking to the king made things worse. As all stiff-necked people do, he justified himself. People in power often have a sense of entitlement that says, "I deserve to be treated a certain way because of my position. I am the pastor; I am the head of the deacon board; I am the policeman."

Nowhere do we have a better example than the three brothers we are about to study. Our word *qasheh*, the word for not being willing to feel shame or bow the head, is applied to them by their uncle, King David. All the translations for the word qasheh are characteristic of these brothers: hard, cruel, severe, obstinate, difficult, fierce, intense, vehement, stubborn, stiff-necked, and battle-hardened.

David's family

David says, *"And I am weak today, though anointed king; and these men, the sons of Zeruiah, are too harsh (qasheh) for me. The LORD shall repay the evildoer according to his wickedness."* 2 Samuel 3:39

Even though David has been crowned king he cannot deal with these nephews, the stiff-necked sons of his sister Zeruiah. As we have already observed, a stiff-necked people take advantage of power, position, opportunity, God's service, family, closeness, trust and deception. They shame others while refusing to accept shame. Qasheh people create their own reality and history to impose on others. Narcissists hurt others when it serves their purpose, but blame the other person for getting hurt. These three nephews of the king fit this profile well.

David had two sisters we will study. The first is Zeruiah, mother of the three nephews: Abishai, Joab, and Asahel. They were three great warriors of David's army. When Jerusalem had to be captured, David told his men, "Whoever captures Jerusalem, I will put him in charge and make him the prince of my whole army." The winner was Joab, one of the sons of Zeruiah. He became a prince and a commander of all the other units of the army.

Joab had been with David ever since the wilderness days. Right from the start, David's nephews led the fight. They were considered the three best fighters in the country. We will see how these nephews take advantage of their relationship to David and his power as they head straight for the top.

David had another sister named Abigail. She is not the same Abigail we saw with Nabal the narcissist in Chapter Five. This Abigail is the sister of Zeruiah and mother of Amasa, another of David's generals. Amasa is a nephew to David and cousin to the three sons of Zeruiah, which brings us to the reason for looking at this detail. We want to see how these cousins got along. We want to note how well they all knew and trusted each other. It is hard to remember that those narcissistic, power-hungry generals clawing their way to the top are a band of cousins.

David's worship did not correct his predatory Winning Warriors Who Worship group identity.

THE THREE NEPHEWS – SONS OF ZERUIAH

Asahel

Asahel's story runs from 2 Samuel 2:8 to 3:39. We meet him as an amazingly fast runner, said to run as fast as the gazelle on the plain. Like his brothers, Asahel wants to win. We will return to his running after more background.

Right after Saul was killed, the kingdom split. Abner, the commander of Saul's army, put one of Saul's sons in power. Abner did not like David and was glad to hunt him down because David was a descendant of Ruth the Moabitess. Abner considered David a half-breed. David did not belong in Abner's Jewish group identity. He was keeping any half-breeds out of power.

As commander of Saul's army, Abner had an ongoing war with David's men led by the three sons of Zeruiah. One day the two armies met at a pond. As they sat on each side of the pond, Abner said to the sons of Zeruiah, "Why don't we just have a fight of the champions? You pick your best twelve soldiers, and we'll pick our best twelve and we'll have them fight each other. Whichever side wins will win the battle and the rest won't have to fight." Abner was looking for a way to save lives.

Each side picked their twelve champions. All twenty-four killed each other on the spot so that place became known as the Valley of Sharp Swords. With no champion, the battle broke out. The sons of Zeruiah were winning. Asahel, the fastest, ran after Abner to kill him. As Abner was running, he realized he was being chased by a really good runner, so he called out, "Is that you Asahel?" When Asahel answered, "Yes it is!" Abner knew Asahel wanted to win the top prize of the day which would go to anyone who killed Abner.

Asahel pursued relentlessly, but Abner knew that war is more than running. He had a way to kill Asahel and said, "Why don't you kill someone else besides me? Why should I kill you and have to face your brother Joab?" Asahel continued pursuing him, and Abner killed him by jabbing his spear backwards, right through Asahel.[1] The Hebrew gives us a gory picture of the fatal blow – a thrust that struck him right under the fifth rib and came out his back. Asahel dropped and died.

---

1   The spear was sharp on the other end in order to be stuck into the ground when not needed.

Abner's side of the dialogue reveals that he did not want to kill Asahel. Abner had already tried to keep the bloodshed to a minimum and now, as he was running for his life, he thought about relationships. He knew Asahel's brothers and did not want to be their enemies. Asahel wanted to win, to kill so his enemy would lose. Asahel was in a predator mode; a narcissist with a sociopathic wish to win.

Some time later, Abner decided to take one of Saul's concubines for himself. Saul's son became angry and condemned Abner. Abner then blasted Ishbosheth: "How can you complain to me about a concubine when I'm keeping you in power? Do you think I am some baboon? You think I'm a puppet for Judah and David? I tell you what I'm going to do! I'm going to take your whole kingdom and give it to David for treating me this way!"

Abner sent a message to David saying, "I'm tired of how I'm getting treated here." David threw a feast for Abner and sent him back to arrange for David to be king over all Israel. Meanwhile, Joab son of Zeruiah arrived and heard that Abner had been there. Joab confronted his uncle the king: "What? You let Abner in here? Don't you know he's here to spy so he can sneak back later and do you in? He's dishonest and not to be trusted!"

This tirade is really very interesting when thinking about narcissists. If there was ever a fellow who was dishonest and not to be trusted, it was Joab. He was sneaky while Abner had considerable integrity.

Joab sent a message to Abner telling him to come back as David wanted to see him. Joab used his position to lure Abner back, then he and his brother cornered Abner and stabbed him under the fifth rib. They killed Abner the way Abner killed Asahel, except one was in a battle and the other in a dark alley.

The sons of Zeruiah won through treachery, all very justified from their point of view. In their minds they were honorable defenders of their country, their king, and their family honor. David disagreed.

> *Afterward, when David heard it, he said, "My kingdom and I are guiltless before the LORD forever of the blood of Abner the son of Ner. Let it rest on the head of Joab . . ."*
> 2 Samuel 3:28

Abishai

The second stiff-necked brother was Abishai. His story starts in 1 Samuel when Saul is chasing David. Three thousand of Saul's troops were all sleeping in a circle around the king. Abner was sleeping right next to the king.

David asked for a volunteer to go with him into the circle of three thousand troops, to the place where Saul was sleeping. Abishai volunteered.

> So David and Abishai came to the people by night; and there Saul lay sleeping within the camp, with his spear stuck in the ground by his head. And Abner and the people lay all around him. Then Abishai said to David, "God has delivered your enemy into your hand this day. Now therefore, please, let me strike him at once with the spear, right to the earth; and I will not have to strike him a second time!" 1 Samuel 26:7-8

Abishai had predator eyes. His immediate desire was to kill the enemy. David was a protector looking for God's presence.

> But David said to Abishai, "Do not destroy him, for who can stretch out his hand against the LORD'S anointed, and be guiltless? . . . The LORD forbid that I should stretch out my hand against the LORD'S anointed. But please, take now the spear and the jug of water that are by his head and let us go."
> 1 Samuel 26:9 & 11

David wants Abishai to see relationships. Abishai wants to win and would kill to win. Like other stiff-necked people, he believed he should not have to suffer when someone else could.

We can see a contrast between Abishai and Abner (who he later killed) after the battle of the twenty-four champions. Asahel was dead, but the brothers did not yet know who killed him. Joab and Abishai were pursuing Abner up the hill of Ammah, and Abner said, "How long are you going to keep killing us? This is brother killing brother. Are you never going to call off the pursuit and stop the battle? You obviously beat us; we're on the run, but the more people you kill the more bitter this day will become in our history. Think of all the people (our identity group)." Abner makes room for loving enemies who are also his people.

Joab responded, *"God only knows what would have happened if you hadn't spoken, for we would have chased you all night if necessary."*[2] So Joab blew the horn and ended the battle. Joab had to be reminded of what Abner knew – hesed is more important than making sure everyone else loses. Abner was thinking about the lives of his people, all dear to him. Relationships mattered to Abner, but if Joab and Abishai had known that Abner had killed their brother, they would have killed everyone there.

Abishai's narcissism showed up when David was chased out of Jerusalem during the insurrection by Absalom (another narcissist). As David and Abishai were fleeing town, a fellow named Shimei, a descendent of Saul, cursed David and threw rocks at him shouting, "You blood thirsty pig! It's about time you lost! God is chasing you out of the country."

Abishai, the narcissist, did not tolerate being shamed. *"Then Abishai the son of Zeruiah said to the king, 'Why should this dead dog curse my lord the king? Please, let me go over and take off his head!'"*[3] But the king answered,

> *"What have I to do with you, you sons of Zeruiah? So let him curse, because the LORD has said to him, 'Curse David.' Who then shall say, 'Why have you done so?'" And David said to Abishai and all his servants, "See how my son who came from my own body seeks my life. How much more now may this Benjamite? Let him alone, and let him curse; for so the LORD has ordered him. It may be that the LORD will look on my affliction, and that the LORD will repay me with good for his cursing this day." And as David and his men went along the road, Shimei went along the hillside opposite him and cursed as he went, threw stones at him and kicked up dust.*
> 2 Samuel 16:10-13

David was trying to see the situation and others as God sees them. "Well, how do I know that God did not send him to curse me? If God did, then we shouldn't take off his head. And if God didn't send him then God is going to take care of him." David accepts shame. "If you want to say something is wrong with me, there might very well be something wrong with me, and I ought to have a look at it and talk with God about it."

---

2   2 Samuel 2:27 (NLT) Basically, "We would have chased you until you were all dead."
3   2 Samuel 16:9

Abishai thinks he knows the right thing to do. "If you are going to say there's anything wrong with my uncle – *slice* – off with your head!" Like most narcissists, Abishai learned nothing from David's response. After the insurrection is over, Shimei fell down before David after he crosses the Jordan and said,

> *Do not let my lord impute iniquity to me, or remember what wrong your servant did on the day that my lord the king left Jerusalem, that the king should take it to heart. For I, your servant, know that I have sinned. Therefore here I am, the first to come today of all the house of Joseph to go down to meet my lord the king.* 2 Samuel 19:19-20

Abishai went another round with David:

> *But Abishai the son of Zeruiah answered and said, "'Shall not Shimei be put to death for this, because he cursed the Lord's anointed?" And David said, "What have I to do with you, you sons of Zeruiah, that you should be adversaries to me today? Shall any man be put to death today in Israel? For do I not know that today I am king over Israel?" Therefore the king said to Shimei, "You shall not die." And the king swore to him.*
> 2 Samuel 19:21-23

David was repairing the group identity with a joyful return. But mercy is not in narcissistic character, and narcissists hold grudges. This brings us to the worst of David's nephews – Joab, the third brother.

Joab

We will pick up Joab's story as King David wants to kill his good friend Uriah the Hittite before Uriah discovers his wife Bathsheba is pregnant with David's baby.[4] Uriah was one of David's mighty warriors and away with Joab at war. David arranged for his nephew Joab to get Uriah killed, and Joab did the ugly deed. Joab was willing to kill one of his friends and colleagues to get ahead.

Let's set the background for another of Joab's plots. This time Joab plotted against David with his cousin Absalom. David's son Absalom is another poster child for a narcissist, and he was gorgeous like his sister Tamar. The plot thickens when their half-brother exploited attachments and weakness to rape Tamar.

---

4   2 Samuel 11 and 12

Absalom wanted to kill him. Absalom (the son of worship leader David) searched for a weakness and used a worship feast to get his half-brother drunk and kill him. We can see that David's children turned into narcissistic predators with psychopathic tendencies.

Absalom did not seem afraid of anything. He escaped to the wilderness of Geshur and stayed with his grandfather, king of Geshur.[5] Absalom stayed with Grandpa for three years, and David missed him every day. This unpurified hesed made David act more like Eli – honoring his sons over God.

Narcissists see attachment as weakness, and Joab thought old King David had gone soft. It was time to replace him with Absalom. Joab planned to exploit David's attachment to Absalom and eliminate weak David while gaining favor with the new king. After all, Absalom was not too sentimental to kill his father. That looked like the kind of king Joab liked.

Joab hatched a plan with a sneaky, tricky, clever, and cunning woman from Tekoa, who was likely a professional performer. She went before David acting like she was in mourning because one of her sons had killed another son and the family wanted the remaining son put to death. Joab instructed her how to exploit David's weakness followed by his faith.

Joab then had her spring an accusation on David creating toxic shame so David would feel like the bad one. Joab used shame, group identity, and hesed in twisted ways in order to win and take David's kingdom if not his life. David dropped his head in shame, looked at her and asked, "Is Joab behind this?"

"Yes, My Lord," she answered. "You are clever and know what is going on. In fact, Joab told me word for word what to say. He put the words in my mouth."[6]

After Cousin Joab brought Cousin Absalom back, Absalom usurped his father's throne BUT made Cousin Amasa head of his army instead of Cousin Joab. Absalom was now on the wrong side of Cousin Joab when he declared himself king and went to kill his father David. Joab was now one angry narcissist when David

---

5   Absalom's mother, Maacah, was the princess of Geshur (2 Samuel 3:3; 13:37-38). Geshur is called Bashan in David's psalms. Giants from Bashan gave Joshua a hard time (Deuteronomy 3:13). Og, king of Bashan at the time had a bed twelve feet long (Deuteronomy 23:11).

6   2 Samuel 14: 19-20

put Joab in charge of his army with orders to capture Absalom without hurting him.[7] Anyone want to guess how this is going to turn out?

During battle Absalom got caught in the tree by his gorgeous hair. Joab finds where Absalom is and, *". . . he took three spears in his hand and thrust them through Absalom's heart, while he was still alive in the midst of the terebinth tree."*[8] Joab's ten armor bearers finish beating Absalom to death then throw him into the trash.

When Joab came back to the city, David was mourning for Absalom. Joab gave David a classic narcissist's speech. "Why are you crying for Absalom when all of us went out to war for you? You should be ashamed of yourself. You're acting like none of your people matter to you. All you care about is your own family, so get out to the gate and start thanking all your soldiers for the win."[9]

More Joab Narcissism
Uriah – 2 Samuel 11
Absalom – 2 Samuel 14
Amasa – 2 Samuel 17:25
Absalom – 2 Samuel 18:1 to 19:13
Amasa – 2 Samuel 20:8 to 23
Adonijah – 1 Kings 1:5 to 53

Joab shows absolutely no shame. Instead, he shames David. Joab follows the three rules of the narcissist game: self-justification, no suffering for me, and show no weakness.

Evidently Joab's killing Absalom and the rant did not sit well with David. David replaced Joab and made Amasa captain of his army, even though Amasa had been the commander of Absalom's army. This was twice that Cousin Amasa came out ahead of Cousin Joab, and he was not going to be replaced.

David's army was soon deployed to stop another uprising. During the deployment Amasa encountered Joab in camp. Joab kissed him, declared they were brothers then at close range stabbed Amasa under the fifth rib and killed his "enemy." Amasa was betrayed by a kiss of false hesed! "Let me kiss you, brother," and while narcissists are kissing you they stab you in the heart!

---

7   2 Samuel 18:5
8   2 Samuel 18:14
9   2 Samuel 19: 5-7 paraphrased

The last story about Joab begins when Adonijah, another of David's sons, tried to become king.[10] When he was caught by Solomon, Adonijah ran to the altar and grabbed the horns so Solomon wouldn't kill him in front of God. Solomon forgave Adonijah.

David was now an old man and as he lay dying he had one last request for Solomon, the next king. David said,

> Moreover you know also what Joab the son of Zeruiah did to me, and what he did to the two commanders of the armies of Israel, to Abner the son of Ner and Amasa the son of Jether, whom he killed. And he shed the blood of war in peacetime, and put the blood of war on his belt that was around his waist, and on his sandals that were on his feet. Therefore do according to your wisdom, and do not let his gray hair go down to the grave in peace.[11] 1 Kings 2:5-6

After King David died, Solomon declared that Joab should be killed. Joab ran right to the altar so he wouldn't be killed in front of God. Cousin Solomon had him killed on the spot for "the blood which Joab shed without cause."[12]

To the end, Joab the narcissist used God to justify himself. He accepted no shame, believed he did no wrong and killed enemies, like his cousins, when they were in his way.

PURIFYING OUR GROUP IDENTITY

From the first kings of Israel to Judas Iscariot, we see that stiff-necked people value winning more than they hesed their identity group. Qasheh people do not see their part of a problem and blame others: "Well, she made me do it." Where did we hear that first? Self-justification nurtures qasheh.

David would often ask God why evil had happened to him. Perhaps he had done wrong. This humble invitation for a healthy shame message is what God looks for in His servants.

At the same time David let his family attachments and "man of war" identity contaminate his hesed and group identity. David's narcissistic family (brothers, children, cousins, and nephews) did

---

10 1 Kings 1:5-53
11 *So don't let him live.*
12 1 Kings 2: 31

not use shame to improve their identities. When David gave shame messages to his relatives he was ineffective. This will always be true – why? Narcissism cannot be corrected by one person – even the king. When purification of a group identity is left to a king, heads will roll but character remains unchanged.

Narcissism is corrected by a group identity not by individual action. Priests and elders like Eli are to guide everyone to act "like our people would act in this situation." Elders and priests should guide the purification of hesed by addressing qasheh. David and Eli both made the family-hesed mistake of making family bonds stronger than their "God's people" group identity.

In this chapter we have learned we must resist qasheh in ourselves and in others. We have more to learn from David's life in the next chapter. We want to create a *people* by raising *hesed* and lowering *qasheh* until we spontaneously love our enemies.

Lord Jesus, we want to continue listening to Your voice. Let us not be too stiff-necked to notice that there might be things wrong with us. Be the one who justifies us, as you did David, over and over again.

If You Are Ready
Group Exercise for Chapter Six

Today's group identity affirmation

Repeat together, "We are a people who remind each other who we really are whenever we forget."

In groups of about five people tell each other why this characteristic matters to you. (5 minutes)

Today's healthy shame message practice

In groups of about five people create a healthy shame message for me when <u>I am ignoring the feelings of others.</u> (5 minutes)

Note: A healthy shame message states "we do not" and then states who we are with a Christ-like character response. "We do not _____, we _____."

Tell each small group's statement to the whole group. (5 minutes)

Today's withstanding self-justification practice

Self-justification: We all have to make sacrifices for this vision to become reality.

In groups of about five people make a list of the weaknesses that lie behind this self-justification. What would a hesed community do to be sure these weaknesses do not prevail? (10 minutes)

Report each small group's conclusions to the whole group. (5 minutes)

Today's loving my enemy practice

This exercise is like texting with God. Write the impression that comes to your mind. Start with something that makes you grateful then your impression of God's response. Next read the question

and write your impression of God's response that gives you peace. (5 minutes)

1. Dear God, I am thankful:
2. My dear child:
3. God, when has someone felt like an enemy to me this week?
4. What do You want me to know about loving them?

Read what you have written in groups of about five people. Do not explain what you wrote. Check for a sense of peace after you read. (5 minutes)

Building loyalty around weakness

1. Gather in groups of about five and pool your experiences with the following questions. (15 minutes)

    a. What are my first reactions to being called "weak" or having a weakness pointed out in a group?

    b. Have you ever seen someone struggling with a weakness and stopped to help them? How was it received?

    c. Have you ever tried to point out a weakness to a leader? How was it received?

2. Pool your experiences with leaders (10 minutes)

    a. How are you impacted by leaders who are consistently positive about their vision, organization, plans, abilities, and goals?

    b. How are you impacted by leaders who are transparent about their weaknesses?

3. Read the passage from 2 Corinthians 11:27-30 (NASB) below and list all the ways Paul illustrates building loyalty around weakness and what we can learn from him. (15 minutes)

    I have been in labor and hardship, through many sleepless nights, in hunger and thirst, often without food, in cold and exposure. Apart from such external things, there is the daily pressure on me of concern for all the churches. Who is weak without my being weak? Who is led into sin without my intense concern? If I have to boast, I will boast of what pertains to my weakness.

4. Report to the whole group what you learned from Paul. (5 minutes)

Repeating today's group identity affirmation

Repeat together, "We are a people who remind each other who we really are whenever we forget."

CHAPTER SEVEN

"I Am Not Alone"

A Bedtime Prayer

I will both lie down in peace, and sleep; For You alone, O LORD, make me dwell in safety.
Psalm 4:8

Mount Everest is not where city folk learn to climb; it is a test of stamina, technical skills, and teamwork. Facing narcissism is not where we learn basic godly character development.

This chapter examines how individuals interact with their group identity to raise hesed and lower qasheh. Raising and purifying hesed develops the spiritual stamina we need to address Pandora problems. When all we do is keep the lid on our Pandora's box we also keep hope locked inside as Pandora did in the myth.

Earlier in this book we studied Psalm 4:2, *"How long, O you sons of men, shall you turn My glory into shame and how long will you love worthlessness?"* By the final verse of Psalm four David is safely at rest. *"I will both lie down in peace, and sleep; For You alone, O LORD, make me dwell in safety."* In this psalm we will discover David's way to escape the narcissism trap.

Psalm 4 is a bedtime prayer as David starts his day with prayer. You may recall that for God, our day starts at sundown. Starting our day with God means giving God the evening hours we often spend lowering our joy with the evening news.

From God's perspective the day starts in the evening with togetherness and rest. Then God works half a day and wakes us up in the morning to join Him for the second half of the day.

The following psalm (Psalm 5) is a morning prayer. These two prayers are among the first things Hebrew children learned as they memorized all of the Psalms.

The reason for studying this entire Psalm is twofold. First we learn how to deal with stiff-necked people. Second we avoid becoming qasheh ourselves. Our people accept being weak and suffer without self-justification.

Psalms are Hebrew poetry. Like all poetry, there can be several meanings for the same line. Translators must pick one of the meanings. Which meaning they pick often depends on how they read the poetic structure. In this Psalm our first puzzle is the key phrase, "turn My glory into shame." (NASB) Who is saying "my" – God or David? Many of the cues come from the poetic structure.

In the NASB translation, "My" is capitalized by the translators indicating they believe this is God speaking. The original does not have capitalization so this is a guess based on context. Since Hebrew poetry rhymes thoughts rather than sounds, every place we have a rhyming thought we have two chances to understand the meaning. Here is an example:

> How long ... shall you turn My glory into shame
> how long will you love worthlessness?

By studying the rhyme we discover that "turning glory into shame" is the meaning of "loving worthlessness."

THE POEM'S STRUCTURE

Translators may not agree about meaning or poetic structure of texts. To place as much text as possible on scrolls, words were not separated by spaces. Separate lines and indentations were not used to lay out poetry. Melodies that might have given hints are also missing from psalms.

So, how does the poetry flow for Psalm 4? The people who added verse numbers (not in the original either) gave us eight stanzas of two lines each. In *The Message*, the translator created six stanzas with three lines each. *The Message* had to split a thought between stanza five and six in order to get three-line stanzas.

I suggest that a better structure would have five stanzas. The first and last stanzas rhyme with each other, matching messages. We will label them "A." In this case both sections marked "A" are talking to God.

The second stanza and the second from the end match ideas. We label them "B." Both stanzas marked "B" address people who need to correct their ways.

The middle stanza combines aspects of "A" and "B" into the main point or resolution of the conflict between "A" and "B." Whenever we find this chiasmic structure in Hebrew, the main point is in the middle. In this case we find advice to speak to God, quiet ourselves, and go to bed without sinning.

Let's look at it as a diagram:

A			(Psalmist talks to God.)
	B		(Psalmist talks to his group.)
		A + B	(Psalmist tells his group to talk to God.)
	B		(Psalmist talks to his group.)
A			(Psalmist talks to God.)

We can indent the text to match this diagram and then look at what we can learn from the song. Here is the poem:

Psalm Four

an evening prayer to start the day

A (v 1) (Psalmist talks to God.)

Hear me when I call,
O God of my righteousness!
You have relieved me in my distress;
Have mercy on me, and hear my prayer.

B (v 2) (Psalmist talks to his group.)

> **How long, O you sons of men,**
> **Will you turn [my] glory to shame?**
> **How long will you love worthlessness**
> **And seek falsehood? Selah**

A+B (vs 3-4) (Psalmist tells his group to talk to God.)

But know that the LORD has set apart for Himself him who is godly;
The LORD will hear when I call to Him.
Be angry, and do not sin.
Meditate within your heart on your bed, and be still. Selah

B (vs 5-6) (Psalmist talks to his group.)

> **Offer the sacrifices of righteousness,**
> **And put your trust in the LORD.**
> **There are many who say, "Who will show us any good?"**
> **LORD, lift up the light of Your countenance upon us.**

A (vs 7-8) (Psalmist talks to God.)

You have put gladness in my heart,
More than in the season that their grain and wine increased.
I will both lie down in peace, and sleep;
For You alone, O LORD, make me dwell in safety.

AN INTERPRETATION

In the first part (A) and the last part (A) the Psalmist is talking to God. The two parts (B) are addressed to people in David's identity group who are not in good relationship with God. Placed together, the two B parts constitute a healthy shame message. Right in the middle (A + B), is how we purify our group identity with God's help.

In the first stanza, the Psalmist remembers times God has been with him and purified his life with righteousness. **Remembering God is with us and purifies our lives is the first step in facing narcissism. Our people purify hesed.** We saw in the last chapter that an unpurified hesed allowed qasheh to win in David's group identity.

The second stanza raises the question of whether God or David is speaking. *"How long will you turn my glory into shame?"* Some commentators say the "sons of men" are mortals and God is speaking, saying, "Listen up, people. How long will you turn my glory into shame?" We have read the text that way thus far.

Other commentators believe David is speaking and reminding the "big shots" that they are humans. These stiff-necked qasheh people that we have been calling narcissists are turning David's glory into shame. Many people were dead-set on humiliating David and saying bad things about him including his generals, wife, children, and Saul.

In the last chapter we observed that one reason Scripture devotes such a huge amount of space to narcissists is because of what happens when God shares rule with people. For God's will to be done on earth as it is in Heaven requires that people share their dominion with God. Under ideal conditions of shared rule, what people request or require would mirror what God requests or requires.

Because the "my" can be read as either God or David speaking, it reflects the reality of shared rule. **To face narcissism we must share rule over our dominion (from as small as our body to as large as our kingdom) with God. Our people are God's people.**

Although the second stanza could be God or David speaking, if we go back to the poetic structure and compare the two sections we have marked "B" we conclude David is speaking. The second stanza marked "B" is clearly David speaking so the matching first stanza marked "B" is also David giving a healthy shame message. "How long will you, O sons of men (you tough guys, you big shots) turn my glory into shame? How long will you love worthless delusions?"

Narcissism and seeking falsehood

How long will you love worthlessness and seek falsehood? Selah

Low hesed people – like Saul who was out to kill David – love their qasheh thoughts about others. Saul saw David as a threat, and what Saul considered safety was a danger to David. Saul threw his spear at Jonathan while making this point.

People who steal glory, demean others, and make themselves look good actively believe falsehoods. David sings, "How long will you try to make me look bad? How long will you love lies? "Selah: Stop and think!" he says and the music stops a moment. **To face qasheh narcissism we must speak up to the people in our identity group, correcting their worthless lies about glory that create shame instead. Our people do not listen to self-justified deceptions.**

Dr. Karl Lehman helps us understand how qasheh people actively desire lies. On the left side of the brain is a function Dr. Lehman calls the *verbal logical explainer* or the *VLE*. We mentioned the VLE in Chapter Three. Logic, words, and reasoning focus our conscious attention on the left side of the brain. The right side of the brain is more relational and leads our hesed bonds, gut reactions, and group identity. If the right brain is blocked then the left brain makes up explanations that justify our reactions and beliefs with whatever explanation keeps us from pain. These are lies we love. Without our right-brain relational circuits, we will believe the lies and justifications from the VLE.[1]

The Psalmist speaks to self-justified thinking. He says something like, "If your thoughts shame others to take away their glory, your worthless thoughts are not what God wants you to think."

Qasheh minds seek falsehood. Stiff-necked narcissists actively support their false reality. They love to imagine ways to make others look bad, make themselves look good, get in a snide remark, or be quick with a put-down. This is an active and intentional mind process. Narcissists like thinking bad things about others. "If they lose I win," is the qasheh (and sociopathic) mindset. Narcissists expend the kind of energy making others look bad that lovers would put into a love affair.

When we want to believe lies and turn people's glory into shame, we will love a good justification for our actions and attitudes. "Of course he/she is a bad person! Of course we should get rid of them, not listen to them, not let them into our identity group." **To face narcissism we must actively stop the lies we love. Our people love our enemies and share their pain.**

Section A/B

The center of the poem combines the themes from Sections A and B into a resolution. Section A is addressed to God. Section B is addressed to narcissists. In Section A/B we find David telling narcissists how to interact with God. He reminds them in verse three, *"But know that the LORD has set apart for Himself him who is godly; The LORD will hear when I call to Him."*

In the next verse, David tells the qasheh, "If you are going to rage, do not sin. Go consult your heart on your bed and be still. Selah. Think about it." The music stops again for a moment.

Remember your group identity when you are angry.

Paul quotes from this bedtime Psalm in Ephesians 4:26, admonishing readers not to go to bed while angry. Talk to God and hear His perspective. God's people (our group identity) need God's perspective before our anger will improve relationships

---

1   For more on the VLE see Dr. Lehman's website kclehman.com.

with God and others. **To face narcissism we need to be sure anger does not lead to sin and we become less than our hesed, joyful identity would require. Our people stay hesed while angry.**

Does building hesed while angry sound difficult or even impossible? It is not impossible but is a learned, relational skill acquired through fellowship with people who still hear God when they are angry.[2] Hearing God while we are angry remains a pipe dream without meaningful fellowship during the moments we are angry.

Consult your heart.

In place of simply raging when things do not go as we want, David wants us to meditate at bedtime. The word *meditate* might be better translated as *speak with your own heart* or *talk to your heart*. **To face narcissism we must consult our hearts. Our people live from our heart connection with God.**

David's psalms frequently describe dialogues between two parts of us – our heart and our soul. While the word "soul" is not used in this passage, David's frequent references to the two parts lead us to the implication that the soul is speaking to the heart.

Why the soul? Our soul contains our emotions and upsets. David is saying, "The part of you that's upset, angry, agitated, raging, and furious must start the day (evening before bed) talking to God and hearing what God says to your heart."

Why the heart? Our heart is where we communicate with God. The heart is our eyes and ears in the spirit. Hearing through our heart how *God* sees our situation is how we can avoid sin. Speaking with God keeps our hesed attachment with God clean and strong. **We need clean hesed to face narcissism.**

David ends with, "and be still." **To face narcissism we must quiet ourselves. Our people seek shalom.** David writes very specifically: "I'm going to call on God, and He's going to answer me, and you better quiet yourself and listen to God, also." Here is the focus of this Psalm and the core of his healthy shame message.

---

2   *Transforming Fellowship*, Chris Coursey, pp. 149-170.

David's second address to his narcissists

In verse five, the Psalmist addresses the second Part B to qasheh people, reminding them that turning to God is the answer. *"Offer the sacrifices of righteousness, (or gifts of righteousness), and put your trust in Yahweh. There are many who say, 'Who will show us any good?' LORD, lift up the light of Your countenance upon us."*

David quotes from the Aaronic blessing in Numbers 6:24-26: *"The LORD bless you and keep you; The LORD make His face shine upon you, and be gracious to you; The LORD lift up His countenance upon you, and give you peace."* This blessing was said over Israel every night and fits with an evening prayer. To David, having God's countenance and blessings is what prosperity looks like. We are prosperous again when God's smile shines upon us.

Gladness in our hearts when alone

In the final Part A David ends by talking with God. In verse seven, he responds to God's presence: *"You have put gladness in my heart, more than in the time that their corn and their wine increased."* David says, "Yahweh's face is the best feast."

David finishes with verse eight: *"I will both lie down in peace and sleep; for You alone, O LORD, make me dwell in safety."* G. Campbell Morgan points out that "You alone" does not mean "the Lord and none other." Instead, Morgan suggests that although *David is alone* in solitude, Jehovah makes him dwell safely.[3] The word בָדָד translated *alone* in this passage does not refer to God, it refers to David. "When I am lonely" would be a good translation.

This same word **alone** is first used in Leviticus 13:46, *"He is unclean, and he shall dwell **alone**; his dwelling shall be outside the camp."* Jeremiah 15:17 also uses this word. *"I did not sit in the assembly of the mockers, nor did I rejoice; I sat **alone** because of Your hand, for You have filled me with indignation."* In Lamentations 1:1 we read: *"How **lonely** sits the city that was full of people! How like a widow is she, who was great among the nations!"*

The Psalmist is saying, "When I am alone, like a widow or forsaken in the wilderness then the Lord makes me dwell in safety." The Psalmist lies down in loneliness, turns to God and says, "This is when I count on You."

---

3   G. Campbell Morgan's Exposition on the Whole Bible. Morgan, G. Campbell. "Commentary on Psalms 4:4". Public domain. http://www.studylight.org/commentaries/gcm/psalms-4.html. 1857-84.

A narcissist is always alone even among people. Low levels of hesed/agape (attachment) create isolation. The three rules of a narcissist's game, 1) self-justification is good, 2) I should not suffer, and 3) weakness is bad, ensure loneliness (attachment pain). David sings that even with loneliness he is not alone.

SAFETY

God directly contradicts the narcissist's rule two that, "I should not suffer." As we look at the last verse of this psalm we should wonder what God means by safety: *"I will lay down in peace, and sleep; for You alone, O LORD, make me dwell in safety."* God does not keep us safe in the ways that people normally consider safety. When a Western ear hears, "God will keep me safe," most hear, "God will keep anything bad or painful or hurtful from happening to me."

What is safety?

The word rendered *safety* in this psalm is the word בֶּטַח *batach*. *"Thou O LORD, make me dwell in* batach." This word can be translated as *safety* or *no cares*. "You make me lie down with no cares (with assurance, with confidence, with hope or unafraid.)"[4]

Jeremiah 49:31 renders batach, *"Arise, go up to the wealthy nation that dwells* **securely**," *says the LORD,* "*Which has neither gates nor bars, Dwelling alone.*" Jeremiah describes an unprotected place, a place with no other gates or bars around it. As David sleeps on the side of the hills with no fortifications he can dwell securely. Meanwhile, King Saul is surrounded by thousands of guards but not secure for no qasheh person will be secure.

A good rendition of verse eight would be, "I will both lie down in peace and sleep, for in You, Yahweh, I trust and have no worries in this isolated and desolate situation."

The passage is a long way from saying that God will keep anything bad from happening to us. It is saying, "When I am isolated, withdrawn, separated or desolate, I have no worries. There is One I can trust. As long as Yahweh is with me, I will sleep."

David's batch story

Let's look at David's actual lying-down-to-sleep story:

---

4   The word *batach* is used in all these ways in the King James Version.

Then Saul sought to pin David to the wall with the spear, but he slipped away from Saul's presence; and he drove the spear into the wall. So David fled and escaped that night. Saul also sent messengers to David's house to watch him and to kill him in the morning. And Michal, David's wife, told him, saying, "If you do not save your life tonight, tomorrow you will be killed." So Michal let David down through a window. And he went and fled and escaped. And Michal took an image and laid it in the bed, put a cover of goats' hair for his head, and covered it with clothes. So when Saul sent messengers to take David, she said, "He is sick." Then Saul sent the messengers back to see David, saying, "Bring him up to me in the bed, that I may kill him."'

1 Samuel 19:10-15

Here is David's life of safety. David sings an evening prayer, "How long, O Saul will you turn my glory into shame – believe false things about me – Be angry Saul, but don't sin. Talk to your heart instead of thinking about how to pin me to the bed – quiet yourself and seek righteousness. Selah."

The nephews

Consider David's safety in reference to the sons of Zeruiah – Joab and Abashai. Abner wanted to bring the tribes from Saul's side over to David. David's glory was turned to shame when Joab and Abashai killed Abner. Imagine David in camp one night. His generals, the sons of Zeruiah, listen to him sing this night prayer, "How long, you sons of Zeruiah, will you turn my glory into shame? You have endangered a kingdom. Be angry and sin not, Sons of Zeruiah! Selah. I will both lay down in peace and sleep. You, Lord, are the One I trust."

PAUL

In the New Testament we see another Saul rail against the Lord and His Anointed. Saul imagines vain things, believes lies, and justifies killing people for God. But something happens that changes Saul to Paul as he stops and listens to God's voice. Saul checks his heart to see if the things he believes are true. Stopping and listening to God changes him. Here we see the transformation of a hardcore qasheh narcissist with sociopathic tendencies into the character of Christ.

Years later Paul writes to the Ephesians saying they have not learned to love deceitful things from Christ. As a group they should put off their former behavior and put on the new identity they have received from Christ. Paul gives their group identity as the reason, "for you are members of one another."[5] Then Paul quotes Psalm 4, admonishing them to change their ways: *"Be angry and sin not. Do not let the sun go down on your wrath."* You are new creatures who are changing from a Saul into a Paul." Change is possible for narcissists.

NICHOLAS RIDLEY

Consider another example from the English reformation – Bishop Nicholas Ridley. He was put to death as a heretic in 1555, but his execution was actually politically motivated. On the night preceding his execution, Nicholas Ridley's brother offered to pass the last hours with him, but Bishop Ridley refused, saying he meant to go to bed and sleep as quietly as he ever did in his life. He said, *"I will lay me down in peace; for You alone, O LORD, make me dwell in safety"*

The next morning he was chained to a stake in the town ditch, opposite the front of Balliol College, Oxford. As the flames rose around him the Bishop declared in a loud voice in Latin and English, "Lord, Lord, receive my spirit."[6]

Ridley illustrates the safety in Psalm 4:8. There is no promise we will not get burned at the stake in the morning. Safety does not mean the king will not catch us, we will not be lonely, or we will be free from pain. Safety means that no created thing, person, or fate can keep our life from accomplishing God's purpose.

When we can look at Ridley and see him as safe, we are ready to lead a team, family, or congregation to face narcissism. Our stamina, technical skills, and team building can face a Mount Everest of narcissism even if we will burn in the morning.

When we are safe, like David and Ridley, we are able to lead our group to face qasheh. If we still fear then we should not lead expeditions – we need to develop godly maturity and character as part of a group identity. Even if a Pandora problem is right in front of us, we need more preparation. Try starting every day

---

5   Ephesians 4:25
6   W. Graham Scroggie, The Psalms (Old Tappan, N.J.: Fleming H. Revell Co., 1973 reprint

(every evening) by reading or singing Psalm 4 aloud instead of watching the evening news. Pray this prayer for 30 days, memorize it, and speak to your heart.

Singing this song did not change David's predatory identity, correct his narcissistic leaders, or keep his sons from becoming narcissistic predators. Changing someone's character cannot be accomplished through highly qualified individuals; it is the combined work of God and a strong group identity in God's people. A godly group identity raises hesed and lowers qasheh in its members.

As we view the group around our personal Pandora problems, we help create a *people* by raising *hesed* and lowering *qasheh* until we spontaneously love our enemies. Lowering qasheh means removing self-justification from the group. Fr. Ubald, whom we met in Chapter One, needed to end self-justifications in his parish in order to see transformations. Perpetrators and victims all had justifications for why they didn't hesed their enemies.

We will focus next on how a group identity can recognize and deal with self-justification.

Hear me, YHWH, and relieve my distress again.
Powerful people may shame me and love lies about me.
You listen when I call no matter how angry they are at me.
If I am angry and want to shame others, I will speak to my heart.
I will trust in YHWH, and You will give me joy.
Although I am lonely, I will lie down and sleep in peace
because I am confident in YHWH.

Facing Narcissism Safely

- To face narcissism the first step is to remember God is with us and purifies our lives.

- To face narcissism we must share rule over our dominion (from as small as our body to as large as our kingdom) with God.

- To face narcissism we must speak up to the people in our identity group correcting their worthless lies about glory that instead create shame.

- To face narcissism we must actively stop the lies we love.

- To face narcissism we need to be sure anger does not lead to sin making us less than our joyful, hesed identity would inspire.

- To face narcissism we must consult our hearts.

- To face narcissism we need clean hesed.

- To face narcissism we must quiet ourselves.

If You Are Ready
Group Exercise for Chapter Seven

Today's group identity affirmation

Repeat together, "We are a people who know we are weak. We help each other grow where each of us is weak."

In groups of about five people tell each other why this characteristic matters to you. (5 minutes)

Today's healthy shame message practice

In groups of about five people create a healthy shame message for me when <u>I continue thinking that others are envious of me.</u> (5 minutes)

Note: A healthy shame message states "we do not" and then states who we are with a Christ-like character response. "We do not _____, we _____."

Tell each small group's statement to the whole group. (5 minutes)

Today's withstanding self-justification practice

Self-justification: I cannot believe the stupidity of what you (they) are doing.

In groups of about five people make a list of the weaknesses that lie behind this self-justification. What would a hesed community do to be sure these weaknesses do not prevail? (10 minutes)

Report each small group's conclusions to the whole group. (5 minutes)

Today's loving my enemy practice

This exercise is like texting with God. Write the impression that comes to your mind. Start with something that makes you grateful then your impression of God's response. Next read the question and write your impression of God's response that gives you peace. (5 minutes)

1. Dear God, I am thankful:
2. My dear child:
3. God, when has someone felt like an enemy to me this week?
4. What do You want me to know about loving them?

Read what you have written in groups of about five people. Do not explain what you wrote. Check for a sense of peace after you read. (5 minutes)

Loving my enemies: Excerise 1

Consider the following situation:

> You meet a Christian friend from your church's small group for a walk or coffee. Your friend is annoyed with George who pushes his opposite political views in group and Jane who can be very irritating and critical. Your friend wants to quit coming to group.

Answer the following questions in small groups of about five people. (30 minutes)

1. What are the usual responses when talking to someone who wants to leave an irritating situation?

2. What do you believe is going on inside your friend's mind?

3. In how many ways does this situation involve loving our enemies?

4. What would genuinely change your friend's first reactions to George and Jane?

5. What needs to change in the small group to create a stronger group identity?

6. When have you seen genuine improvement in loving enemies? What helped?

Gather as a whole group and discuss answers to question 6 – what have you seen that helps Christians love their enemies and have a fundamentally different response to them? Keep answers short and make a list together. (15 minutes)

Repeating today's group identity affirmation

Repeat together, "We are a people who know we are weak. We help each other grow where each of us is weak."

CHAPTER EIGHT

Self-Justification

The Good Samaritan

**But wishing to justify himself, he said to Jesus,
"And who is my neighbor?"**
Luke 10:29 (NASB)

The Good Samaritan is so well known in Western culture that many people do not even realize it comes from the Bible. We immediately think of someone who helps a stranger in need. When Jesus told the parable, however, His main point was not about helping strangers. Let's have another look at how this story can help us distinguish self-justification, making ourselves understood, codependency, and God's justification by grace.

WHAT IS THE MAIN POINT OF THE PARABLE?

For most readers, the parable of the Good Samaritan begins with a lawyer asking, "Who is my neighbor?" We think the parable is Jesus' answer to that question. But Jesus never answers the question, "who is my neighbor." Jesus sidesteps the lawyer's question and goes directly after the lawyer's motives.

Almost every conclusion we have heard from this parable, except for one, can be found in the story itself. Like all of His teachings, as Jesus speaks to one issue He addresses many other topics. What we cannot conclude from the parable is how to justify our actions. We have already seen in Chapter One that it is impossible for the human mind to calculate the right thing to do. This parable will help us respond to self-justification which is the main symptom of qasheh and the main block to hesed.

THE LAWYER

In Luke 10:25-28 a lawyer tested Jesus by asking Him how to gain eternal life. Like lawyers today, the lawyers of Jesus' time never asked a question if they did not already know the answer. This lawyer had memorized the entire Old Testament and knew how it fit together. Jesus answered his question with a question: "What is the greatest commandment?" When the man answered that the greatest commandments were to "*Love the LORD your God with all your heart, with all your soul and with all your strength and with all your mind; and your neighbor as yourself,*" Jesus told him to do this and he would live.

The first commandment quoted was from Deuteronomy 6:5. The second commandment came from Leviticus 19:18. Examining verse eighteen in its entirety reveals a text that begins with a reference to group identity. "*You shall not take vengeance or bare any grudge against the sons of your people.*" Our response to offenses by our identity group should be governed by these two great truths: "*but you shall love your neighbor as yourself; I am the LORD.*" Placed together, God is Lord and loving our neighbor as ourselves reveals our group character. Even when our neighbor acts like an enemy, we will love. This identity is not open for discussion. Our God has this character. What our people do to us does not justify a grudge.

Explaining **is done in order to feel satisfied that we have said what we needed to say for clarity.**

Self-justification **is always at the expense of another.**

This unquoted context for the second greatest commandment is the setting for the parable. God sees that we want to have vengeance, to bear grudges, and to hold things against those who do not love us as we would like. For these self-justified reasons we stop seeing others as our people. We stop our hesed. Narcissists, as we have seen, justify angry responses to those who fail to love them well enough. Holding a grudge, not forgiving, and "giving others a taste of their own medicine" are all self-justifications for not loving.

If you have had a relationship with a narcissist you noticed that narcissists punish those they feel deserve punishment for not loving the narcissists well enough. Punishment is done through shame, anger, blame, and humiliation. A narcissist only loves those the narcissist believes deserve love at that moment.

BEHOLD!

In the last chapter we noticed that the original Hebrew texts did not have either spaces or capitalization. Now we will notice that there were no punctuation marks in the text either. When the Scripture writers wanted emphasis they often used the word "Behold." When reading the story of the Good Samaritan, most of us skip over this important word in Luke 10:25, only noticing the lawyer's question, "Who is my neighbor?"

The text asks us to "Behold a certain lawyer" who, against all God's teaching about self-justification, desired to justify himself (v 27). Can you imagine a lawyer making such an error! There in front of Jesus in the full light of day a lawyer is trying to justify himself. Jesus' response answers a question we have been asking for the last seven chapters – what are we going to do with people who justify themselves?

This pericope is as interesting for what Jesus does not say as it is for what He does say. We may ask ourselves, "What is Jesus going to do – answer the question or speak to the problem?" Jesus picked up the motive: *"Desiring to justify himself."* A man justifying himself by asking who his neighbor might be is not interested in how to hesed!

Jesus himself obeys Leviticus 19:18. Even when the lawyer tries to discredit Him, Jesus treats the lawyer like a member of His identity group. We will notice that Jesus does not follow narcissist's rules and, in fact, challenges them. We can imagine Jesus thinking, "I have this wonderful man here. He wants to have eternal life, but one thing can stop him. He is intent on justifying himself."

Jesus strips off the man's self-justification with a story that would inspire anyone to justify themselves but adds a twist; one person does something that is hard to justify. Jesus does not let the point slip and ends with a direct question to the self-justifier. Let us examine how Jesus handles a qasheh master of self-justification.

SELF-JUSTIFICATION

Self-justification is probably the most consistent, reliable, and definite way to get in trouble with God. God can deal with our sin – a provision is already made and confession will apply that solution. We can sin against our neighbor, have a grudge, and if we do not justify ourselves we can find forgiveness. But when we justify ourselves, we are stuck. Self-justification will keep us out of the Kingdom of God. From one end of Scripture to the other there are no exceptions.

Explaining versus justifying

Self-justifying is easily confused with *explaining myself*. There is a major difference between making ourselves look good and making ourselves clear.

Explaining: making ourselves understandable

Mature people work to make themselves understood. When someone misunderstands what we have said or done we need to work to clarify our meaning. Making ourselves clear is not what Scripture means by self-justification.

Jesus often explained Himself and worked hard to help people understand, even when it was not what they wanted to hear. Jesus, the apostles, and all of us must clarify our meaning. That is not self-justification but part of maturity. Explaining is done in order to feel satisfied that we have said what we needed to say for clarity.

Self-justifying: passing a favorable judgment on ourselves

Self-justification is done for the purpose of making us look right, good, or better than others and goes beyond explaining. Self-justifying goes past simply explaining ourselves in an effort to pass a favorable judgment on ourselves. Self-justification is always at the expense of another.

Self-justifiers try to make what they are doing look righteous, not just understandable, and that is the problem. Jesus said in Matthew 23:27: *"Woe to you, scribes and Pharisees, hypocrites! For you are like whitewashed tombs which indeed appear beautiful outwardly, but inside are full of dead men's bones and all uncleanness."*

Self-justifying narcissists

Narcissists cannot distinguish explaining from justifying. Now that we are distinguishing explaining ourselves from self-justification we can notice that not only do narcissists justify themselves, but qasheh people are very intolerant of those who try to explain themselves. Narcissists read their own motives into other's attempts to be clear.

Let us consider the person in the center of a Pandora problem. A self-justified person will invalidate what others say even when others are clarifying meanings and intentions. Narcissists invalidate by pointing out faults and failings using their good mental notes on the weaknesses of others. Weaknesses are bad! Limitations are unacceptable! (This is narcissist game-rule three.)

We find self-justifiers in all levels of management, education, politics, church leadership, and family life. They do not humble themselves before God and say, "I also have sinned, so I can't justify what I do. It is up to me to love my neighbor as myself rather than passing judgment on him or punishing him for all that I feel makes him weak and inferior." Qasheh people are not looking to expand their hesed love to include enemies but rather to justify themselves so they do not need to share the pain of others.

DEALING WITH SELF-JUSTIFICATION

We begin learning how to deal with self-justification in this passage and will expand the discussion in our next chapter. Let's see what Jesus did:

> *Then Jesus answered and said, "A certain man went down from Jerusalem to Jericho, and fell among thieves, who stripped him of his clothing, wounded him, and departed, leaving him half dead. Now by chance a certain priest came down that road. And when he saw him, he passed by on the other side. Likewise a Levite, when he was at the place, came and looked, and passed by on the other side.* Luke 10:30-31

Most of us already have in our minds that the priest and Levite were bad guys. The listeners of Jesus' time would not think that way. To His listeners, the priest and the Levite had a lot of justification for passing by on the other side. The lawyer would expect a rabbinical debate on the laws governing whether or not these two were justified in passing by. Many factors influence the right thing to do. Self-justification makes a great debate.

The priest's justification

Let's look at the things that justify the priest's actions. Jesus' listeners and the lawyer knew things most of us do not, like the many rules regarding priestly duties. The naked man left for dead by the robbers created difficult choices for the priest to make.

Here lay a naked and possibly dead man who was unidentifiable. People's group identity was established by what they wore. The questions in a rabbinical debate would focus whether or not this unidentifiable person is one of the children of God and dead or alive. The priest does not know and may not be willing to risk becoming unclean for what might be a dead body.

It was not just a matter of touching the corpse; the priest could not approach closer than four cubits of a dead man without becoming defiled. In order to see if this man was dead or alive, the priest would have to get closer than four cubits. The priest and Levite could not cross the road to look without risking a high cost for their compassion as the original listeners knew. We will see that this cost was an important part of the story.

Although priests were not allowed to touch a dead body lest they become unclean, the *mishna,* which was the teachings about the Law, made an exception for neglected corpses. If this was a neglected corpse on the side of the road the priest would not become unclean by going over and helping unless the body was not one of his people, then he would be unclean. This makes a wonderful debate. Theologians love staying up late debating these things over seven or eight pots of coffee.

As the lawyer listened to Jesus, he would have loved this rabbinical argument. The priest and the Levite could have used the Law to justify many options. What a marvelous debate about the Law! Jesus is telling a great parable thus far for someone who would justify himself. The lawyer could discuss this a long time.

Additional justifications

Consider the cost to the priest for becoming unclean. As a priest, doing his duties was how he and his family were fed. The priest in Jesus' story is on his way home from the temple. For a priest to become unclean on his way back from the temple would end the value of his service.

Becoming unclean would mean an immediate return to Jerusalem. The process of restoring spiritual purity was time-consuming and costly. The ritual for cleansing would take a week. This is part of the cost whirling in the priest's mind as he passes by. This brings us to the narcissist rule two: I should not have to suffer. Why should God's work, family needs, and the costs involved be risked? What if this is not my people?

THE SAMARITAN

Now back to the parable:

> "But a certain Samaritan, as he journeyed, came where he was. And when he saw him, he had compassion. So he went to him and bandaged his wounds, pouring on oil and wine; and he set him on his own animal, brought him to an inn, and took care of him. On the next day, when he departed, he took out two denarii, gave them to the innkeeper, and said to him, 'Take care of him; and whatever more you spend, when I come again, I will repay you.'" Luke 10:33-35

For the Samaritan, seeing this man lying there on the ground was a stomach-churning event. It was gut-wrenching – it moved him with compassion. The Greek word for compassion means *to be moved in one's bowels*. We saw this word *splagchnon* in Chapter Three when St. John was teaching about hesed/agape.[1] For St. John, the lack of a splagchnon response was proof that we have no hesed love inside. The Samaritan passed this "gut" test for love.

Jesus goes into great detail to show the cost that the Samaritan paid for his compassion. As He enumerates all the costs on the Samaritan's side, the local audience compares that to the cost of what the priest and the Levite might experience if those holy men crossed the four cubits line.

The listeners did not care if the Samaritan became unclean, but they would notice the cost he paid. The Samaritan bound up the fallen man's wounds, pouring on oil and wine. He gave of his time and energy; he got involved. He gave of his food or possibly his

---

1   1 John 3:17

merchandise. When he put the man on his donkey, he had to walk to the inn. While at the inn he took care of the man, spending money and leaving an open-ended expense account for all additional costs.

WHO HAS NEIGHBORLINESS INSIDE?

Jesus asks the lawyer a question that probes the lawyer's group identity. Jesus deviates from the lawyer's original question – *"Who is my neighbor?"* – and asks, *"Which of these became a neighbor to him who fell among robbers?"* Jesus asks, "Who was neighborly?" This is a question directly targeting the listener's group identity.

Who could look at an unidentifiable man and share pain? "To my guts he is my people!" Looking at the fallen man, the hesed in each of the three did the math and decided, "The cost of this mercy is too high" or, "I'll pay it," depending on whether his guts saw one of his people by the road.

The lawyer answers correctly, *"He who showed mercy on him."* The one with neighborliness inside is the one whose stomach churns. It is the man with hesed.

The lawyer was familiar with discussions in a story format. No one was surprised when Jesus asked, "Which of these three . . .?" Neither were they surprised that He changed questions. Even the issue of what kind of person one is inside was well known to Pharisees and lawyers.

People who do not justify themselves can always find a neighbor.

About the same time Jesus was talking with the lawyer, the Essenes, the people responsible for the Dead Sea Scrolls, were having something like a revival and causing a conflict within Judaism itself. The Essenes taught that it was not enough to follow the Law on the outside. One must obey the Law on the inside, too.

In telling this parable, Jesus has illustrated: 1) not accepting qasheh self-justification, 2) sharing pain, 3) loving our enemies, 4) focusing on the group identities of people who justify themselves, 5) His hesed responses to the lawyer plus hesed by the Samaritan, and 6) placing a call for change on the lawyer.

Jesus ends the parable with a group identity question the lawyer must answer, and then He tells the lawyer to go and do likewise. The man must now consider: Will I continue justifying myself? Will my stomach churn? Do I, like my God and His people, have neighborliness inside? Will I pay the cost?

CAN WE JUSTIFY CUTTING COSTS?

What was it that the lawyer wanted to justify? He wanted to justify avoiding the cost of loving his neighbor. We can see that the lawyer wanted to justify himself for some cost-cutting with neighbors because he did not ask, "How do I love God with all my heart, soul, and mind?" He was thinking, "Love my neighbor as myself? Now that could be expensive. That could be problematic. There are a bunch of people out there I do not like. I need to make this manageable. Let me cut some costs."

A Jewish person would debate what he or she had to do for God, but the cost of pleasing God is never an issue for them. The cost of loving our neighbors is a different matter.

What good reason does the Samaritan have for paying the cost of helping a Jewish fellow who probably despises him? There is no reason in the world that he would be obliged to pay that cost. It is unjustifiable, and that is the shocking part of the parable.

ONLY ONE COMMANDMENT

1 John 4:20 says, *"If someone says, 'I love God,' and hates his brother, he is a liar; for he who does not love his brother whom he has seen, how can he love God whom he has not seen?"*

St. John ties loving God and our neighbor together. Unlike the lawyer, St. John sees only one commandment with two expressions. If we say we love God and do not love our brother we simply do not love God. Christian character only matures as the hesed of God becomes indistinguishable from our agape for others. Loving God is only real when expressed as hesed for our identity group – our brothers and sisters.

It is very easy to justify why we should not be involved in some messy lives: it will take too much time and be too costly. We are all prone to run the numbers and say, "Oh I don't want to get involved. The cost is too high."

Now consider the basic objective of all three of the narcissist's game rules – these rules reduce the cost of hesed for the narcissist. We share this urge with the lawyer and the narcissist. We want to justify deselecting someone as our neighbor.

We are prone to feelings and thoughts such as: "This will not only cost me too much but my family, servants, church, and community will be burdened as well. It will take a whole week to clean up my reputation." We feel the temptation to self-justification.

As a younger minister I found myself thinking just these thoughts when I was invited to do a New Age wedding. The couple wanted a shaman and they wanted a Christian holy man in their wedding. After the ceremony I would be welcome at their big party with an open bar.

I was a new minister in a denomination that totally forbade drinking. It would be easier to justify saying no to the couple than justifying my presence in a New Age party to my bishop. I found myself thinking, "If it gets back to the church that I was in the middle of a medicine circle with a shaman doing a wedding and everyone drinking it will ruin my reputation. (I would go from clean to unclean.) Can I justify myself?"

Yes, you caught me! I was thinking, 1) let me justify myself, 2) let them bear the cost of not having a Christian among them, and 3) I will avoid people who might make me look weak.

How often do we look at the cost of neighborliness and see it as a loss to us. And yet Jesus warns us against false cost savings. Those who do not agape because the cost is too high may justify their savings but risk their own souls. The lawyer wanted eternal life. Jesus seems to believe that if we gain the whole world and lose our souls we have false savings.

COST AND CODEPENDENCE

The group around a Pandora problem may act like a codependent. Codependence is a lifestyle built on false savings. Codependence is a pattern of fearfully trying to avoid big losses through accepting many smaller ones. *I give so I will not lose more.* Codependence looks like giving, but it is actually played by the same rules as the narcissist's game.

Codependents have many twisted variations on the narcissist's rule two – I should not have to suffer. For them, rule two becomes:

- I should not suffer if I make the predator happy.

- Suffering makes me a good person.

- My suffering protects my children.

- Many other variations

These are all false savings and based on defective systems for calculating what will cause the least suffering to the codependent's identity group. In this sense, codependents avoid suffering as much as narcissists do and follow the same rules.

Codependents have more hesed than narcissists. Often their suffering is shared pain from their children, friends, church, and other hostages of the narcissist. Codependency, gangs, cults, and organized crime are actually built with dirty forms of a hesed that has been contaminated by predators.

Codependents have a stronger group identity than narcissists and will often allow a predator to "snack" on them to "protect" the group. However when it comes to self-justification the codependents can be even better than narcissists. The same is true for the belief that weakness is bad. Codependents work like the devil to hide weaknesses in their group identity.

Sinful self-justification falls short of true justification just like money we print ourselves falls short of real value. Hesed motivates us to support true justification and avoid counterfeits.

HOW ARE WE JUSTIFIED?

We have looked closely at reasons for not self-justifying, starting with the total statistical impossibility of being right. Let's look at an opposite question: "How are we justified?" True justification has big implications for the cost we pay for our hesed life. Understanding justification opens the way to face narcissism.

Justified freely by His grace – Romans 3:24

St. Paul has much to say about being justified. First, we are justified freely by God's grace. *Freely* means that God pays the cost. God's grace is totally unjustified by anything except that God sees us as part of His identity group – as His children and occasionally His friends. God sees something special even in those who think they are God's enemies.

Part of God's grace to the world is His salvation. God gives grace directly but a second part of God's grace to the world flows through us. No one opposes God giving grace for salvation through Christ, but when God wants to give grace to somebody through us, we want to justify why we should not suffer.

This parable shows how God pays some of the cost for grace *through* us. God's grace to the world extends to those who are saved and to those being saved.[2] Our group (family) identity says we pay the price for others to receive grace even if they are our enemies. At one extreme we see that martyrs like Bishop Nicholas Ridley pay a cost for the grace that God gives to the world. Yet, when we give grace freely there is a daily cost. As we hesed our neighbors and enemies in spite of the cost to us it becomes God's grace.

Justified by faith without the deeds of the Law – Romans 3:28

In Romans 3:28 we read another aspect of justification. *"Therefore we conclude that a man is justified by faith apart from the deeds of the law."* Faith is about the things we cannot see or sense. We cannot *see* how God's cost or actions are justified. Further, whatever we do does not produce justification. Finally, our results do not seem to justify the costs. We are justified even when we can't see results.

Often God asks us to do things whose cost is difficult to justify. When we think about the places and times we have poured out our lives and what *seemed* to come of it, we are not sure the cost was justified. Part of living by faith and not by sight means letting God say if our suffering was worth it. We cannot provide an adequate justification for the cost to ourselves, to our families, or to anyone.

Justified by His blood – Romans 5:9

In Romans 5:9, St. Paul gives us a third element of justification: *"Much more then, having now been justified by His blood, we shall be saved from wrath through Him."* What does it mean to be justified by His blood? In biblical symbolism we find blood means "life."[3]

---

2   2 Corinthians 2:15
3   Hebrews 9:22, Leviticus 17:11, Deuteronomy 12:23

Unless we receive life from Christ we are all lifeless. We are justified, not by life which is ours (in our own blood) but from the life that is given to us through Christ.

Whatever real life we have is a gift from God through Christ. The life we now live is not our own. What God wants to do with that life is His business. So if we say, "Hey! If I go out there and get involved in this situation, it's going to cost me a little blood," God can say, "Whose blood are we talking about here?" It may not seem justified to us, but we are not the ones who justify.

Justified by death – Romans 6:7

We have all heard that Jesus died to justify us from our sins. Romans 5:10 says, *"For if when we were enemies we were reconciled* (by justification) *to God through the death of His Son, much more, having been reconciled, we shall be saved by His life."* Christ's death reconciled us – brought us back together.

But Jesus was not the only one to die! St. Paul points out in Romans 6:1-7 that we died with Christ and concludes; *"Now if we have died with Christ, we believe that we shall also live with Him."*[4] Our death becomes our justification. *"For he that has died is justified from sin."*[5]

We have died! God wants us to know, "You are dead already. Don't fear what you think is going to kill you. Don't resent your suffering. The life you have is My gift, your body simply doesn't know

Our group identity says we pay the price for others to receive grace even if they are our enemies.

yet that you are already dead. Let's not pretend that the cost to your body is the most important thing in the world."

Our death is a total wipe out to the narcissistic game rules. First, no justification is needed because we are dead. Second, we do not avoid suffering because it isn't our life anyway. Third, is anyone weaker than those who have died? What weakness shall we fear? Are we ready to live our new lives this way and face narcissism?

---

4   Romans 6:8
5   Romans 6:7 Darby Bible

Justified by God Himself Romans 8:33

Romans 8:33 gives us one more way we are justified: *"Who shall bring a charge against God's elect? It is God who justifies."* It is very easy to accept God justifying our sins. But God is also the only one who can justify how He invests our lives, what happens to us, what we suffer, what we lose. Only He can justify how much the bill runs up when we tell the innkeeper, "Whatever else is necessary, I will pay that, also."

WHATEVER THE COST

All of us know a little about open-ended costs from observing marriage. Couples pledge "for better or for worse." Whatever the bill becomes, whatever suffering it brings, whatever it takes, the couple pledges to pay. This is the kind of hesed love God expects from two people in a marriage. God asks us to have this same kind of hesed with Him – for better or for worse, whatever the cost, however it turns out, in sickness or in health.

The lawyer did not like the cost. He was seeking to justify himself. He asked, "Who is my neighbor?" Jesus asked him back, "Which of these three do you think became a neighbor? Who has eternal life inside that comes from God? Who can say, 'My eternal life is not my life but His. My life is poured out however God chooses to pour. Let God be the one who justifies.'"

Lord Jesus, these are difficult teachings. We all struggle with them. We continue to struggle with our tendency to justify ourselves. Reveal Your presence to us so clearly that we may walk with You wherever You lead. Lord Jesus Christ, be glorified in us.

Facing Self-Justification
(learning from Jesus)

- **Show hesed toward the self-justifier.**

    o Our motive is not a grudge or vengeance.

    o Our motives are not self-justified.

    o I treat the self-justifier as a member of my identity group.

- **Don't cost-cut (don't be codependent).**

- **Openly honor people who share other's pain.**

- **Focus on the hesed character of God's family group.**

- **Challenge self-justification without justifying ourselves.**

    o Make ourselves understood.

    o Address group identity.

    o Speak to the motive more than the issue.

    o Be clear and accurate about the cost.

    o Speak of the "stomach test" for hesed.

    o Ask a question of the narcissist to focus the need for hesed action.

If You Are Ready
Group Exercise for Chapter Eight

Today's group identity affirmation

> Repeat together, "We are a people who would rather listen than speak."

> In groups of about five people tell each other why this characteristic matters to you. (5 minutes)

Today's healthy shame message practice

> In groups of about five people create a healthy shame message for me when <u>I get angry when contradicted.</u> (5 minutes)

> *Note: A healthy shame message states "we do not" and then states who we are with a Christ-like character response. "We do not _____, we _____."*

> Tell each small group's statement to the whole group. (5 minutes)

Today's withstanding self-justification practice

> Self-justification: You wouldn't understand in a million years.

> In groups of about five people make a list of the weaknesses that lie behind this self-justification. What would a hesed community do to be sure these weaknesses do not prevail? (10 minutes)

> Report each small group's conclusions to the whole group. (5 minutes)

Today's loving my enemy practice

This exercise is like texting with God. Write the impression that comes to your mind. Start with something that makes you grateful then your impression of God's response. Next read the question and write your impression of God's response that gives you peace. (5 minutes)

1. Dear God, I am thankful:
2. My dear child:
3. God, when has someone felt like an enemy to me this week?
4. What do You want me to know about loving them?

Read what you have written in groups of about five people. Do not explain what you wrote. Check for a sense of peace after you read. (5 minutes)

Giving healthy shame messages: Exercise 2 (45 minutes)

1. Form small groups of about five people.

2. Divide the 26 items from *My Forgetful Moments Feedback Request* on the next page between the small groups.

3. Each small group make healthy shame messages with the items they have been given (as many as possible in 15 minutes.) Write down your healthy shame messages so you can read them to the whole group in step four.

4. Someone from each small group can read your group's healthy shame messages to the whole group. (10 minutes) If there are only enough people for one group then use these ten minutes to keep writing shame messages from the 26 items on *My Forgetful Moments Feedback Request*.

5. As a full group, take one minute to remember silently something that makes you thankful.

6. Silently ask God to help you see which of the 26 items on *My Forgetful Moments Feedback Request* would be most helpful to you. (2 minutes)

7. For the remainder of the time, take turns asking the group to read to you the healthy shame message that would be most helpful to you as an individual person.

8. If someone needs a healthy shame message for an item that no one had time to create, the group can create a healthy shame message together if there is time at the end.

Repeating today's group identity affirmation

Repeat together, "We are a people who would rather listen than speak."

My Forgetful Moments Feedback Request

Have you seen me forget who we are?
Tell me which of these ways you have noticed.

1. Can I put on emotions when it helps me win?

2. Can I be rigid and judgmental about who or what is right and wrong?

3. Do I not take criticism well? (I do not invite criticism or appreciate when it is given.)

4. Am I critical of others?

5. Am I sarcastic especially when alone with people I know?

6. Do I paint an unrealistic picture of how good my accomplishments are or have been?

7. Do I work hard for praise and things that make me look good?

8. Am I very interested in my money?

9. Do I undercut people who might take my power away?

10. Do I want my things right now?

11. Do I seek special treatment without questioning that I deserve it?

12. Am I condescending?

13. Do I dislike being just another member of a team?

14. Do I dominate conversations when I get talking?

15. Do my conversations tend to focus on my life and activities?

16. Do I "drop names" of the significant people I know, understand, or build upon?

17. Am I more likely to take credit for good results than contribute to hard work?

18. Do I seem blind to the needs and feelings of "unimportant" people?

19. Do I try to sound like I know what I am talking about when I really don't?

20. Do I make others feel unimportant?

21. Can I be charming when I want something?

22. Do I want people to be impressed with me?

23. Do I contradict myself but won't admit it?

24. Do I use high status people and their ideas to justify myself?

25. Do I get defensive about my authority when it is challenged?

26. Do I get angry at times others might have compassion?[6]

---

6   Questions based on characteristics listed in Narcissism in the Pulpit https://www. epiclesis.org/2015/05/narcissism-in-the-pulpit-2/

CHAPTER NINE

Avoiding Condemnation

Neither Give or Receive

**"If I justify myself, mine own mouth shall condemn me:
if I say, I am perfect, it shall also prove me perverse."**
Job 9:20 (KJV)

Healthy shame in the fast track of the right brain leads to better relationships and a stronger group identity. Narcissism develops as an avoidance of this healthy shame but comes to depend on toxic shame in the slow track of the left brain. This toxic shame creates condemnation. Condemnation is the biggest club narcissists carry.

- Condemnation is destructive unless left to God alone.

- Human or accusing spirit condemnations will poison a group identity if absorbed.

- The group around a Pandora problem must be highly resistant to condemnation or it will fall into self-justification.

- Lowering qasheh means resisting condemnation.

Self-justification is linked to condemnation.

Self-justification is a failed defense to condemnation. But if we justify ourselves it also implies we know who deserves condemnation. The Bible says this knowledge is absolutely impossible for humans. In Chapter One we saw the impossibility of knowing the right thing to do. We would need to know just as much to condemn anyone. The toxic judgments that condemn and poison us and our identity group are as bad as self-justifications. We need to escape condemnation in order to face narcissism.

Katagnosis **and** *katakrima*

We can avoid some confusion about condemnation by looking at two words that are both translated using the English concept of condemnation. We start with what St. Paul says in Galatians 2:11 (NASB): *"But when Cephas came to Antioch, I opposed him to his face, because he stood condemned."* In St. Paul's judgment, St. Peter (Cephas) is condemned. St. Paul believes he must correct St. Peter in public as this is impacting their group identity.

We have just encountered one of those places where one of two Greek words is translated "condemn." Here, St. Paul is using the word *katagnosis* meaning that St. Peter's failure was *exposed for everyone to know.*

In Romans 8:1 St. Paul uses the word *katakrima,* also translated *condemn,* to say, *"Therefore there is now no condemnation for those who are in Christ Jesus."* This Greek word means something more like "sentenced for punishment."

We are to develop excellent *discerning* judgment but avoid all judgments leading to destruction like the condemnation of someone's value or goodness. Let us consider more examples.

Job and friends

The book of Job narrates Job's encounters with his self-justified friends who condemn him with the attitude, "You must have done something, Job, or God wouldn't be treating you this way." The natural response would be for Job to justify himself, but Job says, *"If I justify myself, mine own mouth shall condemn me: if I say, I am perfect, it shall also prove me perverse."*[1] His response was, "I will not justify myself because that will condemn me. My only hope is God's justification of me."

Job's hope for justification is faith. We are justified by faith not only for salvation, but also in every situation. It may be very difficult to see how God will help us when we feel condemned. Condemnation makes it appealing to justify ourselves. But when we self-justify we bring condemnation on ourselves.

If we justify ourselves in our minds, we will justify ourselves to others.

---

1   Job 9:20 (KJV)

David's response

David also did not defend himself. In Chapter Six, we saw David driven out of Jerusalem while a Benjamite was throwing rocks at him. His response, instead of killing the protestor was, *"... Let him alone, and let him curse; for so the LORD has ordered him. It may be that the LORD will look on my affliction, and that the LORD will repay me with good for his cursing this day."*[2]

Jesus' response

Let's look at how Jesus answered when He was condemned: *"He was oppressed and He was afflicted, Yet He opened not His mouth; He was led as a lamb to the slaughter, and as a sheep before its shearers is silent, So He opened not His mouth."*[3] Jesus did not answer back; He did not justify himself. We all know if anyone had the right to self-justify, it was Jesus – but He did not. The rest of us really have no leg to stand on when we want to justify ourselves.

Even as we look at these examples, we see how extremely hard it is to resist the temptation to justify ourselves. From political parties to family feuds we cannot seem to resist our desire to self-justify, accuse, and condemn. When someone says, "I'm right and you're wrong," the natural tendency is to reply, "No! I'm right and you're wrong." We want to show them what idiots they are. We play right into the narcissist's game. Our minds start contesting with them to see who is most self-justified. Our character is now as bad as theirs. This is spiritual immaturity.

Narcissists condemn others

Justifying oneself leads to condemning others as not good enough. Narcissists say some version of, "You are not doing enough. I am justified in treating you as the bad person until you make up for it. Meanwhile, I don't have to hesed. I can avoid you, shun you, dislike you, and complain to everyone about you, because I'm the one here who is being wronged." The narcissist claims to be hurt, shamed, disrespected, cheated of power, to have rights and be entitled to more. "I'm the good person here and they are the bad ones."

Justifying and condemning according to our understanding must be based on something. If something hurts us, it is unfair. If

---

2   2 Samuel 16:11c-12
3   Isaiah 53:7

something moves us ahead, we justify it. Valuing events according to the cost or gain to us biases human judgment. If someone dies when we don't want them to or lives well when we think they should suffer, we must let God judge them or we must judge God.

If we justify ourselves in our minds we will justify ourselves to others. If we condemn ourselves we will also figure out who else should be condemned. If someone hurts us we may condemn them to the silent treatment, gossip, humiliation or rejection by spreading the word about who is "bad." This condemnation poisons group identities.

No destructive judgments

Scripture speaks to the condemning bent in our human nature in Luke 6:37. *"Judge not, and you shall not be judged. Condemn not, and you shall not be condemned. Forgive, and you will be forgiven."* Jesus is clear that we are not to bring condemnation. Instead we are to forgive and we will be forgiven. In the next chapter we will examine helpful, discerning judgments that restore our identities without condemnation or self-justification.

Self-condemnation

Not only should we not condemn or justify others, we should neither justify nor condemn ourselves. Skunk narcissists condemn themselves rather than attacking others. Whenever skunk narcissists are confronted with a shame message it triggers them into an avalanche about how bad and unworthy they are. They go on about their failures, lack of value, and why they are not fit to be part of the identity group. This self-directed barrage only stops when skunk narcissists create enough guilt in the messenger for the shame message to be withdrawn. Skunk narcissists' self-beating sessions only end after extended reassurances of how special, worthwhile, and desirable they are. Skunks use self-condemnation to gain glory.

Without an "inner skunk" to agree with accusations by peacock narcissists we would go home laughing at the narcissist's game. If it is God who judges us, then it is not our business to either justify or condemn ourselves. It is our business to listen closely to God and see what He wants to say about us.

LIVING LIFE WITHOUT CONDEMNATION

Jesus came to do the opposite of condemnation. John 3:17 says, *"For God did not send His Son into the world to condemn the world, but that the world through Him might be saved* (justified, put right)." So if we are the people of the Good News, the Gospel, we are not here to condemn. We are people of forgiveness and this puts us in a wonderful place to deal with stiff-necked folk; although, we realize they might kill us for it. Yet forgiveness, the response needed for stiff-necked people, is hard to give because we tend to stiffen our own necks rather than forgive. Forgiveness means we see others the way God sees them.

The fastest path to REAL condemnation

John 3:18 tells us how this works when he writes, *"He who believes in Him is not condemned; but he who does not believe is condemned already, because he has not believed in the name of the only begotten Son of God."* Our freedom comes from our hesed life with Jesus.

Understanding that we are not condemned brings us to an important question: If we are not condemned, should we accept condemnation from anybody? The answer is a resounding, "No!" Why should we put another person's opinion about us above God's? We should not. We need to develop a real resistance to condemnation. Condemnation will come at us, but we should handle it like we would bad weather. We shelter ourselves.

When we refuse condemnation from narcissists, they often say, "You think you're always right." This is a subtle condemnation accusing us of doing what qasheh people do. Our best path is to refuse the condemnation. Unless we listen closely to God, we will feel crazy.

Jesus' example

In Isaiah 50:6-7 we see how Jesus refused condemnation:

> *I gave My back to those who struck Me, and My cheeks to those who plucked out the beard; I did not hide My face from shame and spitting. For the LORD GOD will help Me; therefore I will not be disgraced; therefore I have set My face like a flint, and I know that I will not be ashamed.*

Jesus deals with stiff-necked people without self-justification. Because of Jesus' hesed with His Father, He avoids becoming qasheh even when treated badly: *"For the Lord will help me, therefore I will not be disgraced – and I will not be ashamed."* While being publicly humiliated by His accusers, He is resistant and resilient.

Although it is extremely painful, Jesus does not take the condemnation seriously. He knows these people are crazy. If they had any idea what they were doing, they would realize just how stupid, how out of their minds, how foolish they were. But above all, He is relying on God to justify Him.

Isaiah continues with the description in verses 8 and 9:

> *"He is near who justifies Me; who will contend with Me? Let us stand together. Who is My adversary? Let him come near Me. Surely the LORD GOD will help Me; who is he who will condemn Me? Indeed they will all grow old like a garment; the moth will eat them up."*

We forget so quickly and easily God is near. We assume if we are being condemned that God is not with us. We falsely conclude that we have to step up to the plate and justify ourselves because no one else will.

The crowd around the cross said, "If God hears You why don't You come down off the cross?" Jesus responded, "No! You try to condemn Me but you're wearing yourselves out. You will look like a moth-eaten coat when we get done. Don't fight God! Repent instead! I put My trust in God."

Romans 8:1 says, *"There is therefore now no condemnation to those who are in Christ Jesus, who do not walk according to the flesh, but according to the Spirit."* Without this kind of confidence and character we accept condemnation and even attack ourselves.

The life of the Spirit is immune to human and demonic condemnation. Compassion (splagchnon) stays high. We resist qasheh and increase hesed. We love any human enemy who is accusing us.

It requires wisdom to distinguish immunity to condemnation from the "forehead of bronze" that keeps qasheh narcissists from accepting shame. The difference is that healthy shame messages call us back to our highest selves while condemnation insists we are our lowest self. We will return to discuss wise judgment later.

No self-condemnation for St. Paul

Christ was not the only one who refused condemnation. St. Paul has this to say:

> *But with me it is a very small thing that I should be judged by you or by a human court. In fact, I do not even judge myself. For I know of nothing against myself, yet I am not justified by this; but He who judges me is the Lord.* 1 Corinthians 4:3-4

St. Paul was not worried about condemnation from others. "If you don't like what I am doing," he says, "this could hardly be more trivial to me. It's a really small thing even if all the courts get together to condemn me. I am unimpressed. It is only stiff-necked people justifying themselves and condemning others." He continues, "Even if my conscience is clear, I'm not justified by self-examination." St. Paul clearly limits the human ability to judge.

Condemnation we carry with us from the past

Before we contrast *living without condemnation* and the *crucial need for judgment* we need to make one more observation. Most of our feeling "bad" comes from improperly processed past experiences that are now intruding into the present. We will not review ways to process these triggered feelings from the past in this book. Yet, feeling like a bad person (condemnation) is healed by asking for God's perspective. [4] God leads us to a time in the past where we absorbed condemnation, then He heals us. We will need healing from those fiery darts. Leaving that poison in us and our group will damage our group identity.

**Lord Jesus, we thank You that You have come to justify us and not to condemn us.
Even if the rest of the world condemns us, You are greater than the world.**

---

4   The Immanuel Process articulated by Dr. Karl Lehman is one of the most effective means for correctly reprocessing past experiences. See his book *The Immanuel Approach: For Emotional Healing & For Life*.

Facing Condemnation

- **Avoid all condemnation.**

    o Don't give condemnation.

    o Don't receive condemnation.

    o Seek healing for old feelings of condemnation.

- **Develop excellent judgment.**

- **Keep hesed clean.**

If You Are Ready
Group Exercise for Chapter Nine

Today's group identity affirmation

Repeat together, "We are a people who really cannot stand self-justification and will not listen to it."

In groups of about five people tell each other why this characteristic matters to you. (5 minutes)

Today's healthy shame message practice

In groups of about five people create a healthy shame message for me when <u>I am taking advantage of others who cannot defend themselves well.</u> (5 minutes)

Note: A healthy shame message states "we do not" and then states who we are with a Christ-like character response.
"We do not _____, we _____."

Tell each small group's statement to the whole group. (5 minutes)

Today's withstanding self-justification practice

Self-justification: Do I have to go over this again with you? (with contempt)

In groups of about five people make a list of the weaknesses that lie behind this self-justification. What would a hesed community do to be sure these weaknesses do not prevail? (10 minutes)

Report each small group's conclusions to the whole group. (5 minutes)

Today's loving my enemy practice

This exercise is like texting with God. Write the impression that comes to your mind. Start with something that makes you grateful then your impression of God's response. Next read the question and write your impression of God's response that gives you peace. (5 minutes)

1. Dear God, I am thankful:
2. My dear child:
3. God, when has someone felt like an enemy to me this week?
4. What do You want me to know about loving them?

Read what you have written in groups of about five people. Do not explain what you wrote. Check for a sense of peace after you read. (5 minutes)

Opposing self-justification: Exercise 2

1. Form groups of about five people.

2. Turn to *My Forgetful Moments Feedback Request* at the end of Chapter Eight and circle the three that seem to most apply to the narcissism in you. (5 minutes)

3. Take turns by going around the group and tell the group what three items you chose. Ask the group if they think there is another item you should add to your list.

4. When everyone has had a chance to tell their three items and ask the group to add another item (if they see one) reflect as a group about:

    a. What makes it difficult to talk about these topics in most groups?

    b. What self-justifications came to your mind in this process?

    c. What would you need from your group to want to talk about these topics again?

5. Where will you ask others to answer these questions about you? Where will you not?

Repeating today's group identity affirmation

Repeat together, "We are a people who really cannot stand self-justification and will not listen to it."

CHAPTER TEN
Developing Good Judgment
The Limits of Wisdom

**Do you not judge those who are within the church?
But those who are outside, God judges.**
1 Corinthians 5:12b-13a (NASB)

"Don't judge!" is the top of the line in self-justifications. "You shouldn't judge!" is the best trump card for all religious narcissists. Few topics create more confusion than asking a group of Christians whether we should judge others. The immediate response of "No!" is soon followed by contradictory stories of judgment that appear in both the Old and New Testaments. Ananias and Sapphira, for example, both dropped dead in what was clearly a judgment against them voiced by St. Peter.

Why does the Bible say to judge and not to judge? For example, St. Paul commands us to judge those who are in the church but not to judge outsiders. Yet it is exactly the wisdom to know what we must judge and what we must not that is needed to face narcissism. Every Pandora problem requires good judgment. Certain judgments are critically needed for healthy shame messages while other judgments make us incredibly toxic and self-justified.

We must judge.

Dealing with narcissists requires three practical understandings about judgment.

1) There is a range of things to be judged. Some things humans can judge (like if a fruit has gone bad); other things only God can judge (like whether a life should be ended).

2) In the human range we differ in capacity to judge. We could judge what music we like best, but most of us would not be able to judge the best paper on quantum physics.

3) The word "judgment" has several meanings – one is to discern and separate and the other to condemn, punish, and ultimately destroy. We are to get better at the former and avoid the latter.

We must not destroy.

In facing self-justified people we must not make any of the judgments reserved for God. God is intent on destroying the power of evil at some point in the future, but when and how are not in our scope of judgment. There is a final judgment called the "day of wrath" when God will appear and eliminate evil on the earth.[1] God can destroy evil without harming good, but we cannot.

The English word "judge" has multiple meanings.

Every school teacher or professional knows about two meanings for the word "judgment." When writing a report about a child, the teacher must judge many things about the child's academic, social, and emotional abilities. At the same time, the teacher must not judge whether the child is a good or evil person, has value or is worthless. Somehow we know that weak does not equal worthless. Judging a child's worth could destroy a child.

English does not provide good words for the different meanings of "judge." Entirely different words in Scripture are all translated with the single word "judge." When different words in the original language must be translated as the same English word it can be confusing. We can, however separate the two major concepts. We are to judge well (meaning discern), and we are not to judge at all (meaning condemn or destroy.)

Know the limits of wisdom.

Wisdom and good judgment are very related concepts. What we can judge is limited by what we can know. We cannot judge anything we cannot discern. The thoughts and intents of someone else's heart are things we cannot discern clearly. We can discern what is painful or desirable for us, but we cannot tell what accomplishes God's hidden purposes.

---

1   Revelation 19-21.

Wisdom knows the limits of discernment. Wisdom prevents us from doing what is right in our own eyes because we cannot see the whole picture. Biblical teaching on judgment sounds contradictory unless we consider the limits of human judgment.

Judgment is also limited by the boundaries of human dominion. We have a certain amount of dominion over our own lives and thoughts but very little dominion over others. God has not promised to tell us what is going in others. Therefore, wisdom says we cannot tell others how to live each part of their lives.

The "do not judge" instructions from Scripture match our limitations. We cannot judge outside our dominion. We cannot judge what we cannot discern. However, we must carefully judge those things that are under our dominion and within our discernment.

EXCELLENT JUDGMENT IS NEEDED TO FACE NARCISSISM.

> *"If there be a controversy between men, and they come unto judgment, that the judges may judge them; then they shall* justify *the righteous, and* condemn *the wicked."*
> Deuteronomy 25:1 (KJV)

In this passage as well as Exodus 23:6-7, God requires us to justify our judgments. God expects fair judgment when we decide issues that fall in the range we can judge. The words *justify* and *condemn* are used in contrast to one another. We are not to justify the wicked or condemn the righteous. As we remember from Job and his narcissistic friends, self-justification will justify the wicked and condemn the righteous.

Proverbs 17:15 reminds us, *"He who justifies the wicked and condemns the just, both of them alike are an abomination to the Lord."* God's people should not allow bad judgment to prevail. We as a group are not to use bad judgment, tolerate self-justification, or go along with those who insist on justifying themselves. As a people, we are to oppose every stiff-necked, narcissistic, qasheh behavior we see in ourselves or in our identity group. In our jurisdiction, our dominion (where we are in a position of authority), we are to exercise good judgment.

Because we share our rule and dominion with God, as we saw in Chapter Six, there is a shared element to good judgment. We do not share all God's rule and judgment, so God has dominion and judgment over matters where we have no say. For example, we cannot justify or condemn ourselves. Psalm 143:2 says. *"And enter not into judgment with thy servant: for in thy sight shall no man living be justified."* Trying to justify ourselves to God is a losing battle. It is qasheh.

Observing and making judgments

Judging the fruit of people's labor is generally within our ability to observe. We are able to judge the "fruit"[2] of people's character[3] but not the worth of a person. We are able to tell wicked and righteous "fruit" apart and yet, in the parable of the wheat and the weeds,[4] Jesus warns His followers not to pull any weeds but leave that judgment to God and the angels lest we make a mistake.

THE CASE OF THE DEVIL'S ASSISTANT VERSUS THE DEVIL'S HATCHLINGS

Matthew's Gospel contains a story that calls us to make a judgment. Matthew includes all evidence from the case as presented to the original witnesses. This example is very similar to what we will face with narcissists in our group identity. Two sides will face off. Each will claim to be serving God while saying the other side is wrong. Matthew presents this case for us to judge. The question is, who works for the devil? I have called this the case of the devil's assistant versus the devil's hatchlings.

Matthew starts his story telling of a man who was blind and mute because of an evil spirit. Jesus healed him. The crowd began to judge that Jesus might be the promised Messiah. The Pharisees judged that Jesus was a personal assistant of Beelzebulb, the prince of devils. This judgment difference between the crowd and the religious leaders becomes a test for our judgment. Jesus expected the crowd could and must make a judgment as well. Matthew expects the same of his readers. Let us pick up Matthew's narration with Jesus' response to His accusers:

> *If Satan casts out Satan, he is divided against himself. How then will his kingdom stand? And if I cast out demons by Beelzebub, by whom do your sons cast them out? Therefore they shall be your judges. But if I cast out demons by the*

---

2   Not to be confused with "success"
3   Matthew 7:16
4   Matthew 13:24-30

> *Spirit of God, surely the kingdom of God has come upon you. Or how can one enter a strong man's house and plunder his goods, unless he first binds the strong man? And then he will plunder his house. He who is not with Me is against Me, and he who does not gather with Me scatters abroad.*
>
> Matthew 12:26-30

It is important to see that Jesus expects people to be able to tell the difference between God at work yielding good fruit and the devil at work yielding bad fruit. This judgment is not out of range for humans. He goes on to affirm our ability to judge this case and warns us that our decision will determine our future.

> *Therefore I say to you, every sin and blasphemy will be forgiven men, but the blasphemy against the Spirit will not be forgiven men. Anyone who speaks a word against the Son of Man, it will be forgiven him; but whoever speaks against the Holy Spirit, it will not be forgiven him, either in this age or in the age to come.* Matthew 12:31-32[5]

Jesus is saying, "If you look at what God's Spirit does and think it is Satan, you will be stuck forever." Jesus continues:

> *Brood of vipers! How can you, being evil, speak good things? For out of the abundance of the heart the mouth speaks. A good man out of the good treasure of his heart brings forth good things, and an evil man out of the evil treasure brings forth evil things. But I say to you that for every idle word men may speak, they will give account of it in the Day of Judgment. For by your words you will be justified, and by your words you will be condemned."* Matthew 12:34-37

"You brood of vipers" is a way to say "you were hatched from the devil's own eggs." Satan is pictured as a serpent, and when Jesus looks at the religious leaders He sees a nest of hatched snake's eggs. The reader, like the crowd, is left to make a judgment between the devil's assistant and the devil's hatchlings. Which one is it? We must judge and judge correctly. Facing narcissism or any qasheh problem requires this kind of judgment about competing claims and competing realities.

---

5   This verse causes much anxiety among people who are afraid they have done the unpardonable sin. Those who have judged that evil is good, justify themselves and never worry. If you worry you are fine!

Recognize Christian forms of self-justification.

During the first century of the Christian era new forms of self-justification emerged that were uniquely Christian sounding.

- You can't judge me.
- I have faith.
- I am not under the law.
- I am a spiritual being (gnostic).

These Christian-sounding self-justifications (and others) are in constant use today hiding narcissism in Christian circles. Facing qasheh Christians requires us to avoid these traps. Let us consider the first two in greater detail.

You cannot judge me.

We have already mentioned the confusion in Christian circles on the topic of judging others. The proof text is always Luke 6:37a. *"Judge not, and you shall not be judged."* We dedicated Chapter Nine to correcting this error. What makes this all the more amusing is that the person who uses this verse as a self-justification is, at the same time, judging others for acting "un-Christian" for having a judgment. What is rapidly obvious, if we use wisdom, is how often a person who offers this self-justification makes judgments of others.

There could hardly be a greater waste of time than trying to be right with someone who is self-justified. Instead, we need agreement by our identity group that we will judge those in the church. Our judgements will purify hesed and reduce qasheh. St. Paul expects us to judge the church in the quote that begins this chapter.[6]

I have faith.

Until Christianity – and particularly the works of St. Paul – came into existence, no one would have thought to justify themselves by claiming they were saved by faith alone. Now faith is being used as self-justification for bad character and low hesed.

By the time the epistle of James was written, having faith had become a preferred means of self-justification. The tension

---

6   1 Corinthians 5:12b

between St. Paul and St. James disappears when we consider that both writers were opposed to self-justification. St. Paul argued that works cannot be used for self-justification, and St. James argued that faith cannot be used for self-justification. Let us examine the agreement between St. Paul and St. James more closely.

St. Paul says clearly that works of the Law cannot self-justify.

> *nevertheless knowing that a man is not justified by the works of the Law but through faith in Christ Jesus, even we have believed in Christ Jesus, so that we may be justified by faith in Christ and not by the works of the Law; since by the works of the Law no flesh will be justified.* Galatians 2:16 (NASB)

St. James is just as clear that claiming faith cannot self-justify. In James 2:21, 24-25 we read:

> *Was not Abraham our father justified by works when he offered Isaac his son on the altar? . . . You see then that a man is justified by works, and not by faith only. Likewise, was not Rahab the harlot also justified by works when she received the messengers and sent them out another way?*

Martin Luther did not think St. James expressed his argument very clearly – but he did not disagree. Luther defended justification by faith while St. James opposed *self*-justification by faith.

We oppose all forms of self-justification. St. Paul says, "Don't justify yourself by claiming good works." St. James, says, "Don't justify yourself by claiming you have faith."

St. Paul

St. Paul emphasizes faith over good works. Even though Abraham had good works, they provided no boasting rights or claims to be justified before God.

> *For if Abraham was justified by works, he has something to boast about, but not before God. For what does the Scripture say? "Abraham believed God, and it was accounted to him for righteousness."* Romans 4:2-3

St. James

A group in the church was saying, "It doesn't really matter how I live because I am justified by faith." Claiming that faith excuses bad character is as much self-justification as claiming works is going to save us. James 2:17-18 says,

> *Thus also faith by itself, if it does not have works, is dead. But someone will say, "You have faith, and I have works." Show me your faith without your works, and I will show you my faith by my works.*

Religious narcissists justify themselves by their religion, works narcissists justify themselves by their activity, and faith narcissists by what they claim to believe. We will need good, *discerning* judgment.

Judge values by their fruit.

There is some modern and postmodern thought that we should not make value judgments. Really, almost the only judgments worth making are value judgments. However, Jesus and His followers place more weight on the "fruit" of our values than on what values we claim.

Recognize the fruits of self-justification.

Dr. Karl Lehman is quite an ornithologist (and he knows his birds too). Although birds are often small and trees are tall and leafy, Dr. Lehman can find them. Karl knows birds by their calls. When he hears a call he starts looking for that exact bird in the trees. In the same way, when we see the fruits of a qasheh attitude in a group we can begin looking for self-justification. The fruit reveals the tree.

Pandora problems are the fruits of self-justification along with low hesed and high qasheh. This fruit reveals the tree as a group identity that accepts self-justification, does not love enemies, and thinks it is better to say nothing.

Recognize the fruits of genuine justification.

Justification comes by faith and grace. Let's review some verses that speak to this:

> Romans 3:24 – *"Being justified freely by His grace through the redemption that is in Christ Jesus."*

> Romans 3:28 – *"Therefore we conclude that a man is justified by faith apart from the deeds of the Law."*

> Romans 5:1 – *"Therefore, having been justified by faith, we have peace with God through our Lord Jesus Christ."*

Those who have been justified by God have words and works that are justified by faith. Hesed words and works will be peaceable, true, and filled with grace. Jesus amazed people with His words of grace and truth. Grace, peace, and truth are part of His character and should be ours as well – a sign of being justified by faith.

Judging by fruit or words

It would not be a stretch to say that the religious leaders of Jesus' time spent a lot of energy trying to trap Jesus into saying words they could use against Him. Jesus said they should judge Him by the fruits of His ministry. Jesus told His followers that good trees did not give bad fruit.[7]

Jesus told the parable of a son who said no when asked to work but later did as he was told. Another son said yes but did not follow through.[8] Jesus put more weight on what people did than on what they said.

Judging by fruit – Jesus

> *Jesus answered them, "I showed you many good works from the Father; for which of them are you stoning Me?"*
> John 10:32 (NASB)

Jesus put more weight on what people did than on what they said.

Judging by words – religious leaders

> *The Jews answered Him, "For a good work we do not stone You, but for blasphemy; and because You, being a man, make Yourself out to be God." John 10:33 (NASB)*

Religious leaders put more weight on what people said than on what they did.

Words can be judged as fruit.

The pastor of a church was fired after his long-term affair was discovered. A few months later this same pastor reappeared, declared himself rehabilitated, ran the interim pastor out of the building, and installed himself as pastor once again. About 800 members left, but most congregants stayed.

---

7   Luke 6:43
8   Matthew 21:28-32

Suppose we speak with this qasheh pastor about his leadership and he says, "You are trying to destroy my ministry. You yourself teach that we should not destroy. It is wrong for you to speak to me this way."

Does the pastor have us in a corner with his self-justification? If we judge by words we will have more problems than if we judge by fruits. When judging fruit, the answer is clear. The fruit of allowing the pastor's answer to stand will be that the flock under his care will continue to be exploited. This pastor is defending his predatory rights. Is that good fruit?

As we prepare to face narcissism we certainly will want to judge both the words and the fruit if we are to avoid traps. All too often the members of a church group identity listen only to the words and fall for a self-justified spin. We need clear judgment about both words and fruit.

The peace of Christ is to be the gauge for all we hear.[9] People who do not justify themselves respond with gentleness and understanding when they are corrected. Good judgment purifies hesed. Hesed people learn to love their enemies.

We want to create a *people* by raising *hesed* and lowering *qasheh* until we spontaneously love our enemies. In our next chapter we will examine the character needed to confront narcissism in our identity group.

Lord God, help us to live in your peace so that we might hear your thoughts and judge rightly. Amen

---

9   Colossians 3:15

Facing Self-Justified People

- **Develop excellent judgement.**

- **Recognize, avoid, and address Christian forms of self-justification.**

  o *"I have faith."*

  o *"You cannot judge me."*

- **Pay close attention to "fruit."**

- **Look for a sense of shalom when you hear truth and a sense that "something isn't right" when you hear self-justification.**

If You Are Ready
Group Exercise for Chapter Ten

Today's group identity affirmation

> Repeat together, "We are a people who share other's pain even when we have caused it."

> In groups of about five people tell each other why this characteristic matters to you. (5 minutes)

Today's healthy shame message practice

> In groups of about five people create a healthy shame message for me when <u>I use more than my share of resources.</u> (5 minutes)

> *Note: A healthy shame message states "we do not" and then states who we are with a Christ-like character response.*
> *"We do not _____, we _____."*

> Tell each small group's statement to the whole group. (5 minutes)

Today's withstanding self-justification practice

> Self-justification: Jesus is coming back soon, and we must (fill in the blank, e.g., reach every language group on earth).

> In groups of about five people make a list of the weaknesses that lie behind this self-justification. What would a hesed community do to be sure these weaknesses do not prevail? (10 minutes)

> Report each small group's conclusions to the whole group. (5 minutes)

Today's loving my enemy practice

This exercise is like texting with God. Write the impression that comes to your mind. Start with something that makes you grateful then your impression of God's response. Next read the question and write your impression of God's response that gives you peace. (5 minutes)

1. Dear God, I am thankful:
2. My dear child:
3. God, when has someone felt like an enemy to me this week?

173

4.   What do You want me to know about loving them?

Read what you have written in groups of about five people. Do not explain what you wrote. Check for a sense of peace after you read. (5 minutes)

Sharing other's pain: Exercise 2

1.   Individual quiet preparation (5 minutes)

    a.   List the relationship with the top three people whose pain you share regularly.

        i.
        ii.
        iii.

    b.   What person would Jesus have you add to the list for His sake? Write the relationship but not the name.

2.   In groups of about five people (25 minutes – about 5 minutes per person)

    a.   First person: describe anything that makes you uncomfortable or want to withdraw from sharing the pain of the person Jesus brought to mind in 1b. Do not mention their name or your relationship.

    b.   Without giving any advice say together as a group, "Lord Jesus, help us."

    c.   Go around the group so everyone has a chance to share and be prayed for by the group.

3.   As a whole group, read the story aloud of Jesus and the woman sharing pain at Simon's house from Luke 7:36-50. Take the following steps: (15 minutes)

    a.   Pray aloud, "Lord Jesus, show us how You will be with us when we share the pain of others as You ask us to."

    b.   Notice (in silence for a minute or two) what comes to mind that brings you peace.

    c.   In pairs, tell the person next to you what came to mind that brought peace.

Repeating today's group identity affirmation

Repeat together, "We are a people who share other's pain even when we have caused it."

CHAPTER ELEVEN
Dealing with Self-Justified People
Testing Our Character

> **"I tell you, this man went down to his house justified rather than the other; for everyone who exalts himself will be humbled, and he who humbles himself will be exalted."**
> Luke 18:14

Qasheh people often seek positions of leadership and power. The study by Ball and Puls revealed that rates of diagnosable narcissistic disorders were from five to thirty times higher among ministers than in the average population.[1] The question becomes, "What shall we do?"

Facing narcissism and avoiding the traps of the narcissist's game requires more than a one-time encounter like Jesus had with the lawyer. That lawyer walked away from the Master with his neck as stiff as ever. Narcissism, particularly with the psychopathic tendencies present in 15% of the population,[2] cannot be addressed by techniques – it must be addressed through mature character in an identity group context.

Narcissism does not have simple solutions. Ball and Puls state that, "the statistical likelihood of a pastor regaining mental health after NPD [Narcissistic Personality Disorder] is small."[3] In this book we are considering the possibility that facing narcissism effectively

---

1   Glen Ball and Darrell Puls, *Frequency of Narcissistic Personality Disorder in Pastors: A Preliminary Study*, paper presented at American Association of Christian Counselors in Nashville, TN, September 26, 2015. Note that NPD is currently diagnosed as an additional feature for any disorder.
2   See Chapter Two and bakadesuyo.com/2016/10/how-to-deal-with-psychopaths/ This Is How To Deal With Psychopaths And Toxic People: 5 Proven Secrets, Eric Barker, Barking Up The Wrong Tree, ©2016.
3   Ibid page 10.

requires intervention by an identity group – a people of godly character. This people must grow hesed and resist qasheh.

God has faced problems all through the years with people who do not want to feel shame. We have examined Scriptural accounts of stiff-necked, self-justifying people we now call narcissists. Since people do not naturally have high hesed and low qasheh, pastors must teach the flock exactly the skills that narcissistic pastors lack. We can become the dog that chases its tail if we need low qasheh pastors to teach churches to face narcissism so that the church identity group can address narcissistic pastors.

The relationships that develop hesed attachments and a strong group identity are rarely seen in churches. Those who select or appoint pastors are unable to even recognize a stiff-necked leader when they see one. Churches promote pastors and leaders who lack hesed and have high qasheh thus keeping the cycle going. Christians in these churches rarely experience transformation.

The principle reason it is difficult to deal with stiff-necked people is that it requires *good group character*. Dealing with narcissists requires group-wide maturity and spiritual understanding. Christianity, as it is commonly practiced in the West, lacks the relational strength of character needed for dealing with a qasheh character defect.

In this book we have examined how self-justification, avoiding suffering, disdain for weakness, focus on beliefs rather than development of hesed/agape, confusion about the need for good judgment, and fear of condemnation have neutered Christian fellowship to the point that precious little character transformation is ever seen.

We want to create a *people* by raising *hesed* and lowering *qasheh* until we spontaneously love our enemies. We have seen that some important skills include sharing the pain of others, stopping self-justification, exercising wise judgment, avoiding condemnation, seeing from God's point of view, and giving healthy shame messages. Above all these skills, a working sense of God's relational presence in a fellowship community[4]

Dealing with narcissists requires group-wide maturity and spiritual understanding.

---

4   See *Transforming Fellowship* by Chris Coursey.

becomes central for those who desire transformation into the character of Christ.

We should also realize that even the best group identity will do little good without seeing ourselves and others in ways that God sees us. This Godsight allows us to be loyal (hesed) during weakness and see our enemies as people with weak hesed. We learn to love our enemies by sharing the pain of the weak until we can see the weakness in our enemies.

So who watches over group identity? Who is to help communities develop? The biblical answer is that elders[5] lead their group to become a people who love their enemies. Dealing with self-justified people depends more upon mature elders than on pastors. Nowhere is this more important than where the pastor is immature and narcissistic. The narcissists we are trying to correct must be treated like disciples with a decent amount of spiritual parenting included. In this chapter we will learn to render clear judgment in the hesed and humble way that creates disciples.

FACING NARCISSISM TESTS OUR GROUP CHARACTER.

Let us review what we know. In the myth, Pandora opened her "box" and let all kinds of problems loose. Her solution was to slam down the lid and not let anything else get out. Because she focused on how the trouble began, she did not look farther and lost hope inside. We are calling something a Pandora problem whenever we fear that speaking about a situation will only make it worse.

Pandora problems develop when an identity group cannot use shame to develop better relationships. Without healthy shame, narcissists insulate themselves from a group identity. Narcissists develop high levels of qasheh. Narcissists maintain low hesed and have weak splagchnon[6] responses (gut reactions) to the pain of others. Narcissists pay little attention to their group identity and cut costs for themselves in relationships. Narcissists live from the slow track in their brain that justifies everything for them in about two-thirds of a second.

Facing self-justified people requires great compassion and loving attachments from their identity group that is strongly bonded and free from resentments (grudges or desire for revenge) for the hurt

---

5   See *Living With Men* by Wilder for more on elders – soon to be the *Becoming* series!
6   See Chapters 2 & 7

that narcissists produce. The group around a Pandora problem must be learning to love their enemies if the person with character disorders is to change. High hesed character is needed by the narcissist's identity group. A counselor, leader, or family member working alone will almost always fail to disciple a narcissist.

Handling shame creatively

Narcissists insist they are right. Words are the self-justified person's main tool. Our response to narcissism cannot be an attempt to outmaneuver them and prove we are right. Our goal is to activate their group identity through demonstrations of handling shame creatively for the benefit of all.

Narcissists find their power through the words they speak. Speaking condemnation, self-justification, and illusion creates an advantage for narcissists. We must not accept self-justifications. The words we speak should be words that come from God.[7] We will need excellent control of our tongues.

Our words must harmonize with what God would say or we will fall into self-justification. When we begin justifying our judgment of the narcissists then their character defect has pulled us into the narcissistic game rather than our identity group pulling the narcissists into godly character.

Our humble connection with God

We cannot speak words that come from God until we humble ourselves. Stiffening our necks will not help. Jesus reminds us that *"everyone who exalts himself will be humbled, and he who humbles himself will be exalted."* Luke 18:14b

Unlike narcissists who justify themselves while condemning others, we are to humble ourselves and let God lift us up. By humbling ourselves we will be justified. St. James says:

> But He gives a greater grace. Therefore it says, "God is opposed to the proud, but gives grace to the humble." Submit therefore to God. James 4: 6-7a (NASB)

> Humble yourselves in the sight of the Lord and He will lift you up. Do not speak evil of one another, brethren.
>
> James 4:10-11a (NKJV)

---

7   Ephesians 6:19

Throughout Scripture, we find *humility* and *not speaking evil* mentioned together. Speaking evil is condemnation. Those who are humble do not speak evil of other people; they speak words of grace and peace. Humbling oneself without speaking evil is the opposite of being stiff-necked, self-justifying, and condemning.

Control our own tongue

If we are going to deal humbly with the self-justifying narcissists, we must deal with our own tongue. Tongue management is vitally important because the stiff-necked narcissists' favorite weapon is the tongue. It is better not to say anything when facing a Pandora problem precisely because no one's tongue is as sharp as the narcissists'. With their tongues they defend themselves, blame, condemn, and accuse others. Skunk narcissists condemn themselves while peacocks condemn others.

St. James says of the tongue:

> The tongue is so set among our members that it defiles the whole body, and sets on fire the course of nature; and it is set on fire by hell. For every kind of beast and bird, of reptile and creature of the sea, is tamed and has been tamed by mankind. But no man can tame the tongue. It is an unruly evil, full of deadly poison. With it we bless our God and Father, and with it we curse men, who have been made in the similitude of God. Out of the same mouth proceed blessing and cursing. My brethren, these things ought not to be so.
> James 3:6b-10

Elders help establish a group identity as people whose tongues confess our shame, praise God, and build others up without boasting, self-justification, condemnation, or pride. At the same time the group does not accept self-justification in silence but speaks up saying, "We don't justify ourselves." In such a group, stiff-necked, narcissistic, self-justified folk who condemn other people will be ashamed.

Observing what tongues say with wise judgment

As we watch our own tongues we will begin noticing how narcissists depend on their tongues to make themselves look good, be right, and condemn others. That is narcissism. Dealing with stiff-necked people means we cannot justify ourselves nor can we justify them. We cannot agree with what narcissists are saying when they condemn others. If we go along with what the narcissist says or does, we are building their narcissism and bringing unfair judgment on others.

We have to oppose our stiff-necked neighbors. We cannot accept them justifying themselves. We cannot accept condemnation from them. We cannot condemn them in return. We cannot condemn ourselves because they condemn us. Our people just do not act that way.

SEEING THINGS GOD'S WAY

Learning to walk humbly is a long process. We learn to distinguish what God sees from the ways stiff-necked people see others.

Observe first.

The long path to seeing others as God sees them is not learned by jumping into action. First we learn to observe ourselves and others carefully. Yet learning to observe carefully is useless unless we dialogue with God about what we observe and learn how God sees what we have just noticed.

Dialogue about observations with God in our identity group.

Perhaps it sounds strange to the reader to hear about a dialogue with God. Learning to dialogue with God is beyond the limits of this book but it is as essential as it is simple. A good introduction can be found in *Joyful Journey*[8] or *Passing the Peace.*[9] With practice we can notice and test thoughts that God may place in our mind.

By noticing the thoughts that bring us a deeply settled sense of peace and sharing those thoughts with our identity group, we develop a sense of dialogue with God. This process is best done in groups as we have a better chance of avoiding our own narcissism. Dialoguing with God together builds our group identity.

The "peaceful thought test" does not work to protect narcissists from deception when they listen privately for God's thoughts. Narcissists have a way of making themselves feel peaceful and settled by having others agree with their self-justifications. Qasheh people will credit God as the source of their self-justifications. However, when a group who has a hesed relationship with

---

8   *Joyful Journey* by Wilder, Kang, Loppnow and Loppnow, 2015
9   *Passing the Peace* by Life Model Works, 2016

God hears these self-justifications they do not produce peace in the listeners. Therefore, to avoid places where our own self-justification will deceive us, we should make listening to God's perspective a group effort.

Notice all self-justification.

Begin listening for times we justify ourselves or justify others. If we hear others justifying themselves, talking themselves up, or tearing others down, we have spotted the self-justifying process that goes with stiff-necked people. When two parties each claim they are the "injured party" there is most likely narcissism in the mix.

Notice all condemnation.

Whether we condemn ourselves or others, it does not change the diagnosis. Many of us, when condemned or attacked, try to protect from future shame by condemning ourselves before anyone else has a shot. When the condemnation is aimed at ourselves we are watching "skunk" narcissism. Self-condemnation is no prettier than when someone else is doing it.

Notice humble character.

There is another thing to observe before dealing with self-justified people. Our character must be humble. Humility is a sign of listening to God. We wait for God so that we may speak grace to ourselves and others. When elders are building this common Christian character, hesed goes up and qasheh comes down.

When we must judge a conflict, we watch for those who humbly give grace to both self and others. We learn to recognize the humble through their grace and to recognize the stiff-necked through their condemnation and judgment of others.

St. Paul describes grace this way when writing to the Ephesians:

> *Let no corrupt word proceed out of your mouth, but what is good for necessary edification, that it may impart grace to the hearers. And do not grieve the Holy Spirit of God, by whom you were sealed for the day of redemption. Let all bitterness, wrath, anger, clamor, and evil speaking be put away from you, with all malice. And be kind to one another, tenderhearted, forgiving one another, even as God in Christ forgave you. Therefore be imitators of God as dear*

children. And walk in love, as Christ also has loved us and given Himself for us, an offering and a sacrifice to God for a sweet-smelling aroma. Ephesians 4:29 to 5:2

Make wise judgments.

It does not take long, when observing with wisdom, to be able to recognize the narcissists in any conflict in churches, organizations, or families. Listen for condemnation, judgment, and self-justification when helping families or doing marriage counseling. Notice who is humble, admits his or her faults, and shows grace. When we see one person condemning and self-justifying and another swallowing it all, both are narcissists. We can know what we are seeing because we judge the fruit and ask God to guide us.

ARE WE READY?

When we see a humble group, not justifying themselves and waiting on God, we have found people with the character to deal with narcissism within the identity group. Dealing with self-justifying narcissists is principally about *our* character and not about techniques. We do not justify ourselves by our actions, we do not justify ourselves by our faith, and we are immune to judgments coming from the flesh, the *sarx*. We are sensitive to God's voice and what He says about us. We govern our tongues, and we judge wisely by the fruits. We give healthy shame messages. In these ways we lower qasheh, share pain, build loyalty around weakness, see what God sees, and become a people of hesed.

Facing narcissism is a discipleship process. Developing character must be done in community, and a community is a public place. Christian group identity requires a steady flow of healthy shame messages to our people about how we live. Facing narcissism is not a one-time correction of beliefs, behavior, or choices. One-time events do not build a hesed life.

In our next chapter we will examine the way our brain treats enemies differently from "my people."

LORD have mercy. Christ have mercy.
Teach us to pray that we might hear Your heartbeat.

Facing Self-Justified People

- **This task is for a community with mature leaders.**

- **Demonstrate humble character.**

- **Don't try to prove we are right.**

- **Avoid all condemnation.**
  - Don't give condemnation.
  - Don't receive condemnation.

- **Develop excellent judgment.**

- **Recognize, avoid, and address Christian forms of self-justification.**
  - "I have faith."
  - "You cannot judge me."

- **When the group has been impacted, correct the self-justification in front of the group.**

- **Keep our hesed clean.**
  - Don't hold grudges or seek revenge.
  - Keep compassion high (splagchnon).
  - Our goal is discipleship not a one-time correction.

- **See things God's way.**
  - Observe first.
  - Dialogue about observations with God in our identity group.
  - Notice all self-justification.
  - Notice all condemnation.
  - Notice humble character.
  - Make wise judgments.

If You Are Ready
Group Exercise for Chapter Eleven

Today's group identity affirmation

> Repeat together, "We are a people who once were not a people until we learned mercy."

> In groups of about five people tell each other why this characteristic matters to you. (5 minutes)

Today's healthy shame message practice

> In groups of about five people create a healthy shame message for me when <u>I charm others to get my way.</u>
> (5 minutes)

> *Note: A healthy shame message states "we do not" and then states who we are with a Christ-like character response.*
> *"We do not _____, we _____."*

> Tell each small group's statement to the whole group. (5 minutes)

Today's withstanding self-justification practice

> Self-justification: You are bringing up the past. You should forgive and forget.

> In groups of about five people make a list of the weaknesses that lie behind this self-justification. What would a hesed community do to be sure these weaknesses do not prevail? (10 minutes)

> Report each small group's conclusions to the whole group. (5 minutes)

Today's loving my enemy practice

This exercise is like texting with God. Write the impression that comes to your mind. Start with something that makes you grateful then your impression of God's response. Next read the question

and write your impression of God's response that gives you peace. (5 minutes)

1. Dear God, I am thankful:
2. My dear child:
3. God, when has someone felt like an enemy to me this week?
4. What do You want me to know about loving them?

Read what you have written in groups of about five people. Do not explain what you wrote. Check for a sense of peace after you read. (5 minutes)

Building group identity: Exercise 2

1. In groups of about five, describe the identification groups who helped shape your identity. Consider relatives, friends, neighbors, schools, teams, TV, music, clubs, camps, churches, styles, and work. Consider the three age groups below. (15 minutes)

    a. Before age 12

    b. From 12 to 24

    c. After age 25

2. In groups of about five people describe what is taking shape in your mind about the characteristics of "my personal identity group?" Who are you identifying as the people you belong to who can help you become like them? (10 minutes)

3. In groups of about five people describe the aspects of your identity that have been touched in this study group. (10 min)

    a. How much change have you experienced?

    b. Do your changes make you feel more Christian?

4. As a whole group, make a list of the Christian identity characteristics of this study group. (10 minutes)

Repeating today's group identity affirmation

Repeat together, "We are a people who once were not a people until we learned mercy."

CHAPTER TWELVE

The Brain and Loving Our Enemies

Our "Enemy Mode" Weakness

I urge Euodia and I urge Syntyche to live in harmony in the Lord.
Philippians 4:2 (NASB)

"These things have I spoken to you, that My joy may be in you"
John 15:11a (NASB)

Loving enemies is the highest expression of Christ-like character. Loving enemies provides a sufficiently challenging goal to measure the growth of all human virtues across a lifetime. All of us require significant help before we love our enemies spontaneously. We are now talking about the level of character change that is rarely seen in Western Christians.

We have glanced briefly at Fr. Ubald in Chapter One and seen his church members loving those who tried to kill them and who *did* kill their families. But what is equally striking about Fr. Ubald's story is that the killers have also learned to love their enemies, intended victims, and families. We are talking about character change of a magnitude that could change narcissistic and sociopathic character. We are watching people who love their enemies transform. We will return to Fr. Ubald's story and other examples in these last chapters.

It may seem an obvious idea at this point, but the mind can sometimes regard another person as an enemy and then change to see that person as a friend. When in "hesed mode" the brain regards others as *my people*, but when relational connections are missing, the brain can go into "enemy mode." This switch is sometimes slight and sometimes almost absolute. I can be irritated with my wife, children, neighbor, friend, co-worker, or a store clerk and begin to see them as my opposition. This is a slight case of enemy mode. But, should someone attempt to break into my house, the intruder will not be through the door before my mind is strongly inclined to be in enemy mode.

Let us consider the people involved in a Pandora problem. The group is thinking, "Better to not say anything!" Do they think the person in the center of the problem is an ally or an enemy? Of course, our sense of being polite would keep us from calling most people enemies – particularly if it is someone we love. Still, do we anticipate help if we speak about the problem? Are we preparing for opposition? Is the person in the middle reacting as though allies or enemies are pointing out a problem? Most likely, the person in the middle feels attacked by "enemies." Each one is experiencing some degree of enemy mode in their brain.

It is always better to train the brain in the way that the brain learns. Let us consider three specific processes tying enemy mode with changing character. These three topics are no more difficult than the biblical topics we have considered thus far. We are ready to study character transformation.

1. Because people regard each other as enemies in the heat of hurt and conflicts we must consider carefully how the brain enters and resolves its enemy mode.

2. Because correcting enemy mode requires learning new responses, we must understand how the brain uses healthy shame messages.

3. Because our brain develops character from its identity group we need to understand how group identity helps the brain resolve enemy mode.

Altering the parameters of enemy mode in the brain produces a profound change in character. Since loving our enemies is an acquired ability we learn from a group who is learning to love its enemies, how our hesed group deals with enemy mode will be the subject of these last three chapters.

The relational brain

By now the term "the brain's relational circuits" is becoming familiar. This relational network is called the brain's "fast track" in my book with Dr. Marcus Warner called *Rare Leadership*.[1] Marcus

---

1   The relational circuits are also called the "control center" in some Life Model literature.

calls it a "joy elevator" that lifts experiences through the brain in relational ways. Joy, as we recall, is a relational experience of people who share hesed, understanding, and group identity together. One of the strongest indicators of the relational circuits operating well is that we can achieve "mutual mind" with others and with God to see, feel, and live life together in harmony.

ENEMY MODE IN THE MIND

When the brain's relational circuits begin to desynchronize (usually under internal or external overload combined with a lack of attachment) the subcortical amygdala takes the brain into the fight, flight, or freeze reactions of "enemy mode." The detail we will add here is that there are two fight modes using different branches of the vagus nerve.

One fight mode is hot anger; the other is a cold, predatory, "stalking of prey" reaction. Both the hot anger and the predatory coldness are "enemy mode" in the brain. In both hot and cold anger, the brain tracks what will hurt others. In both cases the brain scans for weaknesses. In both cases the brain can tell just how much something is going to hurt the enemy, but there is no sharing of that pain. There is no shared pain because the brain is now focused on an enemy and not one of "my people."

In cold predatory operation, enemy mode can run for hours, days, or years with no loss of energy or decrease in motivation. Once a narcissist, sociopath, or other personality disorder is in a cold enemy mode their mind develops strategies, seeks and exploits weaknesses, and deliberately creates pain in order to make their enemy lose. Occasionally, enemy mode may switch to hot anger if a threat is approaching. Once the hot energy passes, enemy mode resets to cold operation, and the "prey" is lulled into a false sense of confidence that the threat has passed. Nothing could be further from the truth.

If we allow our minds to fall into enemy mode around predatory people, we immediately suffer from impaired function of our own relational circuits. We begin to track what we fear. We soon conclude that approaching anyone who is in enemy mode will set off their hot anger and someone will get hurt. We decide it is better not to say or do anything. We become the circle around a Pandora problem.

When we are in enemy mode ourselves we see others as a threat and therefore "strong." We are actually dealing with a weakness. We are up against brains that drop into enemy mode when they do not have an enemy. While most of us struggle to see narcissism as a weakness, we can see a failure to love our enemies as our moral weakness. When we respond by going into enemy mode ourselves, the battle begins – but an experienced cold predator will always win. If the narcissist's rules govern the hunt, the narcissist wins; yet, enemy mode is a weakness. Our alternatives are to become better predators, to give up, or to love our enemies.

When our identity group is not learning to love our enemies, we easily fall into enemy mode. Let us consider the signs that our minds are going into enemy mode.

Here are some familiar signs of enemy mode:

- Self-justification

- Condemnation received or given

- Lack of judgment

- No pain sharing

- Forgotten hesed (if there was any)

- Loss of group identity awareness

- Disconnection from God even when hearing Scripture

Enemy mode in the mind involves the inhibition of the brain's relational circuits.[2] When we revive our own relational circuits by quieting, thankfulness, and appreciation, we will exit enemy mode more easily. Since the brain's relational circuits have been so extensively covered in other Life Model books and programs we will not say more about them here.[3]

Instead we will consider how to train our people to give healthy shame messages whenever we encounter someone from our identity group in enemy mode. Our people do not justify treating others as enemies.

---

2   Any of the tests for relational circuit function help find enemy mode.
3   ThriveToday.org, kcLehman.com, *Transforming Fellowship* by Chris Coursey or Connexus by Ed Khouri, et al.

How our people escape enemy mode weaknesses

We help our people give healthy shame messages about lost hesed and high qasheh by inviting correction ourselves. "Talk to me if you see me in 'enemy mode.' Remind me if I do not love my enemies."

As we build our Christian group identity we begin to speak to others about "your enemy mode." We remind others with healthy shame messages when they are not loving their enemies. This is the life of real grace. When the weakness of "enemy mode" is taking over their minds, it is essential we remind others about who loves us and that we express love to our people. We quickly restore the sense of being special for those who hang their heads in shame.

The hardest correction is speaking up when we as a group are in enemy mode. Uncorrected qasheh and narcissistic weakness in our leaders puts us all in enemy mode. Allowing enemy mode to continue is not a grace response to a harmful weakness. Group enemy mode creates the silence around every Pandora problem. With silence instead of a loving shame message, we will not learn to love our enemies.

What does a mental "enemy mode" moment look like?

Because part of the brain's relational system is subcortical, it cannot be shut off while the cortical segments are down. The subcortical segments, under the control of the amygdala, are highly defensive. Defenders have a strong propensity to see others as enemies. However, as we have seen, narcissists come in two varieties we have called *peacocks* and *skunks*. Peacocks have defense systems that attack their external enemies while skunks have defense systems that attack themselves as though the enemy was within.

The "enemy within," as Fr. Andrew Miller calls it,[4] is a frequent element in all human conflicts whether internal, between people, or between people and God. Once in enemy mode, we can fight internally as easily as with others around us. While in enemy mode we focus on making the other person lose rather than on what we value. We are now acting like sociopaths even if we usually do not. We have lost track of our people and are becoming qasheh.

---

4   HeartSynch by Rev. Andrew A. Miller is a ministry program for dealing with internal conflicts.

Self-justification extends enemy mode and protects it. Many Christian and pastoral counseling sessions are little more than extended self-justification sessions. The counselor sometimes provides the most biblical justifications. I myself spent the first ten years of my counseling career doing little else. My efforts did not resolve anyone's enemy mode.

Because we are dealing with the same sort of brain systems that control what we call "involuntary functions," once the brain is in "enemy mode" it is very unresponsive to reason or persuasion. **But, all hope is not lost.** Down even deeper than the guardian function of enemy mode (amygdala) in the subcortical brain is the brain's attachment (hesed) system. When our people activate the attachment center of our minds we have reached our deepest self – a self who can even overcome enemy mode with some help. Enemy mode is overcome by hesed and not by persuasion, power, or punishment.

No brain enjoys enemy mode, so to make it stop we must: a) win (at whatever cost), b) find relational joy, or c) withdraw. The responses we have practiced will become the most likely next step. Will we look for our people? Will we go into predator mode and attack to win? Will we play dead and hope the predators go away? Will we use the compassion of others against them and attack ourselves in their plain view? Will we go away thinking, "It will only get worse if I say something?"

Our relational circuits want to know, "What would it be like our people to do now?"

We answer, "We love our enemies."

We ask, "Even when the enemy is me?"

We answer, "Yes! And there is no time more important than when we are in enemy mode to learn to love our enemies. Enemy mode is a weakness that requires our careful hesed. Enemy mode is a harmful weakness and so we give it some special attention because we are protective people."

At the same time, we must recognize that enemy mode is a really hard place to start learning to love our enemies. We tend to see every enemy as "strong" when, in fact, enemy mode is a symptom of weakness. We fall into enemy mode when half of our brain's identity and navigation system is shut down.

Enemy mode is a sort of "half-witted" response – and very harmful. We need to look at people in enemy mode and say, "Father forgive them, they don't know what they are doing." While they understand full well the predatory responses they are perfecting, people in enemy mode will never achieve what they really want or need. **Their hope is in our hesed.**

LIVING IN ENEMY MODE

We notice that life goes on whether someone is in enemy mode or not. Enemy mode can take on a life of its own. Keeping in mind that some people may live their whole adult lives in enemy mode, we may mistakenly accept this malfunction as that person's personality. What we need to realize is that enemy mode is capable of producing a large array of life functions. Home, school, work, marriage, and church life may all be lived in enemy mode. While people in enemy mode have symptoms of personality disorders, they are common in all walks of life. Whole lifestyle patterns can be developed either with or without the relational circuits functioning properly.

Have you ever met a person who was always relational? Few people stay in relational or enemy mode for their entire lives. It is possible (and common) for people to spend part of their lives in relational mode and part of their lives in enemy mode. As a person spends more time in either mode, he or she develops a repertoire in that mode. In the relational mode the person is very pleasant and Christian, and in the enemy mode the person is predatory. These two personality styles develop lives of their own.

The brain is a learning machine, and in either relational mode or enemy mode the brain learns. In enemy mode, the only motive is to win (defined as the enemy will lose.) In relational mode, the motive is becoming part of our identity group. Now the question is how much life experience lies in each of the two modes? In particular, how much life experience does the enemy mode possess?

There is nothing like growing up with condemnation, criticism, self-justification, and related qasheh behaviors to encourage living in enemy mode. Children of Christian leaders, children sent to boarding schools, children of abusive parents, children in foster care, and children of minority groups who live in hostile social environments may spend large segments of their childhoods with their relational circuits disabled. Children who feel threatened can spend much of life in enemy mode and learn to do almost all of life from that condition. Their minds may revert to enemy mode at the slightest provocation.

It is difficult for a mature mind that has spent little time in enemy mode to switch from relational mode to enemy mode. The more extensive our life experience has been in enemy mode, however, the more reasons there are to stay there. An emotionally cold family or boarding school may make triggers out of most life activities. Once activated, enemy mode produces the feeling that people, society, God, and anyone in power do not desire real relationship. Being approached by people can trigger enemy mode for someone who grew up surrounded by people whose relational circuits were off.

Early in his career, Dr. Lehman noticed that people responded remarkably differently when they were triggered. At first Dr. Lehman wondered if there might be an entirely different memory system for trauma memories. What he and many others observed is that once people are triggered they do not act like the same people. Sometimes the responses are defensive, sometimes aggressive, sometimes hot, and sometimes cold. In every case the person is responding as though they are facing an enemy. Relational systems become significantly impaired and enemy mode reactions occur without the person's choice.

Because the activation of enemy mode depends on the amygdala and the amygdala is below the conscious cortex, we cannot say that people "choose" to enter enemy mode. Amygdala operation is "pre-conscious." The location of the amygdala has other important implications we will examine in a bit. For now, we observe that any sort of unresolved emotional memory that leaves the mind feeling threatened and alone can trigger the mind into enemy mode. Dr. Karl Lehman has written extensively on this topic with regard to triggering and the resolution of triggers through Immanuel healing.

What became clear to Dr. Lehman and others is that to resolve a triggered state one must engage the mind while the triggered reaction is active. Since enemy mode is essentially a triggered state, learning to love our enemies must be learned while the mind is in enemy mode. We learn to love our enemies while our mind still thinks we are enemies.

Enemy mode may be obvious or quite camouflaged. Because enemy mode can run like a submarine below the surface it can be hard to engage. This submarine function develops frequently in religious communities where everyone is required to act nice but there is no real hesed. These communities inevitably have high levels of self-justification built into their culture. A Mennonite or Plain People community that would not tolerate hot anger or war might, at the same time, house cold enemy mode under many a head covering or beard. The pastoral staff in large and open-looking churches can attest to sudden strikes from submerged enemy modes within the inner circle of the church.

In the extreme case of BTK, the serial killer from Kansas, Denis Rader was the president of the church council of Christ Lutheran Church who brutally stalked and killed ten people. He wrote notes to the police from the church office and even sent them a CD made on the church computer. He bragged and threatened more murders. He was a dogcatcher and compliance officer with a degree in administration of justice and known for his overly strict enforcement.

Many people with well-developed enemy mode see themselves as God's enforcers and take great pleasure in announcing God's judgment on the sins of others. It should come as no surprise to anyone who understands enemy mode that pastors and leaders who are prone to denouncing sin in others often have religious-sounding enemy modes. Predatory pastors may get away with their sudden strikes for a long time, but they eventually slow down or the sheer number of victims gives them away. Predictably, most of the religious community around them will be in total disbelief.

DETECTING ENEMY MODE IN OPERATION

The brain has two options within enemy mode: "hot anger" and "cold predator." We easily notice when someone goes into hot anger, but when the crocodile-like cold predator mode is running like a submarine most people only have a slight sense they are being stalked until the "strike." The strike can be swift, almost silent, and disappear as quickly as it came, leaving people wondering "did that really happen?"

We can expect to find all combinations of modes, alternating patterns and degrees of awareness of their enemy mode in people. I myself would have honestly insisted at age 18 that I

Learning to love our enemies must be learned while the mind is in enemy mode.

had no enemy mode inside. No one had ever engaged me relationally at a deep enough level for me to see myself change from relational to enemy mode. Marriage would surprise me with some new revelations.

Some people have never experienced relational mode. Without experiencing relational life they have nothing to compare with enemy mode. Our entire discussion makes little sense to anyone without a meaningful hesed experience. Some people – and narcissists often fit this pattern – develop a "social interface" for their enemy mode without ever entering into relational mode. Narcissistic and sociopathic people make arrangements and manage people without leaving enemy mode. Just as the crocodile knows that the wildebeest will need to drink, and the orca knows that the baby whale will need air, the needs and attachments of others become the weaknesses that narcissistic and sociopathic people will use to bring them down. Monitoring weakness in others does not produce shared pain. Therapy and learning about feelings makes them better predators.

While it may be possible to hide the cold enemy mode reaction from untrained eyes, it is generally noticeable to trained predators or trained protectors. Untrained people, church members, boards, and relatives will not believe when told about enemy mode. Not believing in enemy mode neither stops the attacks nor helps the predators change. What we can be quite sure of is that people who are hiding their enemy mode are not learning to love their enemies. Pastors who are hiding their own enemy mode are not helping others to overcome theirs. The group around a Pandora problem will need solutions to enemy mode.

Let's take a look "under the hood" at enemy mode.

If the switch to enemy mode is subcortical, and therefore not a conscious choice, does that leave the conscious brain with no influence? The answer is *no* in two ways. First, as we have pointed out before, people can learn to shut down the cortical segments of their relational circuits. This means people can learn to shut off their relational mode intentionally. Certainly, once the cortical segments are shut down, the switch to enemy mode is automatic in much the same way that if you hold your breath long enough passing out happens automatically.

Second, while the amygdala is subcortical, it is not the deepest part of the brain. The brain's attachment center stands in line before processing reaches the amygdala. This is to say, if we have hesed, the brain has a strong incentive to stay out of enemy mode. When we do not have hesed, the amygdala becomes the strongest force. Hesed also directly affects the amygdala as a good attachment and will always let the amygdala know that this is a good person and not an enemy. When this personal attachment is missing, the amygdala cannot correct any enemy associations in memory. Bad experiences with men, women, dogs, authorities, whites, blacks, Israelis, Palestinians, Muslims, Christians, loud, or quiet people all become a reason for enemy mode to start and run.

A dominant feature of enemy mode is the persistence of negative reactions. After we work hard to resolve a real or imagined wrong with someone, we may think we have been forgiven and worked things out, but what happened was that they emerged from enemy mode. The next time enemy mode is activated it is as though every past fault has been committed again right now. Nothing has changed, the anger is as strong as ever, and everything we thought was worked out is back in our faces with no trace of a previous resolution. Enemy mode has not learned to love its enemies. This is only made worse because the enemy mode has its own version of what really happened, what the "enemy" really meant, what the "enemy" really intended, and what the "enemy" needs to "own."

Enemy mode is not done until you lose. Enemy mode will believe you the "enemy" are also intent on winning and justifying yourself every time you explain.

ENEMY MODE IS SEEN AS WEAKNESS IN SCRIPTURE.

The New Testament gives evidence of encountering enemy mode in Christians. Enemy mode is a harmful weakness. When the Apostle Paul instructs the church in Philippi to help two women get along, he was almost certainly dealing with two minds in enemy mode. While the Bible does not report their brain state, it can hardly be anything but enemy mode. If the conflict was caused by demons, doctrines, or disobedience, St. Paul would have offered different solutions. Demons can easily be cast out, doctrine corrected, and obedience commanded. What we read is:

> *I urge Euodia and I urge Syntyche to live in harmony in the Lord. Indeed, true companion, I ask you also to help these women who have shared my struggle in the cause of the gospel, together with Clement also and the rest of my fellow workers, whose names are in the book of life.*

> Philippians 4:2-3 (NASB)

The women's mutual attachments to Paul, God, and the community are being used to help their community engage with the women while they are in enemy mode and help them out of it. These two are clearly Christian leaders who cannot stop treating each other like enemies. The women's identity group must engage while the women are still stuck. We notice that Paul starts with attachments and group identity when speaking to the community about Euodia and Syntyche. Paul does not lead with a healthy shame message – and he is quite capable of one! This time Paul starts with a reminder of their attachment to him, to Christ, and to their group identity. Paul exhorts them to live in φρονέω (phronéō) – a Greek word that comes about as close to "mutual mind state" as the language can muster.

In a group that is busy learning to love their enemies, Paul's encouragement is all that is needed. The church will help these two leaders to love each other. Most Western churches that never think of loving enemies would have no idea where to start. There is no indication that either of these ladies is narcissistic although I would not be surprised to hear self-justification from their enemy mode thinking. We simply hear of two dedicated and much-loved ladies who both have an enemy mode weakness.

We have been examining simple enemy mode. Narcissism adds an interesting "catch 22" element to the enemy mode weakness. A good technical definition of narcissism is that a narcissist goes into enemy mode when receiving a shame message. We need healthy shame messages to correct our identity. Narcissists drop into an enemy mode weakness every time they hear the message that could save them.

We remember that our attachments (hesed) are deeper in the brain than enemy mode. Because attachment comes first in the brain, an attachment cannot be blocked by enemy mode. The church that builds hesed has a strategic starting point against the enemy mode weakness. Hesed is a basic Christian group identity process and essential for overcoming enemy mode.

Because self-justification extends enemy mode, the church that raises hesed must also lower qasheh. Hesed people find self-justification disgusting and provide healthy shame messages as needed. In order to understand the shame messages, we must first understand how the brain processes shame. We must know how to guide narcissists out of their "catch 22."

RELATIONAL JOY AND RELATIONAL SHAME

God designed our brains for relational joy. Joy means *someone is glad to be with me.* We are relational creatures who want to see someone's eyes light up when they see us. Our brains also have another system built in for the opposite of joy, the feeling that comes when *someone is not glad to be with me.* We call the antagonist system *relational shame.* Shame signals, *I'm just not glad to be with you while you're doing that.* This *anti-joy* warns us something is "off" and not good for relational life.

God designed us to feel relational shame in order for us to become socialized people. Shame helps all of us to learn there is a better way to behave when our behavior is "off." Everyone knows, whether they are Christians or not, that people do not always live like their best self.

All human beings stop acting like themselves at times. We are quite able to pretend to be different outside from who we are inside. Dolphins, dogs, or cats do not masquerade; animals always act like themselves. Humans are unique in this sense that they can fail to act like themselves. When we are not acting like our true selves, we are not pleasing God either. People around us should respond by sending us a relational shame message – a message that starts (though this is only the start) with the signal, "I'm not really happy to be with you right now."

Problems with shame

Shame is a difficult emotion to deal with, even though God wired it into us for a reason. Sometime in the 1970s a change in our culture contributed to our difficulty with shame. Psychologists discovered that alcoholics were living in toxic shame. Culture responded with the conclusion that we should never do or say anything that creates shame. This seemed like a smart idea.

Failing to notice the difference between relational shame and toxic shame meant we could not correct failures in our group identity.

Using shame messages relationally is a learned brain skill. Brain skills can disappear in one generation without use. The irony is that without the learned skill to use a shame message relationally ALL shame messages become toxic. We have seen how this works with

Like all pain systems, shame exists to warn us when we are damaging something important.

narcissists. Any shame message lands narcissists in enemy mode as though the message were toxic. So, as we lose the relational skill to exchange shame messages, we set everyone up to react like narcissists and lose the ability to form a hesed identity group.

It is now common for people to regard all shame messages as toxic. Many people go straight to enemy mode and fight back with anger, blame, and attacks. Angry people will self-justify. People who have difficulty with shame – that is, they refuse to feel shame when receiving a shame message – flip the message around insisting there is something wrong with the messenger.

Instead of attacking the messenger, God would have us say, "Wow! I should look at myself," and ask, "How is it I'm not bringing you joy?" However, we can make this useful outcome much more likely if we give a complete relational shame message. A healthy relational message will have three features. First, it will be a message about group identity – "we don't" and "we do."

The second feature of a relational message is that it identifies the malfunction in identity: "we don't call people names." However, for anyone who is weak with shame skills this part of the message alone is likely to slide into toxic range quickly. We need to add the third element and say, "we (do) like to help others find and recognize their true selves."

The brain needs healthy shame messages.

Shame is one of the brain's hardwired pain systems. Like all pain systems, shame exists to warn us when we are damaging something important. In the absence of a pain signal, the brain will continue what it is doing – such as leaving our hand in a fire. Our pain signals protect us. Shame protects us from things that are damaging our relational joy.

Since everything that is resilient and good about our identities grows in response to relational joy, the brain has a high priority to protect us from anything that would damage the joy we need. It is fine to ignore things that do not bring joy – trimming our fingernails generally brings little joy but needs to be done. What we must avoid and correct quickly are those things that make others wish we were no longer there. Shame – the pain feeling when we are killing the joy around us – is essential.

Let us review quickly what we know about shame. The brain is tuned to watch for negative reactions toward us. Our mind understands these shame pain signals as a sign we are not the people we should be. In heathy relationships, each shame reaction is automatically tied to the positive path back to joy. The formula would be, "We do not (whatever it is). We (act this way)." This formula can be expressed many ways but always with a warm and inviting tone that welcomes one of our people back into joy if they will simply feel the shame and not stiffen their necks. An opening shame message for enemy mode would be, "We do not let our enemies make us become like them, instead, we love our enemies."

Toxic shame is pain with no way back to relationship. Enemy mode obviously neither has nor seeks a way back to relationship. So, victims of enemy mode are often left in the pain of shame. Their conscious mind must then decide if there is something wrong with them or with their enemy. Skunk narcissists begin attacking themselves, and peacocks attack the enemy. Most people only think of toxic shame when they hear the word "shame."

Like all pain, shame is a moment of weakness that brings attacks by predators and protection from protectors. When our mind is in enemy mode we will attack, and when it is in relational mode we will protect. Either way, we will track the pain the other person is feeling. In enemy mode we will use this pain to make them lose, and in relational mode we will feel their pain as ours. Feeling their pain as ours will help the person in shame learn how to build a stronger identity group through the pain of shame. We are people who care about each other even when we must share shame.

TEACHING SOMEONE WHO IS IN ENEMY MODE

Teaching someone who is in enemy mode cannot be done if there is no attachment. People without attachment are beyond the scope of this book. We are in a partnership with God on this venture, so we will notice that deep transformation of character needs an attachment (hesed) to God and to God's people. Since God's people love their enemies, we always offer enemies an attachment to God and to us. Transformation of character will have to wait for attachment to grow.

If someone has an attachment to God or to us we have a starting place to help deal with the weakness of enemy mode. Christians who are busy learning to love their enemies will have many ways to teach someone in enemy mode how our people love our enemies. I believe **learning to love enemies is the key feature of all Christian discipleship and spiritual formation**. At its core, we are learning to see others the way Jesus sees them and respond accordingly.

Many resources are already available to help people share a kind of mutual mind state with God. We have called this an Immanuel lifestyle within the Life Model literature. Living with the active sense of God's presence and communication is an identity group characteristic for God's people. We are looking at helping someone who is in enemy mode with the assumption that the reader is experienced in achieving a mutual mind state with God in order to see others more as God sees them.

What we will consider next is how to help a narcissist learn while in enemy mode. When I say "we" I mean a plural "we" of an identity group. I mean a group that practices relationship with each other. I mean a group who isn't just trying to "intervene" with a narcissist. We are talking about hesed people.

A weakness causes narcissists to fall into enemy mode every time a healthy shame message comes their way. Instead of being corrected, they start to fight. But there is a wonderful flaw in enemy mode. We can "exploit" this flaw to help narcissists learn their way out of enemy mode!

No shared pain

Recall how enemy mode does not a) share pain but b) tracks pain carefully? This feature can be used to teach narcissists with attachments how to deal with shame. Take a moment to consider two things at once:

1. Narcissists go into enemy mode each time they feel shame (even healthy shame messages).

2. Narcissists in enemy mode are not bothered by shame others feel (no shared pain).

Narcissists will listen very carefully to the shame experiences of others and watch what happens, but they do not feel other's shame themselves. If our identity group invites healthy shame messages, gives healthy shame messages, rejoices in the excellent outcomes of healthy shame messages, then the group will have the narcissist's attention for every healthy shame story[5] that is not about him or her – even in enemy mode.

Viper bite

The narcissist experiences shame like a viper bite. So, let's say that an identity group is talking about healthy shame messages they have received and how it helped them reduce their qasheh, increase their hesed, or improve their ability to love enemies. Every place in a story where someone receives a healthy shame message, the narcissist will think a viper has just struck. The person who received the shame message should soon show signs of poisoning and enemy mode but . . . what is this?

What!?

What just happened? Like St. Paul being bitten by the viper on Malta and shaking it off, the storyteller is enjoying better relationships with my people! By the time that fifty stories have been told the narcissist's mind – still in enemy mode – has learned something very interesting about shame and its effects. Shame doesn't kill everybody! Some people get stronger! This is something that every mind exploiting weakness wants to know.

About this point, healthy shame messages no longer mean an automatic switch to enemy mode for the narcissist. If we are in a fellowship that is learning relational skills and loving their enemies we have a new path forward. The narcissist is learning how *my* people do it.

Relational skills (and resources) in church

Any fellowship that is learning to love their enemies will be practicing and developing relational tools. There are a growing

---

5   Good stories are explained in the Life Model literature as 4+ stories. The 4+ refers to the four levels of the joy elevator in the right brain plus the verbal skills of the left brain. See the 4+ story appendix for more detail.

number of teaching tools for these relation skills. Reviewing them all is beyond the limits of this book, but a list of better relational resources can be found at the end of this chapter.

Sequence matters.

It should now make sense that dealing with a Pandora problem requires some character and skill on the part of our group. An identity group that does not practice healthy shame messages or loving enemies will not make progress. We need to know where we are starting and take steps in the right sequence. In general, we deal with enemy mode (in our own people) using this sequence:

1) Attachment (raise hesed)

2) Healthy shame processing (lower qasheh)

3) Loving our enemies (offering attachment to those who are weak on hesed)

We will face various levels of enemy mode: simple enemy mode, narcissist in enemy mode, unattached person in enemy mode, non-member of our identity group in enemy mode, and leaders in enemy mode. For this book we are not considering unattached people or non-members of our group. We are looking carefully at leaders in enemy mode.

Super Q moments

When we read the Bible we cannot miss the very strong shame messages being given to teachers of God's people who are in a super qasheh moment. Teachers are judged by a higher standard, and for those to whom much has been given much is required. When teachers of God's people are in self-justification mode and claiming to speak for God, they are on a collision path with a public shame message. The life of Jesus and the prophets includes many of these public shame messages.

Protecting the "flock" from predators in teachers' clothing means a healthy shame message cannot wait. Those who teach God's people publicly must be corrected publicly if they stiffen their necks. Super Q moments must be corrected without falling into enemy mode and without letting our people be deceived.

Jesus gave the parable of the Good Samaritan in response to self-justification by a teacher. Jesus' parable was to teach, but it did involve feeling some shame by the teacher. Jesus was dealing with self-justification but not someone in enemy mode.

The stories about Jesus make it quite clear when He was approached in enemy mode. Teachers claiming that Jesus operated in the power of Beelzebub are one example. We are told when leaders sought to trap Him, and we can tell they were in enemy mode. A healthy shame message is about to come their way. The key, however, is that we must always offer hesed attachment at the same time as the healthy shame message.

GROUP IDENTITY IN THE BRAIN

About this point, it is very tempting to start figuring out the right thing to do. I will leave that to people with brains larger than the universe. The question is not "when do I have to give a healthy shame message to a leader" but rather "are we building up the group identity for God's people."

Group identity is built up through sharing each other's joys and sorrows and learning how our people express their true selves under diverse conditions. We are motivated by the joy of being together. A sense of "me and my people" is growing in the right prefrontal cortex of the brain.

The brain grows identity through hesed attachments.

The brain develops its identity around strong bonds. These bonds are not created by concepts or goals but rather by strongly felt experiences. Strong experiences can be joyful/loving experiences or fearful/enemy experiences. The consistently intense experiences during the brain's development generally win. The brain can run on either joyful desire or fearful avoidance, and our group identity will help us establish our pattern.

While the joyful motivation tends to bring the mind into harmony with itself and others, the fearful motivation tends to cause desynchronized, modular operation such as living in enemy mode. Fearful motivation creates people who act like different people when they become upset.

Our minds drop into enemy mode with our people way too easily. My mind has dropped into enemy mode at least three times today as I have been writing. Enemy mode loses track of a) group identity, b) acting like ourselves, and c) loving our enemies.

The adult brain looks for a hesed group identity.

While identity is more individual until age twelve, the profound brain changes with puberty bring a life-long need to become a joyful part of a peaceful and protective people. It is fine if people are loyal when everything is going well. The brain wants attachments (hesed) to people who are loyal even when upset. We need loyalty (hesed) when we feel weakest. The test of loyalty comes when there is a weakness.

The brain will not be hesed with everything or everyone. The brain attaches to "my people." Having grown up in a Spanish speaking country, my mind associates anyone who speaks Spanish as "my people." When I see someone looking "gangsta" the reaction is "not my people." People with shaved heads were "skin heads" and "not my people" until my son adopted the look. Bikers changed to my people when another son started riding motorcycles. I feel my attachment response when seeing people with my granddaughter's skin tone. Yet if I smile, their faces usually reflect, "You are not my people."

Hesed loyalty extends to our people. We must begin with the realization that our brain excludes some folks from being our people. In a discourse about rejection, St. Peter said, *"You once were not a people, but now you are the people of God; you had not received mercy, but now you have received mercy."*[6] As people of mercy we learn to love our enemies. We use the brain's learning ability to add newcomers to our people. This means we help each other when we forget who we are and that everyone might be one of our people.

> **If we willingly share the pain of others, we will not be controlled by pain avoidance.**

Our people provide the healthy shame the brain needs. As hesed people, we invite and give reminders when we neglect being God's people. We consider our weaknesses a place to grow. Weaknesses in others are exactly why they need our loving reminders. Once we were not the people of God. Becoming the people of God permits a rather intense transformation.

Hesed group identities share pain. We need to share the pain of others, if only to keep us out of enemy mode. Feeling someone's

---

6   1 Peter 2:10

pain gives us a chance to consider what might be more valuable than simple pain avoidance. If we willingly share the pain of others, we will not be controlled by pain avoidance. For example, removing a splinter may cause pain but have value. Sharing pain is needed for a good bond, but that is not all we need.

Hesed group identities are protective of weakness. What shared pain helps us avoid is unnecessary pain. We do not use pain to win. We protect weaknesses from being exploited or injured. We seek instead to help people be the real person each one was created to become.

The "God-intended person" each of us was destined to become is an incomplete image of Christ. Weaknesses are those places where the image of Christ is missing or just flickers on from time to time. Loyalty means we do not abandon others who cannot find or maintain their "God person" identity. Helping people become a "God person" would be more appealing if each failure of their "God person" identity was not prone to plunge them into enemy mode.

ENEMY MODE IS A SYMPTOM OF WEAKNESS.

So we reach the conclusion of this chapter with the realization that people who think they are our enemies are exhibiting a glaring and obvious weakness. Our enemies are unaware that they are showing a weakness and may even consider their weakness a great strength. People who cannot tell a weakness from a strength have another weakness showing – impaired judgment.

As God's people, we are to develop discerning judgment and to love our enemies. Enemies provide a golden opportunity for everything in us that is "God's people" to show. We need enough hesed to offer attachment to our enemy. Our own qasheh ways will want to justify that the risk is too high, the rewards too low, the pain too possible, and the enemy too real. In spite of our total inability to calculate the right thing to do, we will feel resistance against seeing our enemy as weak. Besides, if this person (who thinks I am the enemy) has dominion and power, this weakness will probably cause me pain.

What comes into play next depends on whether we see what God sees and what we have practiced over and over. Will our people give us healthy shame messages if we forget? Will our people be loyal enough to share our pain and help us in our weakness? A low hesed or high qasheh group will leave us in a flash – often saying "We will pray for you" as they go. I hope they do that, at least.

When we see what God sees in each other, we stay – or we at least come back. What we see through God's eyes is called "grace," but the word has lost most of its original meaning. Most of us would say, "What's grace got to do with it?" We will find out in the next chapter.

Lord, we ask for mercy and grace toward those who justify themselves that we might not respond in the same way.

Relational Tools for Identity Groups

- *Rare Leadership* by Warner & Wilder (2016)

- *Transforming Fellowship* by Chris Coursey (2017)

- *Relational Skills in the Bible* by Brown & Coursey (2018)

- *Joyful Journey* by Wilder, Kang, Loppnow & Loppnow (2015)

- *Passing the Peace* by LifeModelWorks.org (2015)

- *The Solution of Choice* by Warner & Wilder (2018)

- *Building Better Community* by Tom Anthony (2018)

- *Joy Starts Here* by Wilder, Khouri, Coursey & Sutton (2013)

- "Grace, Narcissism, and Small Groups" web course by Ed Khouri

- For more by Ed Khouri see DeeperWalkInternational.org

- ThriveToday.org for training and online courses

- DeeperWalkInternational.org for training and materials

- Kclehman.com for a wide range of resources

If You Are Ready
Group Exercise for Chapter Twelve

Today's group identity affirmation

Repeat together, "We are a people who desire to live constantly in God's peace and joy."

In groups of about five people tell each other why this characteristic matters to you. (5 minutes)

Today's healthy shame message practice

In groups of about five people create a healthy shame message for me <u>when I act as though I understand what others are saying when I really don't listen (but others around me do understand)."</u> (5 minutes)

Note: A healthy shame message states "we do not" and then states who we are with a Christ-like character response.
"We do not _____, we _____."

Tell each small group's statement to the whole group. (5 minutes)

Today's withstanding self-justification practice

Self-justification: "God has put me in charge here."

In groups of about five people make a list of the weaknesses that lie behind this self-justification. What would a hesed community do to be sure these weaknesses do not prevail? (10 minutes)

Report each small group's conclusions to the whole group. (5 minutes)

Today's loving my enemy practice

This exercise is like texting with God. Write the impression that comes to your mind. Start with something that makes you grateful then your impression of God's response. Next read the question

211

and write your impression of God's response that gives you peace. (5 minutes)

1. Dear God, I am thankful:
2. My dear child:
3. God, when has someone felt like an enemy to me this week?
4. What do You want me to know about loving them?

Read what you have written in groups of about five people. Do not explain what you wrote. Check for a sense of peace after you read. (5 minutes)

Loving my enemies: Exercise 2

As a whole group discuss the following.

Where in the news have you seen someone in enemy mode this week? What were the signs you noticed? Make a list of the signs of enemy mode. (8 minutes)

Take two minutes of group silence to think of a time in the last few days that your mind went into enemy mode.

Without naming any names answer the following and make a group list: (30 minutes)

1. What word describes your mental state in enemy mode?
2. How would you describe the change when you came out of enemy mode?
3. What one word best describes what started your enemy mode?
4. Can you identify what brought you out of enemy mode?
5. What relationship is strong enough to usually reach you in enemy mode?

Take two minutes of silence to ask God who He has in mind to help you remember your hesed when you are in enemy mode.

Tell the person next to you 1) who God brought to mind and 2) if you will ask that person to help you this week.

Repeating today's group identity affirmation

Repeat together, "We are a people who desire to live constantly in God's peace and joy."

CHAPTER THIRTEEN
Grace and Loving Our Enemies
Narcissism Is a Weakness.

**Do not answer a fool according to his folly, lest you also be like him.
Answer a fool according to his folly, lest he be wise in his own eyes.**
Proverbs 26: 4-5

There is a contrast between narcissism and Christianity that is about as contradictory as one can get. Narcissism creates huge weaknesses in exactly the areas one would expect Christians to show strengths. Christians should be quietly justified by God, but narcissists are busy self-justifying. Christians should love enemies while narcissists live much of life in enemy mode. Christians should be secure in their sense of being special, yet narcissists are working hard to be special.

Whether we have studied anything about narcissism or not, we know that the big N is all about being special. We all *do* need to be special. The most glaring weakness of narcissists is their foolish way of trying to be special. We cannot let people make such huge mistakes and not help them.

WISDOM AND FOLLY

My neighbor Dick Birkey owned an advertising company. Dick was very innovative. When I was starting my own company, Dick inspired ideas I could never imagine. For all his creative thinking, Dick kept me focused on one thing. Advertising, according to Dick, is how the customer discovers what is special about my product. Dick's ability to highlight what was special gained him amazing clients. Dick worked and worked with me to identify what made my product special. My product was complex, but Dick found the special features that brought value. Dick was wise.

In the last chapter, we established that narcissism is a half-witted weakness. Now we will see that narcissism is also foolish. Chapter

Six tells how David's narcissistic nephews won battles but then killed the man who could bring the rewards of victory.

Asahel was a great runner, probably the best in the country. He thought running made him special but killing a general could make him more special. Asahel chased Abner because Asahel was in enemy mode doing some trophy hunting. Asahel was foolishly over-focused on killing Abner. Asahel's plan to be special left him dead in the road. He was both half-witted and foolish; half-witted because he missed the warning and the thing that would kill him and foolish because neither running fast nor killing generals makes one special. Asahel was trying to be special in enemy mode and it cost him his life. That is foolish!

Narcissism is a very harmful weakness that turns glory into shame. In this chapter we will look at many of the ways that narcissism becomes foolish so that we can help folks with this weakness before they get themselves killed or hurt someone else. Narcissists fall into enemy mode where they can spend the rest of their lives. Like Asahel, they have overlooked the other end of the spear. We must understand the key weakness in the narcissist's mind. Dick Birkey's wisdom will help us find and correct it.

Narcissism is folly.

For all their efforts to be special, over time, narcissists become less special to the group around them. Narcissists impale themselves on the other end of their own spear. For all they desire being special, narcissists don't know how to find specialness. This is foolish.

Narcissists work like the devil to be special. **The key to what makes us special will be the key to every Pandora problem.** This key may not seem obvious, so let's take the Pandora situation apart. What does the person in the middle want most? Why are any negative comments punished? Why must there be people orbiting the center? What messages come out of the center of the circle? Everything is designed to make the one in the middle special, but it does not work.

Neuroscience helps us understand how the brain knows "I am special." Feeling special is a gift from our brains' attachment (hesed) circuit indicating that we are securely loved by the people who know us best. Being special is generated by who loves us and not by what we do. The brain cannot achieve "special," rather it is a gift from those who see and know us.

The foolishness of narcissism now becomes obvious. **Narcissists are trying to create that which can only be received.** Further, when narcissists are in enemy mode, they block the very relationships that could impart specialness. Narcissists who deflect healthy shame messages (when they fail to act like themselves and their people) close the gate on what is actually special about them.

Since specialness is created by hesed, it then follows that we are only going to be as special as whoever loves us. If, by some unlikely chance, a very high status being really knew and loved us, we would be very special. No more effort would be needed, no performance would be required. Our sense of special would be like marrying into royalty, wealth, and power. Imagine joining the royal family and trying to prove we are special by how great we burp, how high we jump, or how we can touch our nose with our tongue? The king's family, horses, and all the king's men would tell us to stop making fools of ourselves and remember who we are. We already are special. **The solution to Pandora problems is found in helping each other remember what makes us special.**

Grace is wisdom.

The Bible tells from end to end how we can find specialness. If we do not grasp the ancient expressions, we will hear the answer but not understand. The Bible uses the word "grace" when talking about being special. In ancient cultures, the expression for receiving special treatment was to "find grace." Saying "if I have found grace" means "if I am special to you." To be *graced* was to be granted special status in relationship to the "great one." So, when an Apostle writes, "Grace to you" it means "You are special."

God's grace should not be confused with mercy. Mercy means we do not get what we deserve. Grace means we get loved. God's grace gives us a status that only those who are loved by God and members of God's family have. Therefore, no one can boast about how they achieved their status, and all comparisons with others are foolish beyond words.

God offers grace to all. Narcissists have been offered "special," but they foolishly try to perform, control, compare, and intimidate their way to feeling "special." Narcissists resemble a brain in enemy mode. To be special in enemy mode is to make everyone else lose.

GRACE IS SPECIAL.

Understanding grace helps us keep a Dick Birkey focus as we deal with narcissism. Dick taught me to find what is actually special and make it understood. We must constantly sort through people's characteristics and select the ones that actually make them special. We will be looking for ways people resemble our identity group. We seek out the image of Christ in everyone. What is special will always be seen first through spiritual eyes. This is grace.

> **When someone forgets who they are, a person of grace will help them remember who God called them to be.**

Grace is the secret key to unlock hesed. Did you ever meet someone you thought was really special? Starting a relationship with this person focused on letting him or her know, "You are special to me!" Looks, smiles, comments, interest, gifts, and focused attention expressed our appreciation of their specialness. **Announcing what is special expresses grace.** If we want to see love grow, we discover and express the specialness of that person. We have become the agents of grace. As grace agents we help others understand grace in relational terms.

When I know I am special and I know others are also special, it becomes painful to see others trying to prove they are special. As a therapist in North Hollywood, I saw a number of performers. These lovely looking people came to my office to disclose how ugly they felt. Blemishes so small I could not see them demolished their sense of being special. It was painful to watch.

Developing what is really special always requires removing the "fake special" with healthy shame messages. Wherever people justify themselves to look special, there will be low hesed. So, if we are able to let low hesed people see what is special about them, we will complete Dick Birkey's mission. We will have helped people find grace and have sparked the growth of hesed. We reveal the person God meant them to be while they are distracted by performance, perfection, possessions, or their poisonous ways.

Being perfect is not special.

Our group identity goal is acting like ourselves. Being "who we were created to be" is God's goal for perfect behavior. Our best efforts bring us up to God's normal. If we reach perfect, we are not unusual people; we are just eliminating malfunctions so we can be like our people – God's family. When a malfunctioning computer gets fixed we do not say, "What an extraordinary computer! It works!"

Jesus spoke of our best being God's normal, saying, *"So likewise you, when you have done all those things which you are commanded, say, 'We are unprofitable servants. We have done [only] what was our duty to do.'"*[1] If we were perfect in every way, Jesus says that is nothing special. Dick Birkey says, "Keep looking for the real grace (specialness)."

Narcissism is anti-special.

Grace and narcissism have exactly the same goal with opposite solutions. Narcissism attempts being special through effort – particularly effort aimed at eliminating the competition. Grace achieves being special through relationships that bring out all that is special about everyone. Grace is particularly powerful when we activate what is special in others. When someone forgets who they are and does something harmful, a person of grace will help them remember who God called them to be. A narcissist full of condemnation and judgment will use that same information to broadcast how rotten the person is.

Grace is the opposite of narcissism. Grace is to narcissism as loving-sexuality is to rape. These two are extreme opposites. Narcissism and rape are all about the perpetrator through actions that harm others. Grace and loving-sexuality are about life-giving, loving, mutual, life-giving encounters with others. When we see little grace, we can suspect we are dealing with a narcissist.

Narcissist's pseudo-special identity

Grace does not aid the pseudo-self but instead helps people discover what is really special about themselves in relationship

---

1   Luke 17:10

to God's people. While there are many pseudo-identities, a popular one comes in a good religious package. We are looking at narcissism among Christians for this very reason.

The inability to use shame messages to build better relationships is the base of the unstable pseudo-special identity built by narcissists. Grace therefore opposes religious narcissism but does not abandon qasheh people to their weakness. Let us examine how this is described in Galatians: *"If we live in the Spirit, let us also walk in the Spirit. Let us not become conceited, provoking one another, envying one another."*[2]

"Let us not become conceited." The Greek word here translated *conceited* is the word for *doxology* and *vanity* put together. This is the only place in the Greek New Testament that this word occurs. A vain doxology sounds like *praise me from whom all blessings flow*. We hear vain doxologies from very religious people who present themselves as the ones from whom God's blessings flow. The passage adds that we should not provoke or envy. Narcissists provoke and envy. The passage continues:

> *Brethren, if a man is overtaken in any trespass, you who are spiritual restore such a one in a spirit of gentleness, considering yourself lest you also be tempted. Bear one another's burdens, and so fulfill the law of Christ. For if anyone thinks himself to be something, when he is nothing, he deceives himself.* Galatians 6:1-3

The "trespass" in this particular passage refers to someone becoming conceited. Verse three says, *"If anyone thinks himself to be something when he is nothing he deceives himself."* The narcissist is deceived and most unlikely to find help unless those who are not deceived help out.

St. Paul guides the church to deal with pseudo-identity in narcissists. St. Paul calls for the "spiritual" rather than elders or some other group to take the lead. People who have "Godsight" in the Spirit can see what actually makes someone special. Spiritual people become the agents of grace.

"Those of you who are spiritual, restore such a one in the spirit of gentleness considering yourself lest you also should be tempted." There are many sins that will not tempt us when we go to correct them. Self-justified narcissism is different. When someone is self-

---

2   Galatians 5:25-26

justified, the temptation to self-justify in return is very strong. When people are stiff-necked, the temptation to get stiff-necked in return is very high. Although we have prepared ourselves and can see what the Spirit is doing, we must stay vigilant and gentle. Without staying gentle we will drop into enemy mode ourselves.

Enemy mode is hateful, dangerous, and strong when it comes to creating harm but powerless, weak, and useless when it comes to creating glory. Narcissism (a qasheh response to weakness) almost cannot avoid enemy mode. Everyone becomes a threat when I am trying to be special. No amount of defeating my enemies will make me secure. Enemy mode is a huge and harmful weakness.

Grace and enemy mode

- Grace (specialness) is always a gift from someone who is hesed.

- Grace from a hesed person can activate hesed in a narcissist.

- Grace is the point of the spear for piercing enemy mode armor.

- Grace undercuts enemy mode because hesed attachments are deeper in the brain than enemy mode.

Like the missing scale on the armor of Smaug the dragon, narcissists' sense of special has a hole in it. Grace (what really makes us special) can pierce the armor of enemy mode. Even when someone is treating us as enemies, we still have a clear shot. But, like facing Smaug, only those whose hesed is stronger than their fear of dragon fire should take a shot.

Grace is the actual path to glory. Since glory comes from who loves us, we cannot work, perform, steal, or compare our way to glory. But how do we realize we are special? Grace reveals who God wants us to become as seen by our identity group. As Christians, our identity group contains all the aspects of Jesus' character that could be found in us. Once we pass puberty, our brain expects to find all that is special about us reflected by our identity group. The brain is poised to receive grace from our people.

A mind filled with grace (a hesed response to weakness) almost cannot enter enemy mode. Since we love our enemies, even when others are in enemy mode, the Spirit can reveal to us what is special about our enemies. Grace is never so clearly seen as when it is really not deserved.

What is special about us emerges as we begin to love our enemies. Likewise, we discover what is most Christ-like about us as we learn love for our enemies. Loving enemies surprises us all. That is grace.

Enemy mode requires healthy shame messages.

As grace discovers, shapes, and trains all that is special in us, grace also points out when we miss. Grace says, "Not so good. Try again. We have fallen short of who we can be." Without accepting shame we cannot appreciate grace. Qasheh narcissists cannot see they are special because their minds have made enemies of anyone who gives them shame messages. Yet, narcissists need a shame message that says, "We are not people who compare ourselves to others in order to be special. We are special because of who loves us. We express our specialness by loving others – even our enemies. In fact, our specialness (grace) shows through best when loving our enemies."

Healthy shame messages express what we see through Godsight. Grace sees a situation or person as God sees. Toxic shame messages tell people they are bad. People who will not accept a healthy shame message are listening through their *sarx* rather than hearing God's perspective. Scripture calls those people *fools*.[3]

Fools inevitably get angry with anyone who tries to correct them. Without learning the relational skill to use shame relationally, any shame message, even a good one, will activate enemy mode in narcissists who then become qasheh. To be helpful to narcissists, we must be quite certain that we can give and take shame messages without falling into enemy mode ourselves. Even good words given from enemy mode become foolish.

How we process shame shapes how we understand Scripture.

Passages that deal with God's judgments do not read like a hesed God to minds that do not process shame relationally. Instead, reading Scripture creates toxic shame; the feeling that God does not love them. Reading Scripture leaves them feeling alone and unwanted. Rather than finding a hesed God they find condemnation and feel depressed. Even Scripture becomes corrupted in the minds of narcissists. How will narcissists receive correction that shows them how to receive grace and live?

---

3   Galatians 3:1

Keep relationships bigger than problems.

We must address why a person cannot read relationships correctly. If we are teaching someone whose brain was trained incorrectly we will have to deliberately pay attention to their relational dyslexia. Owning a Bible does not help non-readers. When we notice that someone cannot read, we can teach them how to read. Likewise, reading the words in the Bible will not create better character for those who cannot read relationships enough to process shame relationally. God's people can overcome the relational deficiencies caused by inadequate relational training if we keep relationships bigger than problems. We can extend grace and mercy when others start to feel like enemies.

Whenever we focus on problems and not the person's real identity, shame messages become toxic. Dick Birkey would remind us to practice grace and find the special person God would like to call forth from the grave. Relationships are more important than if someone can handle shame. Relationships are very important to our identity group. We reassure others of our relationship. We are hesed with weakness, including the inability to process shame relationally.

Jesus lived among us to bring relational joy. "I have not come to condemn the world, but that the world through Me would be restored and be put back to the way God wants all of us to live."[4] We need to teach people how to hear shame messages and show them a better way to live. Our people are learning to act like our Father.

God's hesed can overcome any problem. We may not know the way back to closeness, but if we want to stick to God, He will find a way. We offer this mercy to others. Keeping our relationships with others central is what God asks us to do when He says, "Love your enemy."

GRACE IS THE POINT OF THE SPEAR.

The group around a Pandora problem needs Dick Birkey's focus to see what is really special about us. The person in the middle needs to discover the special character of his or her people. But learning character starts with a hesed attachment, and life around narcissists is rather low on hesed.

---

4   John 3:17 paraphrased

When hesed is low we start with grace. Our group identity reveals that we are the people of grace. God's character is grace. God makes us special though knowing His great love for us. Is it any wonder that when my friend Ed Khouri began developing a church discipleship program that could face narcissism, he built his program around grace?[5]

When qasheh is high, grace pierces enemy mode by revealing what is truly special. The point of our spear when dealing with those who refuse to hang their heads brings God's hesed character into direct contact with the narcissist's need to be special. We have already said techniques will fail. God's gracious character built into us is required. We remember God's character from Exodus 34:6-7:

> And the LORD passed before him and proclaimed, "The LORD, the LORD God, merciful and gracious, longsuffering, and abounding in goodness and truth, keeping mercy for thousands, forgiving iniquity and transgression and sin, by no means clearing the guilty, visiting the iniquity of the fathers upon the children and the children's children to the third and fourth generation.

Revisiting iniquity, sin, and transgression

Iniquity, sin, and transgression provide categories for the different ways people become narcissistic: iniquity – deformities of character; transgression – deliberate disobedience; sins – failing to meet the standard. Everything that could be twisted or wrong about us can be overcome. Across history, we see God restoring the joy of salvation to those who fail but accept shame and admit their failure.

Revisiting iniquity

Narcissism can result from iniquity – the way our life has shaped us. It is difficult to get un-twisted. People who are narcissists because of iniquity can barely see the problem because "It is just who we are." Their childhood identity group was full of immature reactions and deformities. God forgives the iniquity, but we have to confront our problems and work to overcome them.

Just as a physical deformity may send us for long, hard work in physical therapy, the same is true in the spiritual realm. Working on these deformities from our childhoods requires retraining our minds because we were trained to do relationships the wrong way.[6]

---

5   Ed Khouri's materials on church and narcissism can be found at DeeperWalkInternational.org.
6   Romans 12:2

I learned tennis from my dad and was a happy tennis player until a college tennis class. The professor said I was holding the racket wrong, standing wrong, and hitting the ball wrong. Everything I did had to be retrained. I could not get a ball over the net after that. Finding a strong deformity can cause frustration.

Many of us have been taught how to play life (how to do relationships) by people who had the wrong patterns that they taught us thoroughly. Our bodies adapted until everything in our brain said, "This calls for enemy mode. I need to justify myself." In families where everyone figured out whose fault things were, those who could not justify themselves lost. Grace didn't exist when there was trouble. An iniquity was formed.

Revisiting sin

Some people are narcissistic because they sin. Although they would really like to be hesed, they blow it when they try. Sin is different from transgression in that we really do not want to be stiff-necked; there are just moments when we are. We know we do not want to be proud; we don't want to be narcissistic; we don't want to be defensive, but sometimes we are. So we tend to either condemn or justify ourselves in those moments. We vacillate between acting narcissistic and not acting that way. At times we just blow up when someone gives us a shame message. We did not want to get so mad, but we did. We justify that the other person was a creep or an idiot. We are trying to get the other person to stop their shame message. We feel there is no alternative to justifying or attacking that is going to work. Let us examine three of the contributing factors.

My relational circuits switched off: When it feels like my people will not help me and it is up to me to make this stop, my relational circuits can fade. I may also turn off my relational circuits as a way to avoid sharing the pain others feel. As soon as I really need to get results and people are in my way, I switch. When I have time to think it over later I am sorry for what I said and did. I lost grace.[7]

I fall back to enemy mode: At times I think, "God's plans are not working for me. I'm going to have to take over and run things myself." This is a bit narcissistic. There are moments of self-justification when someone hurts me and I justify my reaction.

---

7   Relational circuits are described in detail in Life Model resources listed at the end of the previous chapter.

Whole families can get into the cycle of, "They hurt me, so I will hurt them," and, "You hurt me, so I'm going to make sure you know how much I hurt," until everybody in the family is hurting. "They started it;" "They deserve it;" or "Everyone does it," justify at this moment that it is all right to be narcissistic.

I live by the sarx (the flesh): We sin when we are guided by our own understanding, insisting that our explanations have to be what everyone accepts. This often sounds very spiritual, as we try to convince others that our way is how God sees it, that this is what He would have said about it, and that's why He is on our side and not theirs. We do not share other's pain or offer grace.

Revisiting transgressions

Some people are narcissists because of transgressions. Threatening in order to get results is an example of a transgression.

Transgressions are when we disregard direct instructions through omission or commission. As an example, look at what St. Peter said about Jesus not threatening:

> *For you have been called for this purpose, since Christ also suffered for you, leaving you an example for you to follow in His steps, . . . and while being reviled, He did not revile in return; while suffering, He uttered no threats, but kept entrusting Himself to Him who judges righteously;*
> 1 Peter 2:21, 23 (NASB)

We know that St. Peter says Jesus never threatened anyone and neither should we. This verse is clear about what we should not do. Yet, we ignore the command because we need to get results. We are committing a transgression. We know we are doing something God does not want us to do. We justify our intentions and do it anyway.

Jesus says quite clearly, *"Bless those that curse you."*[8] What part of *"Bless those that curse you"* is not clear? Do we justify that we do not have to bless someone whose guts we cannot stand? We understand the commandment to bless. We just don't.

Deliberate enemy mode

A deliberate cultivation of enemy mode creates the most poisonous narcissism. Some narcissists and sociopaths clearly

---

8   Matthew 5:44

know they are being poisonous and harmful. They know this is not what God wants, and they do it anyway. Chronic transgression that develops enemy mode as a way of life fits what Scott Peck called *malignant narcissism.*[9] Malignant narcissists actually enjoy hurting others. They are happy that others suffer while they do not have to suffer themselves. Exploiting weakness makes them feel powerful and free.

Malignant narcissists hurt others just to watch pain happen. Those on this path of narcissism do not care what God has to say. When a person reaches this point, they have reached foolish wickedness. We can think of wicked examples from history: some were serial killers and others were narcissistic rulers. They did not care about man or beast. This hardened state is the farthest end of narcissism with the coldest hearts. This is enemy mode that has no attachments. Both the narcissist and others have become like objects in a cold heart and mind. People can be killed the way we throw a rock in the lake to watch the splash.

Hopefully we are not in association with these coldest hearts, but **if narcissists around us are abusive, we have to remove ourselves from their vicinity.** We do not stay in a situation that is dangerous. If neither the narcissist nor our people will protect us, we find a sheltered place to retreat. **It is not hesed love to allow anyone, even our people, to damage others.** We don't do that.

Knowing we might be in danger from an abusive narcissist and leaving that situation is not self-justifying, though we might be accused of that if we leave. When a truck runs a red light and we swerve to avoid it, we are protecting ourselves from damage. We are not justifying our right-of-way or driving. We are reducing harm as protective people do.

The many works of grace

Moses clearly heard from God that God is gracious. God's grace does not *overlook* that which is evil. God's grace corrects iniquities, sins, and transgressions. God deals with the "footprints" of evil as iniquities are transmitted from generation to generation. We also will not leave people in their messes. Being gracious means we deal with wrongs. We see that people's current state does not express who they really are.

---

9   *People of the Lie* by M. Scott Peck, Simon & Schuster, Inc; page 80

If we let someone do evil and allow them the illusion that evil is good, we are not gracious, rather we are foolish. We address foolish people lest they think they are wise. At the same time we are careful to not act foolish ourselves. Graciousness means we confront others about their foolishness so that they may have a chance to understand what God sees. We hope to bring repentance.

Grace values life more than comfort. Unfortunately, confrontation is often viewed as not nice. When we equate being nice with being gracious we conclude that grace does not confront. We tend to think being gracious makes others comfortable, but that is politeness. Grace does not always make us comfortable; grace preserves what is really special! Grace values life more than comfort. When Jesus died giving us grace, He was not comfortable or creating a way to make people comfortable. Grace seeks Dick Birkey's goal of finding what is really special.

Grace and shame

We can now see that the brain's wiring for shame is a protective circuit guarding all that is special about us. Grace gives and protects all that is special to God. The more diligent we are to keep our "special" special, the greater the activity in our shame system. Monitoring shame signals provides a constant and careful course correction for our identities. The more damaged our identities, the more shame messages we will need from our identity group, but the harder it will be to receive them. Since most damaged identities have been exposed to toxic shame, we must be very gentle. Grace makes sure to point out what is really special about us (and our people) with every healthy shame message.

Grace and loving enemies

As we already mentioned, the brain will not make a correction without a pain signal that says, "Don't do that again." When we share the pain of others it helps us learn. However, when the brain goes into enemy mode we stop sharing what others feel. Instead we use their weaknesses and pain to make them lose. Grace sees no enemies. Grace sees in each one the special work of God that needs to be saved. Therefore, how we love our enemies is both the work of grace and the measure of what grace we have.

Grace toward weakness and narcissism

If we have been in the Pandora's circle we must now face ourselves. Do we not feel the urge to abandon the harmful narcissist in the center? Do we not feel tempted to despise that person's weakness and hope sometimes that the narcissist will lose? Do we fail to see what is special about others when we are faced with a Pandora problem? It seems virtually certain that no narcissist will be able to self-rescue. It is equally certain that every narcissist will be harmful, so he or she will feel like our enemy at times. Will we show them that our people live grace? Will we find and protect all that really makes us special?

RESTORING THE NARCISSIST

Narcissism is a weakness that can mix with other problems to reach sociopathic and psychopathic levels of harmfulness. Those who are qasheh become both foolish and half-witted from efforts to be special using methods that do not work. Qasheh people attack anyone who might provide a healthy shame message that could correct their folly. While in enemy mode narcissists track but do not share the pain others feel as they use the weaknesses of others against them. Narcissism is high in qasheh and low in hesed.

Both the evidence from history and from around the world suggests that restoring a serious character failure requires a hesed attachment with both God and God's people before significant change can be seen. The evidence that one-on-one interventions are ineffective is quite persuasive. Therefore, restoring the narcissist is a) grace from the people of God toward b) someone who is becoming one of God's people.

We will examine how we apply grace for the rest of this chapter.

Bonds with both God and identity group are needed.

Effective restoration requires a clear idea of who we are and enough hesed to hold us steady. Without a significant attachment to God by both narcissist and identity group, there will be no transformation for the narcissist.

While hesed levels will not be high, there must be enough love for God for everyone to want to see things as God sees them. But, never fear, if the narcissist does not accept God's grace, this practice will still be good for the identity group. At the least, the identity group will have their hesed purified and learn to love enemies.

Grace bonds us through undeceived acceptance.

We might think that seeing someone from God's point of view means we accept them completely the way they are. We know everyone malfunctions. Spiritual life involves discovering who we were meant to be. We do not want to confuse sinful pseudo-self with someone's real identity.

In 2 Corinthians 5:16 we are told in the King James Version, *"Henceforth we know no man after the flesh"* (Greek word is *sarx*). The Revised Standard Version reads, *"From now on we regard no one from a human point of view."* We are no longer going to deal with people based on human comparisons.

We will look at each other according to how the Spirit of God sees us and see what makes each of us special. This is grace in action. We direct everyone back to who God created them to be. We provide examples through our lives for everyone in our identity group – God's people.

Bonds use Godsight.

How God sees people in the Spirit we call *Godsight.* God does not see according to the flesh. We find St. Paul contrasting the flesh and Spirit in Galatians 5:14-18.

> *For all the law is fulfilled in one word, even in this: "You shall love your neighbor as yourself." But if you bite and devour one another, beware lest you be consumed by one another! I say then: Walk in the Spirit, and you shall not fulfill the lust of the flesh. For the flesh lusts against the Spirit, and the Spirit against the flesh; and these are contrary to one another, so that you do not do the things that you wish. But if you are led by the Spirit, you are not under the law.*

Biting and devouring one another is a good way to describe the predatory nature of enemy mode. When that sin pattern is running, we cannot do the things we wish to do. The alternative to narcissism is doing the works that God has laid out for us.

Character that will not make us special (not like our people)

St. Paul immediately makes clear what is like our people and what is not.

Now the works of the flesh are evident, which are: adultery, fornication, uncleanness, lewdness, idolatry, sorcery, hatred, contentions, jealousies, outbursts of wrath, selfish ambitions, dissensions, heresies, envy, murders, drunkenness, revelries, and the like; of which I tell you beforehand, just as I also told you in time past, that those who practice such things will not inherit the kingdom of God. Galatians 5:19-21

Typically we overlook the middle of that list where there are things we tend to justify. We would say idolatry and sorcery are not us but what about quarrels, envy, and rage? Justifying condemnation, accusation, rejection, humiliation, withdrawal, contempt, threats, *sarx*-based living, judging others according to the flesh, and unforgiveness all need a healthy shame message. This is not like us as God's children. Grace helps us be clear; these are not expressions of the love that makes us special.

Character that will make us special (like our people)

What expresses our special attachment to God emerges in verses 22-23: *"But the fruit of the Spirit is love, joy, peace, longsuffering, kindness, faithfulness, gentleness, self-control. Against such there is no law." Fruit* is singular because it is Christ's character. This is a single identity not a list of good things to do.

Exhibiting the fruit of Christ is not dependent upon responses from stiff-necked, self-justifying people. Fruit is not a tool to make narcissists change. Our love may provoke an attack on us. Alternately, we may find someone who will listen and change.

God guides us when we are speaking grace to a narcissist. God gives wisdom to help restore them. The burden is on God, though our stomachs may churn. Our part is to give grace, grow in hesed, speak when prompted, and allow the fruit of the Spirit to flow through us.

Bonds need self-quieting skills.

To maintain Godsight we need to practice quieting. Grace flows from quietness and trust.[10] After quieting, we can see the other person clearly, understand God more distinctly, and remember who our people are. As we quiet ourselves, we can better see who we were meant to be. Quietness helps us share, comfort, and validate the pain caused by shame messages for people who do

---

10   Quieting skills are taught through the THRIVE training and materials. See thrivetoday.org.

not know how to understand shame relationally. In order to deal with shame, narcissists need quieting skills as well. Quieting can be learned from our people. Quieting helps grace shine through our eyes even with a shame message.

Grace and hesed together overcome an enemy mode weakness.

Enemy mode is the opposite of what Jesus commanded in Matthew 5:44: *"Bless those that curse you."* Jesus did not encourage humiliating those who do not love us well enough. Blessing others is a special thing about our people that even those who curse cannot remove.

Grace will say, "There really is no reason whatsoever, at any time, or any place to humiliate anyone. Raging at others is never going to be justifiable. We are people of blessing. If we don't want to stop cursing, we tell God, 'You know I have no desire to keep Your commandment. Everything in me wants to do exactly the opposite and I know that's wrong. If You don't do something for me I'm going to keep on this terrible path. I need You to do something with me that I don't know how to do myself. You're going to have to change my desires because I don't know how to change them. You're right. There's absolutely no time I should curse those who curse me. There is no place for rage and dumping shame on another person.'"

Without the hesed to have this dialogue with God, there is no way to change. Grace helps us to see we were meant for better things. Grace digs in to find our "special."

Both grace and hesed are needed to love our enemies.

Narcissists have a huge problem understanding hesed love. They believe love is their slave to please them. Narcissists reason, "I won't love you unless you love me well enough. If you don't treat me right then I don't have to treat you kindly. You will receive my contempt." Love becomes performance.

Narcissists who are not loved the way they want to be loved punish anyone who disappoints them. Instead of love that shares the pain of others, qasheh people switch to rules, roles, performance, and punishment after receiving a shame message.[11] They do this methodically, knowing where to hurt others. Narcissists use their

---

11   For more on narcissism or borderline personality see Track III THRIVE Lectures at thrivetoday.org.

own sensitivity (in enemy mode) to find what will hurt others most. Narcissists use insults to lower self-worth. Narcissists block contact with family members as a punishment. This contempt and deliberate hurting of others is low hesed in action.

Another narcissist tactic is to humiliate and overwhelm anyone they want to control. Humiliation is a complex emotion that combines rage and shame together. The method is, "I will rage at you in a way that causes you shame, and I won't let you get away so you'll have to sit there and feel rotten."

Rage and shame activate opposing nervous systems in the body. The parasympathetic system (shame) is like brakes on a car trying to stop us from doing something harmful. The sympathetic system (rage) is like the accelerator pushing us to do something. During humiliation, we feel as if we are braking and accelerating at the same time. By creating humiliation, the narcissist prevents rest and empties our capacity in a very painful way.

Narcissists expect that if they humiliate someone, that person will comply. "If I humiliate you, you will not correct me and make me angry, because you don't want to get on my bad side. If you don't want humiliation then do what I want." This is the way of life around narcissists.

We see humiliation in action during Jesus' trial. The Chief Priests and the Roman soldiers did all they could to humiliate Jesus. Grace proved to be stronger. In the end, a soldier declared, "This must be the son of God." We also can love our enemies. With grace we can remind narcissists they are our people. The way we are special is revealed as we love our enemies.

What we have learned so far about narcissism

We have looked at the Scriptures and found that qasheh people have recognizable characteristics that have been around a long time. When narcissists are shaped in early life it becomes an iniquity (deformity). Other narcissists try to live as God wants but keep slipping back into sin. Some people justify their narcissism and live defiantly in transgression. **All these malfunctions are forgivable.** Grace sees through these false identities while offering an attachment to God and God's people. Transformation is open to those who accept a healthy shame message.

Narcissists want to manage their image so they can continue to hide from shame. This creates a false identity, but grace says, "If anyone thinks of himself to be something when he is not, he is deceiving himself."

God sees us through His loving kindness (hesed). However, God knows some people cannot get themselves out of enemy mode. God directs those who are Spiritual to restore them.

Restoring is done in fellowship and community with other people who help us see what God sees and give us healthy shame messages when we forget. To begin restoration, we express our shame to God and to His people, saying in repentance, "I'm really sorry. I know I justify my reactions and I shouldn't. I don't know what else to do. Will you show me another way?"

No self-justification is from the Spirit. We are the most deceived when we are self-justified. If we live by self-justification we will miss the Kingdom of God. Let us live in a way that God can justify. Let us be justified through Christ. When He justifies, He takes whatever we did that was wrong and uses it for good.

Transformation through healthy shame becomes the theme of our *4+Stories.*[12] Whatever is or was wrong in our life, God can use as an example of His love and grace. Whatever we may be ashamed of, He can use as an example of unending hesed love.

We are the people who receive and give grace. Through us and through His Spirit, God restores people to hesed. We become people who offer grace to our enemies. We live in the Spirit, so let us also walk in the Spirit, bearing one another's burdens and thus fulfilling the law of Christ.

Lord, help us love our enemies. Let us see in "enemies" what you see. May we find Christ's love in our "guts" when we are tempted to make others lose. May we help each other out of our enemy mode and into Your hesed.

---

12   See Appendix

If You Are Ready
Group Exercise for Chapter Thirteen

Today's group identity affirmation

Repeat together, "We are a people who create belonging."

In groups of about five people tell each other why this characteristic matters to you. (5 minutes)

Today's healthy shame message practice

In groups of about five people create a healthy shame message for me when <u>I only pay attention to things that involve me.</u> (5 minutes)

Note: A healthy shame message states "we do not" and then states who we are with a Christ-like character response. "We do not _____, we _____."

Tell each small group's statement to the whole group. (5 minutes)

Today's withstanding self-justification practice

Self-justification: We feel the Lord leading us to (something that could hurt others).

In groups of about five people make a list of the weaknesses that lie behind this self-justification. What would a hesed community do to be sure these weaknesses do not prevail? (10 minutes)

Report each small group's conclusions to the whole group. (5 minutes)

Today's loving my enemy practice

This exercise is like texting with God. Write the impression that comes to your mind. Start with something that makes you grateful then your impression of God's response. Next read the question

and write your impression of God's response that gives you peace. (5 minutes)

1. Dear God, I am thankful:
2. My dear child:
3. God, when has someone felt like an enemy to me this week?
4. What do You want me to know about loving them?

Read what you have written in groups of about five people. Do not explain what you wrote. Check for a sense of peace after you read. (5 minutes)

Building loyalty around weakness: Exercise 2

1. Pool observations about the following: (30 minutes)

   a. What weaknesses (vulnerability or exposure) do I always notice? What predator and protector reactions do I have in response?

   b. What weaknesses do I notice more often since I began this study?

   c. What weakness would I like to be able to speak about more openly with my identity group?

   d. Is "enemy mode" starting to look like a weakness to me?

2. Review the following actions: (15 minutes)

   a. When have I stepped in to help someone with a weakness recently?

   b. How am I working to help change attitudes about weakness in my identity group?

Repeating today's group identity affirmation

Repeat together, "We are a people who create belonging."

CHAPTER FOURTEEN

Group Identity and Loving Our Enemies

Facing a Harmful Weakness Together

"Brood of vipers! How can you, being evil, speak good things? For out of the abundance of the heart the mouth speaks."
Matthew 12:34

We picture lions as predators, yet humans are the top predators of the planet. The normal process of human maturity takes us from being born as tiny predators to mature as peaceful protectors. As we mature we go from eating everything we can grab to not eating most of what we want. It is quite a process learning that the world is not there for us to eat. Practices from waiting until dinner to fasting teach us to wait and resist the lion within.

Being fed develops attachment (hesed) while learning to wait develops protectiveness. There is a direct connection between our feeling attached and our protectiveness. As strange as it sounds, being fed by hesed people helps us resist taking advantage of weakness. With maturity, we learn to protect weaknesses rather than exploit them. Weakness brings out our protection when we belong to a protective people. We need to practice building hesed around weakness.

Some weaknesses are caused by a failure to develop. Immaturity is a weakness (deformity, i.e. iniquity) of identity. Taking advantage of the weaknesses in others is a sign of weak identity. We are still predatory when we should have developed protectiveness. The older we are, the more harmful predatory weakness will become. The more harmful the weakness, the more we need our people.

Maturing hesed protectors is a normal function of the church. Yet, the question will immediately be raised by many readers, "How do we find or grow a hesed church community? Where are these people you are talking about?"

Levels of narcissism are up to 3,000% higher in the pulpit than in the general population.[1] Churches tend to seek successful pastors, people without weakness, amazing church growers, great expositors, and powerful worshipers as leaders. We find what we seek. Pastors hide weaknesses lest church members, the board, or the community drop them.

It is time that we take some responsibility for the leaders we have, because we seek and grow them ourselves.

NARCISSISM IS A HARMFUL WEAKNESS.

The word qasheh means *to harden*. Weakness will either make us harder or make us tenderer. Hardening ourselves is a dangerous weakness. Avoiding weakness through hardening ourselves is an iniquity of identity. Hesed makes us tender. Becoming tender to weakness is a strength. We are a people who raise hesed and lower qasheh. We avoid hardness through tenderness, and we face harmful weaknesses together.

People who harden themselves develop a strong enemy mode. Enemy mode exploits weakness. Enemy mode is harmful. Enemy mode is predatory. Enemy mode attempts to become big and strong. Enemy mode grows Goliath-sized monsters. God's enemies are portrayed as super-sized in Scripture. Enemy mode creates lions who "bite and devour one another" as St. Paul describes it.[2]

How we deal with narcissism depends on how we see the weakness that causes qasheh people to justify themselves. We noticed that across history God has a hard time with people who self-justify. Often they believe they are right and God is not. Painful life experiences are used to justify that they do not have to love God, that God has not loved them well enough, that God's commands make them angry. Angry people often enter enemy mode and become harmful. Narcissists see people who cause them trouble as not deserving love. Do we see this as a harmful weakness without falling into enemy mode ourselves?

In the end, narcissism is little other than enemy mode dressed to kill. Enemy mode will dress up in anything sexy, attractive, powerful, or impressive. Enemy mode can dress as a pastor, priest, police officer, protestor, professor, progressive, politician, business

---

1   Ball and Puls study – see Chapter Eleven
2   Galatians 5:15

person, activist, actor, or aviator if that outfit looks good at the moment. It takes wisdom and Godsight to see their weakness.

Harmful weaknesses can erode hesed.

Let us review what the Bible says about qasheh. Narcissists are rebellious, do things their own way, don't listen, are jealous, rough, corrupt, rude, fierce, heavy, grievous, severe, burdensome, cruel, treacherous, punishing, pursuing, harsh, obstinate, impudent, disruptive, and hardhearted.[3] These words give some sense of the Hebrew word *qasheh*.

We can see that qasheh is a weakness that erodes hesed. We are people who face harmful weaknesses together. Let us consider six harmful features of narcissism that we must face.

1) Narcissists use weakness against others.

Narcissists keep a very close eye on other people, not because they are interested, but because they seek something they can use against the person later. Qasheh people ask dishonest questions to find weakness and not because they want answers.

This active predatory activity is harmful to hesed and presents a harmful weakness in the narcissist we must face together.

2) Narcissists shift reality.

In order to get their way, narcissists shift reality and spin stories to look the way they want things to look. Justifications may almost sound right, but if we were there, saw what happened, knew the motives, we know deep inside their story is not right. This makes dealing with narcissists extremely difficult.

About ninety days after an event the brain moves memory from long term storage into permanent memory. If we actively deceive our brains for those ninety days, we will believe the story in permanent memory is what really happened. If self-justified people deceive themselves for three months, they will believe their version of reality and forget anything else. When confronted, the narcissist will say, "No! That's not what happened. Here's how it really was. You say I hurt you, but that's not what happened. You hurt me." Narcissists so believe themselves that they are very convincing.

---

3   See Chapter Five for Bible references for each word.

Dealing with a narcissist's false reality drives people crazy. We expect the person has cooled down and will think more reasonably. Instead, we find their version of the event is in cement. Narcissists will ask, "What's wrong with you that you can't remember the facts properly? You must have a mental problem." People that justify themselves ultimately believe themselves.

We cannot be loyal to falsehood. Altered reality is a harmful weakness we must face together.

3) Narcissists are hard-hearted.

The heart, in Scripture, refers to our spiritual sensitivity – what we have been calling *Godsight*. Being hard-hearted means we have spiritual cataracts and cannot see. Stiff-necked narcissists have really bad spiritual vision. Qasheh (hard) people think they have seen God when they have seen nothing.

Spiritual cataracts are a harmful weakness that our people cannot ignore.

4) Narcissists are proud.

Narcissists depend on their tongues to make themselves look good, to be right, and to talk down to others. It is important to them to be on top and make sure others are on the bottom. Qasheh people take advantage of power, position, opportunity, weakness, God's service, family, closeness, and trust. Narcissists shame others while refusing to show, share, or feel shame themselves. They hurt others when it serves their purpose but blame the other person. Narcissists will insist that we back them and be on their side. We fear saying anything to them for fear it will tear apart the family, hurt the children, sink the business, or divide the church. Inevitably, others are to blame for all that went wrong while the narcissist remains proud.

Our people do not ignore this weakness.

5) Narcissists are immature.

Maturity is wholeness at our current age. We can act like our people and stay relational regardless of emotions. Our maturity level – and there are five levels[4] – may not match our age. Immaturity is a weakness. People who are unable to deal with a

---

4   For more information on maturity levels see *Living From the Heart that Jesus Gave You,* lifemodelworks.org

healthy shame message relationally lack maturity. Narcissists are not whole for their age. But, remember, emotional immaturity does not lower our value. We are special because of who loves us.

Maintaining maturity depends on our capacity for joy. When joy is too low we may not act like ourselves. Healthy shame is the guardian of joy. People who are immature and not living in the Spirit will hear condemnation even with a healthy shame message.

Knowing about maturity helps us understand narcissists. Immaturity is always tied to weakness. Iniquity (deformity) has slowed their emotional growth. Narcissists' behavior is partly from a lack of maturity.

We are a people who face such harmful weaknesses together.

6) Narcissists like power.

We tend to push our leaders to be large, powerful, driven, without normal weakness, and bigger than life. The church wants great leaders like those in every successful enterprise around us. We might remember that when Israel wanted a king like all the nations, God gave them a king like all the nations named Saul.

We have already seen that he was head and shoulders taller than others, handsome, and very qasheh. Saul was the God-anointed christ[5] they requested, but he was still a predator. Their next king was a Winning Warrior Who Worshiped. David's predatory nature was only partially controlled. He exploited weakness, killed one of his mighty men, had an affair, and kept his murderous relatives in power.

If churches want to be like the nations, God provides blue-ribbon narcissists as leaders. We will have winners who worship. What we call "moral failures" are glimpses of the predator that hides inside Winning Warriors.

Our people face these harmful weaknesses together.

Our Christ was born as predatory as anyone.[6] Born a lion, He overcame to become a lamb.[7] According to the elders of Heaven, such a victory represents God's purposes in the world and is worthy of worship. Should we not seek leaders who become

---

5   I Samuel 26:11
6   Hebrews 4:15
7   Revelations 5:5

lambs although they were born lions? Isn't this what the prophet Isaiah foretold about the Kingdom of God? Predators will not hurt or destroy. Children (weakness) will be valued, protected, and play with transformed vipers.[8]

Jesus announced this Kingdom is already present. He said to qasheh religious leaders, "You brood of vipers, who warned you to feel the wrath to come!"[9] These were vipers no child should play with because they have not been transformed by the Kingdom. We will soon examine how we deal with qasheh leaders among our people.

Kingdom community turns lions into lambs, or it is not the Kingdom. Scripture shows us that lions become lambs by learning to love their enemies and sharing the pain of others. The big problem is that many Christians make no real effort to turn lions into lambs. We are happy to flee the wrath to come and catch a ride to heaven.

BUILDING LOYALTY (HESED) AROUND WEAKNESS

The real struggle is to create a Christian group identity with enough hesed to be of any value.[10] One obvious factor is the lack of identified enemies. When enemies are obvious, serious Christians realize the need to love enemies and grow hesed. By recognizing when our minds (or the minds around us) are in enemy mode, we can learn to love our enemies.

Every Pandora problem creates an opportunity. By carefully focusing on loving anyone who, even in passing, feels like an enemy, a hesed community can help transform qasheh people with serious character disorders.

We have now gathered enough characteristics of a Christian group identity to put these elements to work. We are looking at a group that knows it is becoming a new kind of people. The group builds hesed loyalty that allows the exchange of healthy shame messages. The group reminds each other who we really are. Hesed forms around weaknesses because that is where we need each other.

---

8   Isaiah 11:8
9   Matthew 3:7 (see also 12:34 and 23:33, Luke 3:7)
10   Growing a local hesed community is a field of its own. Dr. Timothy Johns rocktribe. com, Ed Khouri, DeeperWalkInternational.org, and LifeModelWorks.org are among those developing model groups.

Qasheh refusals to accept good shame messages become a very visible weakness. Welcoming healthy shame messages from those who see us as Jesus sees us brings vitality. Unlike many weaknesses, qasheh self-justification is harmful because it switches the brain into "enemy mode." When in enemy mode, the brain's relational circuits are impaired. Rather than being governed by hesed, people act like sociopaths. Our people love (hesed) our enemies, so falling into enemy mode is a major identity meltdown.

Hesed people use their judgment to evaluate qasheh events and respond tenderly to weakness. Tender responses do not mean that this people tolerate qasheh or listen to justifications! Tender responses mean that God's people do not allow a brain melt-down to do damage where it is within their power to avoid it.

We are a people who face harmful weakness together.

Enemy mode is a weakness.

All our enemies are people in the throes of a major weakness. People with their minds in enemy mode are not looking out for their own best interests, rather they are working to make others lose. We must be wise when confronted with such a harmful weakness. If we cannot take healthy shame messages from our friends without going into enemy mode, we will not withstand the toxic shame messages from our enemies.

We practice by giving and receiving healthy shame messages. When one of our people goes into enemy mode we flood them with grace. We help friends recover from a harmful weakness before we try hesed on enemies who are not our people.

How weakness builds hesed

A study of the word *hesed* in the Bible gives a tour of human weaknesses. "Show me lovingkindness" is the request from people in trouble. Joseph in prison, slaves in Egypt, people in the wilderness, Moses praying for the people, Rahab with the spies, Naomi with Ruth and Boaz all asked for hesed when in need.

All good things start and grow from weakness. Seeing babies, puppies, and flowers, we say, "You're so cute!" Their weakness does matter as we see something special and bubble up inside. Frail elderly people, children struggling with cancer, horses loaded with more than they can carry inspire hesed.

Where there is grace and splagchnon for weakness we find hesed growing. Weakness is where hesed and grace kiss. Seeing someone's vulnerability to an avalanche or forest fire make us hope and pray for their escape. We do not want anyone left behind because they were small, wounded, or weak. We feel hesed.

Some weaknesses are both harmful and hidden. Iniquities are particularly harmful and likely to be hidden. If the owners of a weakness are trying to look powerful, hardening themselves, self-justifying, slipping into enemy mode, taking control of leadership, acting predatory and monstrous, it takes a lot of grace and Godsight to see their weakness as a need for our hesed.

OUR GROUP IDENTITY RESPONSES

As we return to our Pandora problem at the end of this book we begin to see a weakness in the middle of our circle. While things may only get worse if we speak, our objective is to love our enemy and teach our enemy to do the same. We cannot abandon anyone to be consumed by such a harmful weakness.

I can almost feel some readers saying, "Finally here is what to do." I will give you the summary. Dealing with narcissistic people is about God growing our hesed. We remind everyone who we are with words of grace. There is no formula to follow because we are simply acting like our people act. The reaction we receive will test our character and not our technique.

Tender-hearted readers have already been thinking, "I have some narcissism inside." Completing the study guide by Barbara Moon[11] and joining a discussion group are practically all that is needed for tender-hearted readers to start a change. As your group gets serious about loving enemies it will organically reduce narcissism and raise hesed.

Some tender-hearted people will have identified a narcissist individual in their lives. This is a Pandora problem. The "If You Are Ready" exercises help develop a group character around an isolated narcissist or two in a group. When a group begins to exchange healthy shame messages, correct self-justification, and love their enemies, isolated narcissists will learn a better way or leave.

Later in this chapter we will consider the issues around narcissistic spiritual leaders. For now we are speaking of qasheh group members.

---

11   This is a sepearate study guide you can find at DeeperWalkInternational.org.

What is left to address are qasheh group identities. What happens when the whole identity group goes qasheh? Now we have a solitary prophetic voice sounding in a narcissistic world. God's messenger faces a group in enemy mode and those groups will kill. Such groups will also have qasheh leaders.

God wants to speak with qasheh people.

From one end of the Bible to the other, God spends a lot of time and effort speaking to qasheh people. Sometimes God speaks directly, many times through prophets, consistently through Jesus, and finally through the Apostles. We are not far into the human story before we find someone in enemy mode over a healthy shame message. The story of Cain practically opens with:

> But He did not respect Cain and his offering. And Cain was very angry, and his countenance fell. So the LORD said to Cain, "Why are you angry? And why has your countenance fallen? If you do well, will you not be accepted? And if you do not do well, sin lies at the door. And its desire is for you, but you should rule over it. Genesis 4:5-7

God's responses help us see how to speak to angry narcissists. God sees that Cain is really angry at Him and at Abel. God does not back off nor does God ignore the situation. Instead, He engages Cain. God talks with, restrains, and counsels Cain. God actively shows him a way out. God gives a healthy shame message.

God has witnesses.

Moses leading a qasheh people out of Egypt is a central Bible narrative. God sets up a plan for those reality shifters knowing that narcissists will twist reality. Near the end of his life, Moses prepares witnesses and announces to the people:

> For I know your rebellion and your stiff neck. If today, while I am yet alive with you, you have been rebellious against the LORD, then how much more after my death? Gather to me all the elders of your tribes, and your officers, that I may speak these words in their hearing and call heaven and earth to witness against them. Deuteronomy 31:27-28

God stays flexible.

Once in the Promised Land, God changes His direction to deal with stiff-necked narcissism. God cancels something He promised.

> *Then the anger of the LORD was hot against Israel; and He said, "Because this nation has transgressed My covenant which I commanded their fathers, and has not heeded My voice, I also will no longer drive out before them any of the nations which Joshua left when he died, so that through them I may test Israel, whether they will keep the ways of the LORD, to walk in them as their fathers kept them, or not." Therefore the LORD left those nations, without driving them out immediately; nor did He deliver them into the hand of Joshua.* Judges 2:20-23

We may also need to change what we promised when someone is narcissistic and stiff-necked. We made our promises under other conditions. To keep our agreement would help promote rebellion against God and His reality instead of achieving God's purpose.

God prepares us.

Studying the prophets reveals how God prepares us to speak shame messages to angry people. God explains what the prophet Ezekiel will face:

> *Then the Spirit entered me when He spoke to me, and set me on my feet; and I heard Him who spoke to me. And He said to me: "Son of man, I am sending you to the children of Israel, to a rebellious nation that has rebelled against Me; they and their fathers have transgressed against Me to this very day. For they are impudent and stubborn children. I am sending you to them, and you shall say to them, 'Thus says the Lord God.* Ezekiel 2:2-4

Done in the Spirit

Preparing to deal with impudent, stubborn narcissists has to be done in the Spirit of God. The Spirit of God is not going to be stopped by human hardness. God says to speak and not be afraid, whether they hear or they refuse. The most common excuse for not speaking to a narcissist's behavior is "It won't make any difference." That doesn't change God's plan.

> *As for them, whether they hear or whether they refuse – for they are a rebellious house – yet they will know that a prophet has been among them. And you, son of man, do not be afraid of them nor be afraid of their words, though briers and thorns are with you and you dwell among scorpions;*

do not be afraid of their words or dismayed by their looks, though they are a rebellious house. You shall speak My words to them, whether they hear or whether they refuse, for they are rebellious. Ezekiel 2:5-7

Done in a briar patch

God says speaking with obstinate narcissists will be like walking through briers and thorns while surrounded by scorpions. "You will get those fierce, angry looks, but do not let that stop you! We are going to speak to them."

Receiving condemnation in return

God's grace does not let narcissists fool themselves. We may wonder if we are giving grace by telling qasheh people, "You are like a scorpion." Grace will feel and sound like a toxic shame message to them. Narcissists will hear condemnation and condemn the messenger. Grace reveals their enemy mode and points out how poisonous they are when that is not like God's people at all.

Bringing bad news

Ezekiel is given a hard message of woe and instructed to take this message to qasheh people. *"So the Spirit lifted me up and took me away, and I went in bitterness, in the heat of my spirit; but the hand of the LORD was strong upon me."* Verse 14

Even when God prepares us, dealing with narcissists feels like bitterness and burning. This discomfort makes it difficult to believe God is directing us. God sometimes calls us to do things we do not like. But if we refuse by self-justifying, we have just become narcissistic. We are not learning to express grace to our enemies.

Our responsibility speaking to narcissists

Ezekiel was sent to say something God considered urgently important. It was not up to Ezekiel to make people listen or change. Ezekiel still carried a very serious responsibility.

Now it came to pass at the end of seven days that the word of the LORD came to me, saying, "Son of man, I have made you a watchman for the house of Israel; therefore hear a word from My mouth, and give them warning from Me: When I say to the wicked, 'You shall surely die,' and you give him no warning, nor speak to warn the wicked from his wicked way, to save his life, that same wicked man shall die in his iniquity; but his blood I will require at your hand. Yet, if you warn the wicked, and he does not turn from his wickedness, nor from his wicked way, he shall die in his iniquity; but you have delivered your soul. Again, when a righteous man turns from his righteousness and commits iniquity, and I lay a stumbling block before him, he shall die; because you did not give him warning, he shall die in his sin, and his righteousness which he has done shall not be remembered; but his blood I will require at your hand. Nevertheless if you warn the righteous man that the righteous should not sin, and he does not sin, he shall surely live because he took warning; also you will have delivered your soul." Ezekiel 3:16-21

This passage is often tied to evangelism, but God is speaking to His own people. God's people seem to justify themselves thus becoming the hardest to reach. If we do not deliver the message, we become qasheh. Evangelism was when God sent Jonah to Nineveh where the people would repent.

God sees that some narcissists will respond while others will justify themselves and will not repent. Ezekiel will not know which is which. We also will not know the outcome of loving our enemies ahead of time. We call everyone to become one of God's people.

God's people have a long history of seeing narcissists transformed and become saints. Their stories combine encounters with God and encounters with God's people. Moses started as a murderer. Rahab, Ruth, Matthew, and Peter all needed changed character. Paul, the persecutor of the church, was a real hard case who spent seven years with God before he could be with God's people.

St. Augustine, the hedonist, had a godly mother who would not stop pursuing him. St. Mary of Egypt thought a holy pilgrimage would help her prostitution business. Blessed Bartolo Longo was a sociopathic youth whose community was hesed. Upon conversion Bartolo joined the Dominicans and changed his character.

St. Angela of Fognio was a strong narcissist who encountered God and then a Franciscan group identity shaped her character. St. Olga was a poster child for enemy mode and massacred almost an entire tribe in revenge. St. Francis of Assisi, St. Palagia, St. Callixtus,

St. Vladimir, St. Ignatius of Loyola were once qasheh people whose stories reveal God's interest in loving His enemies.

What our people do

Where God once gave the Spirit to a single prophet, the Holy Spirit is now given to all God's children. This makes it all the more tragic when Christians build high levels of narcissism in their communities and leaders. Narcissism is enemy mode dressed to look sexy, spiritual, and successful. Enemy mode is a false self. We are people who build hesed attachments. We teach each other how God sees us and remind each other when we forget who we are. Can you believe we forget we are God's people?

We teach narcissists our group identity.

Hesed attachment creates a people out of those who were not a people. Narcissists may drop out of being part of a people when corrected. Even healthy shame messages can make things "worse." Grace surrounds this weakness with God's reality.

Our people give glimpses of what truly makes us special. These lessons in relational skills allow us to learn to be the selves that God is creating. We can teach narcissists who want to be God's people how we love our enemies because a) hesed enters the brain earlier in the process than enemy mode, and b) group identity still operates during enemy mode.

We defend the narcissist's victims.

We are dealing with a harmful weakness, so our people are protective. King Saul was one of our clearest qasheh narcissist case studies. His son Jonathan defended David against his own father. Jonathan's attachment to David covered a weakness his father wanted to exploit.

> *But if it pleases my father to do you evil, then I will report it to you and send you away, that you may go in safety. And the LORD be with you as He has been with my father. So Jonathan made a covenant with the house of David, saying, "Let the LORD require it at the hand of David's enemies." Now Jonathan again caused David to vow, because he loved him; for he loved him as he loved his own soul.*
>
> 1 Samuel 20:13b-17

Jonathan defended a victim from the narcissist in his own family vowing before the Lord to help David. Jonathan elected God's family hesed over natural family loyalty. Family loyalty, denominational loyalty, and company loyalty are abused by narcissists in power. Their victims get run over without a sign of loyalty in return by the narcissist. Saul's narcissism cost him his son's loyalty. This is a natural consequence of narcissism.

We follow Jesus' culture-challenging example.

Niceness is a very high value in American culture. We like "nice" more than justice, love, and grace. Jesus calls people a *"brood of vipers"* then says, *"How can you being evil speak good things?"*[12] Jesus was not nice. This claim could start a fight with many nice Christians. Christians in every culture face a challenge to become more like Jesus than they are like their culture. When we follow Jesus, we identify with a new reference group as our people. We face harmful weakness together.

We judge fruit in order to know trees.

It is not difficult to distinguish good or bad fruit. When the Pharisees said that Jesus did the works of the devil, He knew that they were unwilling to recognize good works. The Pharisees could not speak good things because they did not have goodness inside. What came out when Pharisees opened their mouths was poison. Jesus pointed out their fangs and poison with compassion. Like Ezekiel, Jesus warned leaders about their bad fruit, so they would know they were not the righteous trees they claimed to be.

We speak although it might only get worse.

We do not allow the response or anticipated response to keep us silent. We have grace on our tongues that builds our group identity. We ask ourselves, "For them to live as our people do, what would they need to hear?" We face harmful weakness and speak.

Knowing ahead of time that angry people will not listen to us does not make it any easier. We think, "It will make him/her mad, and it won't make any difference." Speaking to angry people can be like landing in thorns, thistles, and scorpions. We may consider the cost too high like the lawyer who asked Jesus, "Who is my neighbor?" We may simply be uncomfortable because speaking

12   Matthew 12:34

correction does not feel "nice." But, it is like God and God's people to engage even when we know the listener is in enemy mode.

Are we going to be rebellious and qasheh, or will we love our enemies? Will we go into enemy mode ourselves? What God is calling us to do is not easy. It takes hesed, grace, and mature character by our people. Involvement with narcissists in our culture, families, and churches will not be well received. If we speak with a bad attitude then we get our own reward. If we speak with grace, there is a chance some will hear. Jesus spoke with "grace and truth" so those who want to be like Him speak truth with grace.[13]

We speak words that come from God.

Jesus is pictured in the book of Revelation as doing battle with a sword coming out of His mouth. A physical sword would be in His hand. The sword from His mouth is words that come from God. We either speak words like a venomous viper or words like those that come from God. Jesus said, *"For by your words you will be justified, and by your words you will be condemned."*[14]

What comes out of our mouth is very telling. If we put on the whole armor of God, we find truth, righteousness, peace, faith, and *the words that come from God.*[15] These words are not Scripture (*logos*) but words that God gives us to speak every day. Our people say what God would say. Speaking the words from God is an on-going way of life. If our people have God's Spirit, Gods' words are going to come out of our mouths. God's words give anyone who will listen a chance to repent. Poisonous words will only make things worse.

We guard our tongues.

> And the tongue is a fire, a world of iniquity. The tongue is so set among our members that it defiles the whole body, and sets on fire the course of nature; and it is set on fire by hell. But no man can tame the tongue. It is an unruly evil, full of deadly poison. With it we bless our God and Father, and with it we curse men, who have been made in the similitude of God. Out of the same mouth proceed blessing and cursing. My brethren, these things ought not to be. James 3:6-10

13   John 1:14
14   Matthew 12: 37
15   Ephesians 6: 13-17

We cannot speak poison for people and have love for God. Enemy mode and hesed do not work together. God is grace, splagchnon, and hesed. With God's Spirit inside what comes out of our mouths is not cursing. Cursing comes from snakes in our bellies. Grace and mercy tell people when they are poisoned and acting like scorpions and vipers.

One spirit is always glad for us to get into the fight with a narcissist. We will gain the devil's assistance finding something self-justified, condemning, and stinging to say. Without God's Spirit we will be fooled by the other one.

We don't fear death.

Enemy mode in predators wants us to lose. Small attacks can kill our reputation. Ultimately a self-justified and qasheh community will kill us if they can. In the case of Jesus and almost every prophet, a qasheh community justified killing them. Didn't we think that if we say something it will only get worse?

The benchmark for Christian character in disciples of Jesus is how we love people who will kill us one way or another if they can. We are talking about predators. This is enemy mode, the center of all the character disorders we have considered. I win when you lose. All of us have been there.

We were all born lions and predators, and our group identity goal is becoming like lambs that have been killed. We want to live like we have already been killed. Half-witted and foolish people who want to kill us don't understand.

> *For if we have become united with Him in the likeness of His death, certainly we also shall be in the likeness of His resurrection, knowing this, that our old self was crucified with Him, in order that our body of sin might be done away with, so that we would no longer be slaves to sin; for he who has died is freed [justified] from sin. Now if we have died with Christ, we believe that we shall also live with Him, knowing that Christ, having been raised from the dead, is never to die again; death no longer is master over Him.*
> Romans 6:5-9 (NASB)

Because we attached (hesed) our lives to Christ, we died with Him, we were raised with Him, and we are seated with Him in the

Heavenly places.[16] Our bodies have not yet grasped that truth. (We still have to work with our bodies on that count.) Knowing we died with Christ changes how much weight the judgments from stiff-necked people carry with us. They do not know that we died, but we know that their judgments have no influence on someone who is dead.

Narcissists can kill our reputations, make painful accusations, and blame us for troubles. Qasheh groups might even be able to kill our bodies – a very unpleasant idea that none of us like. These things will hurt. We do not let the pain or fear deter us.

This is how our people are. We love our enemies and attach to them bringing grace and building hesed. Are you in?

An example

We met Fr. Ubald from Rwanda in Chapter One. The beginnings of the genocide killed his father when he was a child. He escaped the first attempt on his life during minor seminary when Hutu students attempted to kill the Tutsis. Ubald then lived as a refugee in Burundi. When Ubald was called to be a priest he returned to Rwanda teaching love for ten years before the next outbreak of genocide. Fr. Ubald again escaped, but 45,000 of his parishioners were killed at the parish by other parishioners.

When I talk with Fr. Ubald, I am always amazed at the ease and clarity with which he hears from God. I think it puzzles him why others (including religious leaders) do not seem to hear God's thoughts clearly. Many clear conversations with God led Fr. Ubald back to Rwanda and revealed what God and the church community would do next.

Fr. Ubald returned, teaching forgiveness and hesed. The Christian truths that Fr. Ubald had taught for ten years before the genocide had not produced an end to enemy mode or a change of character. Fr. Ubald was about to try again. Both the perpetrators of the genocide and the families and victims who escaped were still in churches and the community. It was clear that their character was unchanged.

In 1998, Fr. Ubald went to the parish in Mushaka where he found a way for perpetrators and victims to be united as a spiritual family.

---

16 Ephesians 2:6 and the first chapter of that book

Since he arrived, over 200 enemies have become family. Seven groups are now active. The Mushaka Program takes half a year.[17] The first week Fr. Ubald has one day each for:

- Leaders of the parish (elders)
- Charismatic renewal members (Godsight team)
- Victims
- Perpetrators
- Everyone together

Six months of teaching and healing for perpetrators teaches them their Christian identity. True, most thought they were Christians all their lives, but they never learned to love their "enemies" or God. Now for six months they examine themselves, confess their sins, and learn to share the suffering of their victims. The victims participate during the final three weeks. Victims discover they are people who forgive.

At the end of the six months, the perpetrators and victims come before the whole congregation and reconcile with the church community. After a church ceremony the community has a big feast. The former enemies become family and help each other. They also tell others about their stories and what becoming the people of God has done in their lives. You can hear some of their stories in the film *The Secret of Peace: A documentary on the Life and Work of Fr. Ubald Rugirangoga*.[18]

We may not see our enemy mode as clearly as people who meet the families of those they killed or families who meet those who murdered their loved ones. But, in Rwanda no self-justifications are allowed, pain must be shared, God's point of view discovered, hesed offered, and enemies loved. Lions lie down with the lambs and neither hurt or destroy any longer.

What our people do with qasheh leaders

Earlier in the chapter we discussed how to deal with narcissistic group members. Now let us consider three conditions that involve leaders: a) a leader is qasheh but the people are not, b) the people are qasheh but the leader is not, and c) both leaders and people are qasheh. The answers are now simple.

---

17 Fr. Ubald Rugirangoga, Forgiveness Makes You Free, Ave Maria Press, Notre Dame, Indiana, 2018.
18 SecretofPeace.com

Consider the first case where a leader is qasheh but the people are not. Before Jesus gave all His followers the gift of the Holy Spirit, a prophet full of the Spirit spoke for God. Now, God's people are a prophetic voice of grace and hesed. We remind each other who we are and how we act. A group that reminds each other to love enemies, refuses self-justification, and shares the pain of others has accomplished most of what needs to be done with a narcissistic leader. The leader will hear healthy shame messages very regularly. The leader will experience hesed around the leader's weakness.

On those occasions where the leader is publically self-justified and narcissistic in the name of God, those who are spiritual (can see what God sees) will correct the leader publically lest God's people are deceived. These Super Q moments require character that has been growing for some time plus the power of the Spirit in the moment.

In the second case, the leader sees that the people are qasheh. The people desire a leader like all the nations have – someone powerful, free from weaknesses who will successfully lead the church to victory as winning warriors who worship. Without healthy shame messages that teach who we really are, there will only be biting and hiding.

Leaders must lead each new generation though building hesed around weakness. Every generation must learn to love enemies. Every generation must learn to share the pain of others. Every generation must learn not to pick narcissists for leaders. Every generation must learn they were born lions and must become lambs. It is particularly discouraging when the generation that has retired, paid off the building, and pays the church bills has not yet learned these things. But, the work of the shepherd is to teach his flock who we are and how we act like ourselves. This involves teaching the flock to be tender with weakness including those of the pastor and old people.

God's people are the hardest.

The third case we consider is that where both the leaders and the people are qasheh. This problem appears to be common in churches. Of all the qasheh people in the world, those who claim to be God's people are the hardest. Having heard God they didn't listen. God instructs Ezekiel on this topic.

For you are not sent to a people of unfamiliar speech and of hard language, but to the house of Israel, not to many people of unfamiliar speech and of hard language, whose words you cannot understand. Surely, had I sent you to them, they would have listened to you. But the house of Israel will not listen to you, because they will not listen to Me; for all the house of Israel are impudent and hard-hearted. Behold, I have made your face strong against their faces, and your forehead strong against their foreheads." Ezekiel 3:5-8

God tells the prophet, "This is not a failure to communicate. They understand your words. If it were just about language, surely they would listen to you. If I sent you to people with whom you can barely speak, they would repent after hearing words that come from God. The house of Israel will not listen to Me, so they will not listen to you either." This is ultimately the problem with religious narcissists. If God cannot get them to listen, what do we think we are going to do? If fearing that things will only get worse takes over, we have a Pandora problem.

3,000 years of watching God indicates that when God's people start to dress up their enemy mode in spiritual robes, God removes His protection. Religious narcissism is enemy mode quoting Scripture and citing God for self-justification. God lets people in enemy mode who call Him "Lord, Lord!" see what real enemy mode is like by allowing enemies to strike.

Predators with generations of practice exploiting weakness are ruthless. If we think we can kick butt, God warns us that there are enemies who will drag us butt naked for 1,000 miles before they even get started.[19] The Bible has severe warnings so graphic that my parents would not read the passages to us as children. The point is that we are not to fool ourselves about narcissism and enemy mode done in God's name.

God makes us "harder."

When we are the sole voice speaking for God in a situation where the people and leaders are all self-justified and qasheh "hard," we need strength (Hebrew *chazaq*) that is harder than flint.[20] This strength has to be God's work; otherwise, we become half-witted and hard-headed. There is no technique to achieve this, but rather

---

19   Isaiah 20:4
20   Ezekiel 3:8-9

it is the character of God formed in us. Fearless grace can face a self-deceived people. Led by God we call out our people's true identity before a group in enemy mode dressed to sound spiritual.

THE SIX THINGS WE HAVE LEARNED

In facing narcissism in our leaders and ourselves we have come to learn six things. Perhaps we knew them all before. There is very little new about these six truths that reflect our identity as the family of God.

1. We are a people.
2. We share the pain of others.
3. We exchange healthy shame messages.
4. We combat self-justification.
5. We love our enemies spontaneously.
6. We build loyalty around weakness.

What we have concluded from these six truths can be summarized in two processes.

1. We raise hesed levels.
2. We lower qasheh levels.

Our progress can be measured by one thing.

1. How we love our enemies

All human brains come wired with the desire to be members of a joyful, peaceful, and protective people. How we love our enemies, therefore, becomes the effective focus for communities who are creating disciples of Jesus.

Born as lions we become as lambs.

I went to the most amazing place. I was instantly surrounded with more glory and power than I have ever seen. What a view! God with every saint and amazing creature was there.

One huge angel held up the book with all human history and asked, "Who can deal with this?" No one could, so I started weeping uncontrollably.

*Then I **heard**, "The Lion CAN!" and I looked up.*

*Then I **saw** a Lamb who looked like he had been killed.*

The Lamb took the book and we went wild.

There wasn't a stiff neck anywhere. We were bowing and singing for as far as the eye could see. Every kind of creature was ecstatic.

The song went like this:

You did it!

You made a people out of all the enemies on earth!

You made them into a kingdom of priests to our God!

People full of the Lamb's life now reign on the earth!

Every form of life in the universe and beyond was amazed and kept repeating, "The Lamb did it! Even better, the Lamb will never stop!"

Revelation 5
(paraphrased)

Summary of Dealing with Narcissists

- We watch our own character.

- We establish witnesses to the truth.

- We state our intentions and plans.

- We let hardships test the narcissist's motives.

- We express our disapproval.

- We befriend and defend the narcissist's victims.

- We fight the narcissist's reality with truth.

- We do not give way to fear but let God harden (*chazaq*) us.

- We fill ourselves with God's thoughts.

- We are moved by God's Spirit in the confrontation.

- We do not let the narcissist's response or anticipated response keep us silent.

- We speak the words that come from God.

- We do not accept condemnation or fear judgment.

- We control our tongues.

- We give grace (what they need to hear in order to live).

- We do not make it easy for narcissists (by being nice).

If You Are Ready
Group Exercise for Chapter Fourteen

1. Retake the assessment on the next page titled "My Group Identity Awareness Level." You took this assessment in Chapter One, and we can now compare results.

2. Gather in groups of about five people to discuss the answers to your questions.

3. After you discuss your answers to the assessment consider where this group has changed on the following issues:

    Do we notice who we are more carefully?

    Did we share each other's pain?

    What effect did sharing pain have on me?

    How well do we currently practice healthy shame messages?

    How well do we currently notice self-justification?

    How well do we notice when our minds are in "enemy mode"?

    How do we respond to weakness and, in particular, character weakness?

4. Gather as a whole group. What characteristics of a Christ-like group identity have improved since you started this study?

5. As a whole group decide your next steps.

My Group Identity Awareness Level

1. Group identity

How many times in the last week have I felt I belonged with a group? _____

How many factors can I name right now that make the group where I belong unique? _____

How many times in the last week have I thought of ways to strengthen my group? _____

2. Shared pain

How often in the last week have I felt the pain of someone who is important to me? _____

What three things most make me uncomfortable and want to withdraw from others?
    1.
    2.
    3.

What one thing most makes me think "They had that coming (deserved it)?

3. Exchange of healthy shame messages

How many healthy shame messages have I received this last week? _____

How many healthy shame messages have I delivered this last week? _____

How many times have I expressed appreciation for a healthy shame message this last week? _____

4. Combating self-justification

How many self-justifications have I noticed myself make this last week? _____

What seems to be my main area of self-justification this week? _____

How many self-justifications have I noticed others give this week? _____

5. Loving enemies spontaneously

How many times this week did I notice my mind switching into a less than loving state? _____

What most made me feel that someone was against me this week? _____

How long does it take me to become consciously aware that I (or someone else) have switched into a mental "enemy mode"? _____

What relational weakness causes the most "shutdowns" with people I usually like? _____

6. Building loyalty around weakness

How many times this week have I noticed someone had a weakness and I stepped in to help him or her? _____

This week did I do more to hide my weaknesses or to let others see my limitations? _____

How many times this week did I have helpful conversations about weakness? _____

7. How would I change the way I answered these questions in Chapter One given what I know now?

FREQUENTLY
ASKED QUESTIONS

1. Isn't all shame bad?

Answered by Chris Coursey

Shame can certainly feel bad, but that doesn't mean shame *is* bad. In its purest state, shame is the response we feel when people are not glad to be with us because something about us needs to change. In this way, shame is designed to be the corrective measure to help us discover who we are when we forget.

When we lack relational connection during our shame state, we will feel alone. When we lack relational attunement during our shame, we will feel stuck. When we lack brain skills to return to relational joy from our shame, we will want to avoid and make the emotion stop. In this way, an important distinction must be made between healthy shame (that serves a restorative purpose because it is instructive) and toxic shame (that is simply destructive). All of us have been on the receiving end of toxic shame, and it is safe to say we do not want to touch that hot stove again.

Healthy shame addresses unwelcome behavior or deformed character and says, "This is not who you are; let's get you back. There is something to learn and correct here." Toxic shame focuses on identity and serves no redemptive purpose, saying, "You are bad!" How can we work with that? We can't! Making this distinction helps us embrace healthy shame as an opportunity to learn and grow while also recognizing the presence of toxic shame that serves no useful purpose for the brain and relationships.

> **Rev. Chris M. Coursey** is a speaker, author, and trainer who collaborates with Dr. Jim Wilder designing THRIVE Training, the premiere training format for learning the 19 relational brain skills. Returning to joy from shame is one of the six unpleasant emotion responses we need relationally. Chris and his wife Jen speak, write blogs and books, run Joy Rekindled marriage retreats and weekend True Identity events for communities to practice the 19 relational brain skills. Online curriculum combines with books like *Transforming Fellowship: 19 Skills to Build a Joyful Community*, *Relational Skills in the Bible* with Amy Brown, and *Joy Starts Here* to help build hesed leaders and communities. Learn more at thrivetoday.org.

2. What if there is a narcissist in our group/church/leadership?

Answered by Ken Smith

First of all, it shouldn't surprise us to find narcissistic tendencies in our leaders, even our church leaders. Thankfully the task of forming healthy group and individual identities is one that God joins us in, we merely need to remember He is with us and to listen for Him. Secondly, facing narcissism is the kind of task that can only be carried by a group. Learning to move together in sync with God is just what the church is to be doing anyway. Thirdly, our own weakness, rebellion, and corrupted heart must be dealt with in the process. In our journey of becoming fully alive, fully mature, and fully like Him, He is the only one we are to look to, the only one able to transform what we see when we look in the mirror into what He saw for us to be.

Of course we will struggle with all this in the church, in our home, and in our work. Yet none of it can be ignored, just as we can't be silent any time we see sin, iniquity, or rebellion of any kind, lest we become complicit in it. Learning to receive and give healthy shame messages no matter what the cost is just one of the ways we are to be His people. It is part of how we submit to one another. The strongest and most mature people in a group, often called the elders, have the greater part of this task of reminding the group how to act and correcting it when it veers off the path. Only when elders collectively model healthy shame messages, personal humility, lack of self-justification, and are prepared to accept the consequences for being life-giving can narcissism really be addressed, especially when the pastor is the narcissist.

When church leaders fall short of this, we encourage them and pray they will find the strength needed from God. Individually, we pursue growth in our own maturity. We grieve with God about the narcissism we find where life-giving leadership is needed. Sharing God's pain is one of the ways we love our enemies, which replaces our tendency to grumble about the shortcomings we see in others. Until we stop to see what God sees about others, it is as if we are walking around with a plank in our own eye.

Kenneth Smith has been a part of equipping God's people to become the church and to be fully alive all across the globe, including several unreached people groups. Currently, he and his wife reside in the Philadelphia area and serve through CityNet Ministries. He can be contacted at ken.smith@citynetphilly.org

3. What if I am married to a narcissist?

Answered by Barbara Moon

Narcissists are wounded, immature, and difficult. Spouses have a difficult path living with the pain that narcissism causes. Narcissism comes packaged in different forms and intensities ranging from grouchy and verbally hurtful all the way to psychopathic and dangerous. If a dangerous abuser is not willing to get outside help to create safety, a separation may be necessary. For those married to – or who are themselves – a narcissist who is grouchy and verbally harsh, other options are open. How teachable, emotionally mature, and humble a narcissist is will greatly determine degree of change.

The first order of help for either spouse is becoming part of a community that is high in *hesed*, God's sticky love. We also call this kind of love, *agape love*. Here are some ways I have been building high-*hesed* community in my area. As multi-generational groups, we are working on our fear – fear of speaking to a narcissist's behavior, fear we will be attacked, and the fear that changes are impossible.

Working on our fear starts with a close, intimate, trusting relationship with Immanuel. A relationship that constantly asks Him, "Where are You right now?" and "What do You want me to know?" Living the Immanuel lifestyle includes going to Jesus for healing of unresolved painful memories. We are learning that all relationships require the Relational Circuits [RCs] in our brain to be "on" and functioning. We cannot relate to anyone as Jesus has taught us with our RCs "off." Along with other relational brain skills, our groups are learning how to fill in the holes in our emotional maturity. All of the above require us to learn what to do with emotional pain, to stop avoiding pain as we discover that we can make it through what we call "Pain Lab."

In my hesed communities we are seeing huge transformations with parents (who have acted like narcissists) and teens (who often act like narcissists) as the parents incorporate relational brain skills into their everyday interactions. When parents stop trying to control their teens, start seeing them as God sees them, think good thoughts about them (which shows up on faces), and become gentle protectors of weakness, changes have happened within weeks.

Through the resources we have, the modeling of relational skills, and the stories we share, people are becoming more like Jesus. For learning what to do with emotional pain, we use my book, *Re-Framing Your Hurts*. For helping parents we have *Handbook to Joy-Filled Parenting* and *Joy-Filled Parenting with Teens*. I have videos on YouTube for parents. For learning how the brain works, how to synchronize, build joy, and grow maturity we use my book *Joy-Filled Relationships*. We can spend up to three months just going over Life Model's maturity stages.

Every week in all groups we share appreciation moments and then do listening prayer with Immanuel. People go home and practice then share their victories and failures next meeting. Many are on texting groups where we share ups and downs and prayer requests during the week. The flavor of our *hesed* communities is that it's OK to have weaknesses because our group identity is about being gentle protectors to weakness.

Because we see narcissism as a weakness, not something to reject, we know what to do with it – we give gentle shame and grace responses and help narcissists see that how they are behaving is not like our hesed community. If a narcissist is not willing to get into a group (or a family is not willing to be the group), changes will be more difficult. If the spouse grows hesed/agape and begins to relate differently, this can be the catalyst that moves the narcissist to consider help. So, the person married to a narcissist needs first of all to concentrate on growing their *hesed* with Jesus and getting their own brain retrained with God's people. A narcissistic spouse (or child) might notice something different and might even ask if they can join the group.

Barbara Moon developed the separate study guide accompanying *The Pandora Problem* and has collaborated with Dr. Wilder for many years. Barbara has learned to trust Jesus with her fears of interacting with narcissists. Barbara leads small groups (including one for teens and young adults) and does Immanuel Prayer in the Atlanta area. Her books and blogs are at barbaramoonbooks.com and amazon.com.

4. Can a church really form a hesed group identity?

Answered by Dr. Tim Johns

I have great news. Not only is it possible for a church to cultivate a hesed group identity, it is essential. Only God's love, manifested through God's people, will convince the world that the gospel is real. Do we really want to live beneath this kingdom opportunity? Unbelievers really do want to see an authentic expression of Christ's love in skin form – the ultimate apologetic. Creating a hesed group identity is a matter of life or death. The world must see hesed love-bonded groups to believe Christ is real.

A hesed group identity starts with Christ, who is the personification of hesed "sticky" love. Christ-centered people are progressively transforming into the likeness of Christ. When we are in Christ, the incarnation of hesed-love, we become like him. Any people who are in Christ and stuck together in Christ's body by the glue of love, will radiate the love of God. The exchanged love with God and for one another will emit out of them to a lost and dying world, even toward their enemies.

When we started the Rock Tribe, an international family-of-churches, one of our top core values was to be a people who loved well. God formed us to be a trans-local, multi-generational, interracial spiritual family who love God with all our hearts, who love each other, and who selflessly demonstrate God's love to our neighbors. Of course, we still have a long way to go. However, many who come into our midst testify that they experience an overwhelming sense of God's love and affection when they are in our presence.

Finally, I think we need to go to the heart of the matter and acknowledge that we are facing a highly destructive root problem – the god of "self." What Jim Wilder is addressing is a global epidemic which has deeply infected the body of Christ. Christ predicted that in the last days "the love of many would grow cold" (Matthew 24:12).

The Pandora Problem is exposing this cancer and letting us know just how rampant and embedded self-absorption has become. Systemic root problems require radical solutions. What is the cure? Death to our false selves, both individually and corporately. "We have been crucified with Christ, it is no longer we who live, but Christ who lives in us" (Galatians 2:20). Our responsibility is to "reckon ourselves dead" and to "put to death the deeds of the flesh" (Romans 6:11, 8:13; Colossians 3:5). For us to have a hesed group identity, we must invite our church family to die on three levels:

1. To see God, our false self must die. There is only room in our hearts for one God, and we are not Him (1 Corinthians 1:29-31; Genesis 3:8-10; Matthew 6:24; Romans 8:8).

2. To belong to one another in a hesed, covenant-bonded family, our false self must die. We belong to one another, and not just to ourselves alone (Romans 12:5-10).

3. To advance Christ's kingdom and reach a lost and dying world with the gospel, we must die to our false selves, sell all and follow Christ. We seek first the kingdom of God. We deny ourselves, pick up our crosses, and follow Christ (Matthew 6:33, 13:44-45, 16:24-26; Luke 9:23).

Dr. Timothy Johns is a church-planter, author, and business man. He and his wife, Janet, are the founders of the Rock "Tribe," an international family-of-churches. Tim started All Nations College, an accredited leadership training degree under Family of Faith Christian University. He also launched a ministry called "Jesus Tribes" – a catalyst to inspire high quality relationships in churches and the marketplace. He is an author, speaker, and consultant. He has written a book entitled "Micro-Church Families On Mission." He earned his Master's degree from Fuller Theological Seminary and Doctoral degree from Regent University. Tim and Janet have been married for over 43 years, have two married children and six grandchildren.
www.rocktribe.com | www.allnations.college
www.JesusTribes.com

5. Is my church small group an identity group?

Answered by Dr. Marcus Warner

Simply being in a church small group does not mean you are in an identity group. Small groups can function as identity groups, but they often do not. Most small groups are focused on creating relationships in which you feel like you know the names and stories of a core group of people. Some add content to that agenda.

An identity group is a place where you get to know people's hearts. By getting to know the hearts of those in your group, you can help them understand who they are and grow their capacity to stay that person even when they experience emotional pain.

Here are a few of the objectives of an identity group.

1. Get to know the heart characteristics of those who attend. When you know someone's heart characteristics, you can help them act like themselves, recognize why certain things cause them more pain than others, and help them understand when they are not acting like themselves.

2. Help those who attend practice Godsight to see themselves and their circumstances through God's eyes. Immanuel prayer is one tool for doing this. Sensing what God is showing you and sharing that is another way of helping people practice Godsight.

3. Protect the weaknesses of those who share. It needs to be safe to share weakness, which means predatory behavior needs to be confronted. However, the goal of an identity group is not to stay weak and be honest about it. The goal is to help people move beyond their weakness and grow in their capacity to live from the heart Jesus gave them.

To assemble an identity group, it helps to establish these objectives up front. As you practice these principles yourself, however, you can help the church small groups you are in transition toward functioning like an identity group.

Dr. Marcus Warner is the president of Deeper Walk International. He has co-authored two books with Jim Wilder, *The Solution of Choice* (2018) and *Rare Leadership* (Moody, 2016). A former pastor and Old Testament instructor, Dr. Warner has earned three degrees from Trinity Evangelical Divinity School (M.Div, Th.M., and D.Min.). He has also written many other books, including *Understanding the Wounded Heart* (2013), *What Every Believer Should Know About Spiritual Warfare* (2010), and *Toward a Deeper Walk* (2006).

Deeper Walk International is devoted to heart-focused discipleship that helps people identify and overcome the obstacles to a deeper walk with God.

6. Can a church group deal with character issues?

Answered by Ed Khouri

As Christians, we'd all like to think that becoming part of a group at our church would automatically lead to character transformation. That is very much like hoping that going to a hamburger chain repeatedly would turn us into a hamburger! Proximity to well-meaning and sincere Christians does not necessarily lead to transformation.

The sad truth is that most small group activities in church do not lead to lasting character transformation. Groups that are organized around strong or gifted leaders tend to have their bonds and identity centered around the leader. Groups organized to study books or other helpful information produce bonds around information. Groups designed to facilitate sharing pain and problems tend to grow an identity rooted in pain and problems. While these groups might be helpful at times, they do not lead to lasting transformation of character.

Character change in a small group is possible when a group is rooted firmly in grace, growing stronger attachments with God, and growing a strong, stable, healthy group identity. These groups actively help members experience God's presence and share responses to grace. Grace bonds enable members to see each other through God's eyes of grace. Group members discover their own unique, God-given identity, and learn to see other group members as God does.

Transformational groups gently remind members who forget their God-given identity and wander from grace who they really are. These groups share the joys and pains of life together. Rather than expect overnight character change, identity groups continue calling each other back to life.

> **Rev. Ed Khouri** is pastor, speaker, author, and trainer who creates, tests, and directs programs for discipleship and recovery. His web course "Grace, Narcissism, and Small Groups" is available through Deeper Walk International at deeperwalkinternational.org. Much more about narcissism, leadership, and small groups is found in his series "A Place for Grace" with a projected release in early 2019. These groups are designed to establish a grace-based foundation for character transformation.

7. How do I help my children deal with shame relationally?

Answered by Jen Coursey

As parents, we must learn how to let our children feel healthy shame. This may sound strange, but I welcome opportunities to give my sons a healthy shame message when they are not acting like their true selves. I convey, "Son, this behavior is not acceptable. What do we need to learn here?" This response helps children learn what is appropriate and distinguish appropriate behavior from inappropriate behavior.

At the same time, I do not leave my children in their shame with no way of returning to joy. Such a response would be like trying to teach your children to swim by throwing them into the deep end of the pool. Rather, I join them in their upset as I convey, "This behavior is not okay" and affirm, "You can do better than this." I stay relationally connected with them while they feel shame. My staying connected makes the shame experience relational. We establish and strengthen the return to joy pathway in their brain. These many trips from shame to joy (and the other big six negative emotions) solidify return to joy pathways and ensure children will have this skill throughout their lifetime. Strong pathways back to joy from each of the big six negative emotions build resiliency and strengthen emotional stability.

How do we build this emotional resiliency in our children? It starts with the parents. We the parents must learn to be comfortable with our own emotions so we can help our child learn to quiet his or her emotions as we are listening to each other. In THRIVE relational skill training this is *Skill 11: Return to Joy.* Practice quieting our mind, emotions, and body as a shared experience keeps us in relationship with the people around us.

I practiced quieting myself when things were going well so that I could use this skill when things were upsetting then I could quiet the distress I felt watching my child become upset. If we fear our own feelings of shame, we will shut our child down from learning to feel and recover from negative emotions. When we learn how to recover from our own emotions, we can also model this for our children and we can be their example.

I needed to learn how to quiet my own distress when I felt shame before I could teach my children. I needed examples to learn this. I found friends who comfortably used shame to improve family relationships. I observed how they handled themselves with big shame feelings. I asked my friends to tell me stories about moments they recovered from their upsets. These are all skills we learn and practice at THRIVE Training.

> **Jen Coursey** is a speaker, author, and trainer who blogs about how to apply the 19 relational brain skills in parenting and marriage at thrivetoday.org. Jen and Chris authored *30 Days of Joy for Busy Married Couples* and workbooks designed to strengthen relational skills. They lead THRIVE training and develop resources so individuals and groups can learn the 19 relational brain skills and begin to act like themselves.

8. How are codependency and unconditional love different when facing narcissism?

Answered by Ed Khouri

Codependency and unconditional love are two very different things. Unconditional love is more focused on what is best for another person, and codependency is more focused on what feels better for me.

Unconditional love is the kind of sticky, unwavering, intelligent and hesed love God has. People who love unconditionally are committed to doing what is best for those they love, even when it requires sacrifice or might involve pain. Unconditional love allows others to grow and learn from mistakes without attempting to rescue them from the consequences of foolish choices.

Codependent behaviors are quite different. Codependent behaviors tend to be rooted in fears like rejection, loss of a relationship, making someone angry/upset, or the fear that another person will make poor choices. Codependent people have difficulty trusting that God will be faithful to others, even when they make very bad decisions.

For transformation to occur in the life of a narcissist, unconditional love is non-negotiable. Transformation simply will not take place without persistent, sticky, hesed love showered intelligently upon a narcissist by God's people acting together. It is the intelligent and unselfish nature of God's unconditional love that makes it so essential when facing narcissism. Unconditional love suffers long, even when narcissists bite. It does what is best for someone else and is not rooted in fear.

Codependency is completely unhelpful when responding to narcissism. Because it is a fear-based set of behaviors, codependency actually helps feed and perpetuate narcissistic behaviors. Narcissistic behavior thrives when others are afraid. Narcissists are experts at spotting fear in other people and using those fears against people who try to "help" codependently. Responding to narcissists codependently will unwittingly enable narcissism. Because it is so easy to slide into codependency without realizing it, we must stay strongly connected to our group and our group identity when facing narcissism. Our groups can help us love together without falling into unhelpful codependency.

Rev. Ed Khouri is the co-founder and director of Equipping Hearts for the Harvest ministry to empower leaders to skillfully serve the addicted community globally. He created the Restarting and Belonging Modules of the Connexus program that contain more guidance about codependency and joyful recovery. Ed's resources are available through deeperwalkinternational.org.

9. Why so much emphasis on loving our enemies?

Answered by Jim Wilder

Dr. Dallas Willard proposed loving our enemies as the test for our progress in becoming students of Jesus. The Life Model is built around shifting the "fuel" that runs our lives from fear to love. Where we see Christianity changing character we inevitably find people learning to love their enemies. Where Christians are content to think about loving neighbors there is little change.

At the center of personality disorders like narcissism is a failure to love enemies and anyone with a weakness easily slides into the "prey" category the brain uses to hunt enemies. When the Kingdom of God is described in Scripture, the image of predators who no longer hurt or destroy but now play and rest with their previous enemies is the image given. I find that captivating, don't you?

Jim Wilder is suspected of contributing to this book.

UNDERSTANDING
TERMS & CONCEPTS

UNDERSTANDING
TERMS & CONCEPTS

Agape: Greek translation of the Hebrew "hesed" attachment love of God and God's people.

Batach: Hebrew for the sense of well-being and security that results from having someone in whom to place confidence.

Change agents: people who desire more growth, maturity, and transformation into the likeness of Christ than they have experienced so far.

Character change: developing a fundamentally different response style to others. Desirable change creates responses, attitudes, and actions that are like Christ's.

Character disorder: inability to share pain, respond kindly, live in integrity, and relate unselfishly with others.

Condemnation: decreeing or desiring punishment for anyone who fails to be good enough.

Dominion: authority over a territory, person, or situation – the one who has the last word.

Enemy mode: relationally disconnected state of hot or cold anger.

Explaining myself: making the truth about myself, my circumstances, and my actions clear enough for others to understand while leaving the judgment up to them. Contrast with self-justification which seeks to make a favorable judgment for oneself or persuade others of one's goodness.

Fast track in the brain: the right hemispheric identity process that functions relationally, non-verbally, and faster than conscious thought.

Gentle Protectors: people who respond kindly to weakness and see weakness as something to defend, heal, and nurture in order to create growth.

Godsight: Being able to perceive with understanding what God sees in a person or situation.

Grace: means "you are special." People are special without regard to performance or failure due to who loves them.

Group identity: the group we grant the right to tell us who we are and how we act. Christian group identity should be the Church with high hesed and low qasheh that shares our joy and pain.

Healthy shame messages: correct a person's behavior so we can be glad to be close to them again by stating a) what was done that is not like our people and b) how our people would act. A healthy shame message expresses our group identity and generally takes the form of, "We don't ____. We (do) _____." Saying "you" tends to isolate the hearer and disconnect the group identity center in the brain, so we phrase it with "we."

Hesed: Hebrew for attachment love that is secure, enduring, and bonds us forever. God is hesed.

Joy: a relational state when someone is glad to be with me or I am the sparkle in someone's eye.

Judgment: can have two meanings: a) to discern or separate and b) to condemn, punish, or destroy. Scripture tells us to a) discern well but not to b) condemn or destroy.

Loving enemies spontaneously: the test for real hesed/agape love. We will become the kind of people who love others rather than having to suppress our first reaction to our detractors.

Maturity: completeness and wholeness at a given stage. Increasingly staying relational and acting like oneself in spite of intense emotions. Life Model has six stages with needs and tasks: unborn, infant, child, adult, parent, and elder.

Mindsight: the ability to know there is a human mind behind a face and to be able to perceive what is going on with that other person at that moment.

Narcissist: a person who cannot hear a correction to their identity without provoking self-justification and sometimes hostility or attack. The narcissist uses fear and self-justification to avoid correction (healthy shame) and win.

Pandora problem: a group situation greeted by silence because all those involved fear that if the problem "gets out" in the open it will only make things worse.

Peacock narcissism: a response to correction that does not own faults but pushes the problem on whoever makes the best target. Attacking, self-justifying, and blaming are often used to control others and win.

Predators: people who exploit weakness for self-gain and do not share the pain of their victims.

Protector (gentle): someone who can see the weaknesses in others but prefers to help others heal and grow rather than to take advantage or allow others to take advantage.

Psychopath: People who lack attachment, fear, guilt, or remorse and are unperturbed by others' suffering.

Qasheh: Hebrew meaning stiff-necked, stubborn, obstinate, cruel, defiant, hard-hearted, or self-justifying.

Safety: generally understood by people to mean nothing painful will happen to me. The Hebrew word "batach" is often translated "safety" although the outcome may be injury or death. Safety in Scripture suggests that although the body may be killed what is of value for us cannot be harmed.

Sarx: Greek word often translated "flesh" or "old nature" that refers to the human illusion that we can figure out the right thing to do in spite of the moral and mathematical impossibly of the task.

Self-justification: attempting to prove that we and our actions are good.

Shame: the opposite of relational joy, a sort of inner pain and revulsion in response to unbefitting behavior.

Shame message: an invitation to more joyful relationship for those with relational skills, or an axe to produce misery for the relationally unskilled.

Sharing pain: staying emotionally attuned with a person who is hurting until we experience their distress as our own. Sharing pain is crucial for pain we have caused.

Sin/transgression/iniquity: Three aspects of human failure to act like "God's people." Sin is when we try but fail. Transgression is when we do not try. Iniquity is any deformity of body, soul, or mind that interferes with our attempts.

Six unpleasant emotions: pain signals in the brain that are common to all cultures – anger, sadness, fear, disgust, shame and hopeless despair.

Skunk narcissism: a response to correction in which a person attacks him or herself and continues self-attack until the shame message is withdrawn and replaced by much assurance and praise.

Slow track in the brain: conscious thoughts managed by the left hemisphere of the brain that processes more slowly than the right brain (the fast track). The slow track focuses on details at the cost of the whole picture but uses details for greater analysis and explanations.

Sociopath: a person who lacks concern for the impact his or her actions (or inaction) has on others.

Sons of Belial (worthlessness): people whose foolish and self-justified way of life produces nothing of real value but they think otherwise.

Splagchnon: Greek for one's inner parts (abdominal) that should "move" or turn over when we feel the pain of others. The word is often translated as compassion.

Toxic shame message: condemnation that a person is bad. Painful displeasure is expressed about someone's identity or action without a clear and true message of how to restore their valued identity.

Transformation: becoming someone new that we were not before. Healing and growth are ways to improve the existing self. Transformation creates something new. Desirable transformation produces the character of Christ where it previously did not exist.

4+ STORIES FOR RELATIONAL SHAME

In order to learn a path back to joy from shame, someone must show how it is done. Telling a story with the right details will show others the way. The storyteller has to have the right words to describe the feeling. Our story helps them see what it feels like in our bodies. Shame stories should be rather brief and to the point.

In order to help narcissists learn a better way, we have to know how to return to joy ourselves. In order to tell a good 4+ story that will allow a listener to follow us to shame and back to joy we need the following ingredients:

• The story should show a moderate feeling level of emotion, not too intense. We do not tell the most intense shame story in our life because it will blow their circuits. We train before trying an intense challenge.

• It should be a story we have told before. Otherwise we may say something we did not mean to say.

• We tell a story that we do not have to be guarded about.

• We are involved in the story and how it affected us. The person has to know how it affected us and how we acted when feeling the shame.

• It focuses on how we got back to joy and discovered what God meant us to be and what that looked like.

• The story focuses on the specific emotion of shame that we can name, and it shows on our face and body language. We maintain eye contact.

• The story is concise, under three minutes. Too long a story will lose the audience.

APPRECIATIONS

Thank you to Barbara Moon who transcribed the Sunday School class talks on which this book is based. Barbara then tested the materials with her groups for seven years, created a study guide then revised and tested each version of this book. Without her insistence I would not have written the book at all.

Great appreciation to the Shepherd's House Board of Directors and Jim Martini for giving me a sabbatical this year to complete this and other writing projects. Without your support this book would also not be finished.

My wife Kitty has read and revised every version of this book and coordinated the study group materials. Together with her sister Karen Mertes, they have provided proofreading, correction, commentary, application testing, and support for my writing.

I thank my study group members: Walter and Nancy Short, Dr. Tim and Janet Johns, Amy Pierson, Tamela White, John Lamb, Michel and Claudia Hendricks, John and Linda Miakowski, and Sandie Godsman for reading rough drafts, trying exercises, adding clarity and practical applications. Paula Nolls also participated in the study group, but, in addition, she recorded and distributed the original lessons on which the book is based.

My writers group of Ed Khouri, Chris Coursey, Ken Smith, and Shelia Sutton faithfully reviewed the concepts, exercise design and theory behind the book. This faithful crew has worked with me for years clarifying, testing, and developing both theory and applications for the Life Model.

Stephanie Warner has been my inspiring and helpful editor at Deeper Walk publishing for several projects. It gives me great confidence to have her guidance toward a clear presentation.

Thank you to Dr. Karen Struble who invested a great deal in moving the material from a transcribed talk to something that resembled a book.

Father Ubald and Katsey Long provided much of the inspiration and hope for transformation that you will read in this book. They have breathed life into the Kingdom of God and are teaching lions to become lambs.

Ed Khouri, Chris and Jen Coursey, Ken Smith, Tim Johns, Marcus Warner, and Barbara Moon contributed answers to frequently asked questions. I gave them each three paragraphs to cover each of the really hard topics. These friends represent a wealth of resources you should discover and use.

I would like to acknowledge all the unnamed pastors, professors, colleagues, family, and friends who contributed to my understanding of narcissism. This book creates a conflict for you. You desire to be acknowledged but not here. May I say that your true selves will one day be known and loved.

Finally, thanks also to all the little people – whoever they might be.

DR. E. JAMES WILDER

Jim Wilder (PhD, Clinical Psychology, and MA, Theology, Fuller Theological Seminary) has been training leaders and counselors for thirty years on five continents. He is the author of over ten books with a strong focus on maturity and relational skills for leaders, including his co-authored book *Rare Leadership*. His co-authored book *Living from the Heart Jesus Gave You* has sold over 100,000 copies in eleven languages. Wilder has published numerous articles and developed four sets of video and relational leadership training called THRIVE.

He has extensive clinical counseling experience and is the chief neurotheologian of Shepherd's House Inc., a nonprofit working at the intersection of brain science and theology. He is also the lead developer of the Life Model, which is building contagiously healthy Christian communities through equipping existing networks with the skills to thrive.

Deeper Walk International is a 501(C)(3) nonprofit bringing together biblically-balanced teaching on emotional healing and spiritual warfare that helps people who feel stuck break through to new levels of freedom in their walk with God.

We teach about God's grace, life in the Spirit, spiritual warfare, and authentic community. What sets our training apart is how we bring it all together, then make it simple and transferable, so that people understand what it takes to walk in freedom and grow in maturity. We call this approach to ministry "heart-focused discipleship."

Find us at DeeperWalkInternational.org.

Printed in Great Britain
by Amazon